Here's to
Transforming the
field!

Chris

Palgrave's Frontiers in Criminology Theory

Series Editors
Matt DeLisi
Criminal Justice Studies
Iowa State University
Ames, Iowa, USA

Alex R. Piquero
School of Economic, Political, and Policy Sciences
University of Texas at Dallas
Richardson, Texas, USA

Frontiers in Criminology Theory advances contemporary theory and research on two broad areas of criminological scholarship. The first focal area is on conceptual content areas that seek to explain the etiology and developmental course of antisocial behavior. The series conceptualizes antisocial behavior broadly to acknowledge and incorporate research from multiple disciplinary perspectives including criminology, developmental psychology, sociology, behavior genetics, social work, and related fields. Works in this focal area include book-length developments of extant theoretical ideas, edited volumes of leading research within a specific theoretical area (e.g., self-control theory, social learning theory, general strain theory, etc.), and, of course, new theoretical ideas on the causes and correlates of anti-social behavior. The second focal area encompasses the criminology theory of the juvenile justice system, criminal justice system, and allied social service providers. Like focal area one, the criminal justice system is conceptualized broadly to include multiple disciplinary perspectives that advance research on prevention, psychiatry, substance abuse treatment, correctional programming, and criminal justice policy. Works in this focal area include book-length developments of extant topics, edited volumes of leading topics in criminal justice, and, of course, new theoretical and conceptual approaches to the prevention, treatment, and management of criminal justice clients.

More information about this series at
http://www.springer.com/series/14562

Christopher P. Salas-Wright • Michael G. Vaughn •
Jennifer M. Reingle González

Drug Abuse
and Antisocial
Behavior

A Biosocial Life Course Approach

palgrave
macmillan

Christopher P. Salas-Wright
Boston University
Boston, USA

Michael G. Vaughn
Saint Louis University
Saint Louis, USA

Jennifer M. Reingle González
School of Public Health
University of Texas,
Texas, USA

Palgrave's Frontiers in Criminology Theory
ISBN 978-1-137-55816-9   ISBN 978-1-137-55817-6 (Ebook)
DOI 10.1057/978-1-137-55817-6

Library of Congress Control Number: 2016951435

Cover illustration: © zodebala/ Vetta/ Getty

Printed on acid-free paper

This Palgrave Macmillan imprint is published by Springer Nature
The registered company is Nature America Inc.
The registered company address is: 1 New York Plaza, New York, NY 10004, U.S.A.

"To Javier, Carina, Leighton, and Julio"

Foreword

This book is rooted in the conviction that human biology plays a critical role in understanding drug abuse and antisocial behavior. In the same breath, however, it fundamentally affirms the importance of the many social and environmental factors that influence our behavior across the life course. The book provides an overview of the scope of the problem of drug abuse and crime, as well as an in-depth examination of cutting-edge research on the genetics and neurobiology of addiction and antisocial behavior across the developmental periods of childhood, adolescence, and adulthood. It concludes by exploring the implications of a biosocial, life-course approach in terms of drug abuse prevention and by looking at what lies ahead for drug abuse and criminological research.

Preface

Drug abuse and antisocial behavior are major issues that impact the lives of millions of Americans and their communities on a daily basis. Many people struggle with alcohol and drug use and many others take part in (or are impacted by) behaviors that demonstrate a fundamental lack of concern for the welfare of others and the rules of society. And, as we repeatedly note throughout this text, a substantial proportion of the population is impacted by both of these behaviors at various points in their lives. We know this from our empirical research in the areas of drugs and crime, but it is also something that we understand on the basis of our own experiences working with individuals who struggle with drug abuse and those who have come into contact with the criminal justice system. We have come to appreciate the tremendous impact of drug abuse and antisocial behavior in our own lives as ordinary individuals, parents, family, and community members, and simply as people who open the newspaper on a regular basis. Fundamentally, we are troubled by the tremendous toll that drugs and crime take on our communities. These issues remain the driving force for why we chose to author this book.

In this text, we aim to provide a unique contribution to the literature on drug abuse and antisocial behavior by rooting our analyses in a conjoined biosocial and life-course theoretical lens. At its core, biosocial logic affirms that an appreciation for the role of both biological and social factors is essential in order to understand complex behavioral phenomena such as drug abuse and antisocial behavior. Indeed, drug use and crime are behaviors that are influenced by our genes and our brains, just as they are impacted by the familial, educational, community, and social environments in which we are embedded. Similarly, a life-course perspective is situated in the assertion that our behaviors are best understood by looking not at a narrow window of time, but rather by taking into account the twists and turns that play out over a lifetime. Without any doubt, our understanding of drug abuse and antisocial behavior is enhanced immeasurably by looking carefully at our early life experiences and by considering the long-term trajectories that can only be seen over the course of decades. Taken together, we feel confident that an analysis of drugs and crime that takes seriously the impact of biological and environmental factors across the life span sheds new light on often-explored questions.

We have done our best to put forth a coherent argument that builds upon itself in examining both the biosocial and the life-course elements of drug abuse and antisociality. In Chap. 1, we begin by providing an overview of the scope of the problem of drug abuse and antisocial behavior, and examining the intersections between substance use and criminal behavior in the United States. In Chap. 2, we provide critical background information related to the state-of-the-art understanding of drug abuse and addiction within the framework of chronic disease and as it related to the human brain. Next, in Chaps. 3 and 4, we delve into cutting-edge research on the role of genetic and neurobiological factors in the etiology of both drug abuse and antisocial behavior. Having laid a solid biosocial foundation, in Chaps. 5 through 7 we examine the role of biological and social factors in the development of drug abuse and antisocial behavior across the spectrum of childhood, adolescence, and adulthood. In Chap. 8, we pull the text together by reflecting on the significance of a biosocial, life-course perspective with respect to the prevention and treatment of drug abuse and crime. And, finally, in Chap. 9, we conclude with a look at what we have done as well as what lies ahead in the world of drug abuse and criminological research.

We want to make clear that this text is not intended to answer every question or to provide an exhaustive description of all that is known in the world of drugs and crime. For example, we have focused relatively little on the policies and laws that influence the intersections of drug abuse and antisocial behavior. Rather, we have aimed to look at drug abuse and antisocial behavior in a way that breathes new life into these topics that have been so frequently examined. We affirm that human biology plays a critical role in understanding drugs and crime while—in the same breath—maintaining a consistent awareness and appreciation for the impact of social and environmental factors across the life course. Ours is a biosocial, life-course approach to understanding drug abuse and antisocial behavior, and we hope that it is an approach that can prompt new questions, provide fresh insight, and serve as one small step towards addressing the challenges of drugs and crime in our world today.

Contents

About the Authors

Christopher P. Salas-Wright is Assistant Professor in the Boston University School of Social Work. His research on drug abuse and crime has resulted in more than 100 scholarly publications and has been featured in *The Washington Post, Los Angeles Times,* and *USA TODAY.*

Michael G. Vaughn is Professor and Director of the PhD program in the School of Social Work at Saint Louis University. He is an internationally recognized scholar in the areas of drug abuse and crime and has contributed more than 300 scholarly publications across a wide range of areas.

Jennifer Reingle Gonzalez is Assistant Professor of Epidemiology at the University of Texas School of Public Health in Dallas. She has published more than 75 manuscripts on drug abuse and crime, and has authored a leading textbook on criminology research methods.

List of Figures

1

The Scope of the Problem

Introduction

The use and abuse of illicit drugs and alcohol are widespread and constitute an important social and public health problem in United States (Danaei et al. 2009) and beyond (Rehm et al. 2006). More than half of arrestees have one or more drugs in their system at the time of arrest, and drug users have some of the highest recidivism, or re-arrest, rates for violent and non-violent crime. In the 1980s, the already well-documented relationship between drugs and crime was thought to be causational and uni-directional (Gropper 1985), with some drugs in particular (e.g., "street heroin") being directly associated with criminal behavior. Results from this body of research implied that if treatment and education to reduce drug use among *the most frequent users* was provided, drug-related crime would decline (Gropper 1985). Forty years later, there no doubt that drug use, and drug addiction, is more common among offenders when compared to the general public [for a recent text on this subject, see *The Handbook of Drugs and Society* (Brownstein 2015)].

© The Author(s) 2016   **1**
C.P. Salas-Wright et al., *Drug Abuse and Antisocial Behavior*,
Palgrave's Frontiers in Criminology Theory,
DOI 10.1057/978-1-137-55817-6_1

Despite the breadth of literature now available on the drug–crime nexus, we have made little progress towards our understanding of the causal processes associated with the link. Emerging conceptualizations of the "addiction" process may be instrumental in expanding our understanding of how the cycle of drugs–crime begins (and, correspondingly, how it can end). Rather than conceptualizing drug use and dependency as a rational choice (Becker and Murphy 1988), the term addiction is now being used to refer to chronic, relapsing brain disease caused by repeated exposures to drugs (Kalivas and Volkow 2005). Under this addiction model—one that has is widely accepted across an interdisciplinary field of researchers—drugs modify the cellular structure of the brain. As stated by the pioneers in this domain, Kalivas and Volkow (2005), these cellular modifications, "[P]romote the compulsive character of drug seeking in addicts by decreasing the value of natural rewards, diminishing cognitive control (choice), and enhancing glutamatergic drive in response to drug-associated stimuli (1403)."

As a result of this research in neuroscience, drug addiction is now being viewed increasingly as a disease, and crime may be conceptualized as a side effect. This indicates a need for lifelong support for people suffering from addiction, which should indirectly prevent a great deal of drug-related crime. However, despite this advancing knowledge that addiction is less a conscious choice and more a chronic disease, persons suffering from addiction are stigmatized and discriminated against even more so than those suffering from severe mental illnesses (Barry et al. 2014). The public remains skeptical of drug treatment and its effectiveness, thus opposing policies and resource allocation towards treatment for persons suffering from addiction (Barry et al. 2014).

This ongoing public sentiment could indicate that dissemination of recent findings in support of addiction as a chronic disease has been limited. This book represents an attempt to aggregate and disseminate the most recent research on drugs and crime; particularly, how the intersections of biology and social behavior can converge to enhance our understanding of the causal processes associated with addiction and criminal behavior.

The arguments presented in this book are built upon seven guiding principles related to addiction and criminal behavior. Below is a brief description of each principle to provide context for this chapter and the remaining text.

1. There is no gene for drug use and crime, but there is a genetic vulnerability that underlies both substance use disorders and antisocial behavior. A number of genes, such as GABRA2, CHRM2, and MAOA (among several others) have been implicated as playing an important role in addiction. Many of these genes overlap with externalizing and antisocial behavior.
2. Drugs of abuse hijack the brain's reward pathways. This leads to compulsive drug-seeking and, in turn, crime. As discussed by Kalivas and Volkow (2005), acute drug use triggers a dopaminergic response, even despite long-term use.
3. Addiction alters brain function long-term. These cognitive modifications could explain ongoing criminal behavior. Addiction alters the prefrontal cortex, the brain center responsible for behavioral regulation and decision-making abilities, to over-activate when presented with drug-related stimuli. Rational decision-making becomes limited in the presence of long-term drug-seeking motivation and craving.
4. Early manifestation of childhood behavior problems that persist into adulthood could result from a combination of biologic susceptibility and social conditioning. There is no inherent gene that causes delinquent or criminal behavior. However, alleles linked to deficits in neurocognition and antisocial behavior have been identified (Beaver et al. 2009; Vaughn et al. 2009). In the presence of environmental risk factors (e.g., limited parental supervision or peer drug use), life-course-persistent criminal behavior may occur.
5. Delayed onset of drug use is critical, as developmental neuroplasticity among adolescents and young adults is easily disrupted by substance use. This could result in long-term harm. If normal development of impulse control and reasoning is impaired, long-term deficiencies in executive function, and corresponding criminogenic impulsive behavior, may persist throughout the life course (Crews et al. 2007).
6. Crime and antisocial behavior are asymmetrical. That is, a small subset (approximately 5 %) of individuals account for the lion's share of offending. Further, many of these chronic offenders have

had troublesome histories with psychoactive drugs and, at various points in their criminal careers, possess diagnosable substance-use disorders.

7. All substance use and crime-prevention or treatment strategies are inherently overlapping and biosocial. Not all persons suffering from addiction will criminally offend; however, an exceedingly large proportion do. Principles 1 and 2 tell us that prevention and treatment strategies will be unsuccessful if they ignore the biology of addiction or the social context of the person suffering from addiction. Treatment strategies that ignore family, friends, significant others, and pharmacological (or behavioral) treatment of brain disease will be ineffective and result in relapse of either drug use or crime (or, commonly, both).

Drug Abuse, Dependence, Use Disorders, and Addiction

What is the Difference?

Before we can begin to understand how each of these principles relates to crime, a historical review of the terminology surrounding substance use, abuse, dependence and addiction is needed. The (recorded) origins of modern addiction date back to 1641 (Wassenberg 2007), when Calvinist theologians made the first attempts to explain "compulsive" alcohol use as "sinful" behavior. In the 16th century, "addict" was defined by the *Oxford English Dictionary* as "attached by one's own inclination, self-addicted to a practice; devoted, given, inclined to." No reference to drug addiction as a psychiatric condition appeared in the *Diagnostic and Statistical Manual of Mental Disorders*, 2nd edition; however, "nicotine dependence" emerged in the 3rd edition of the Manual (DSM-III-R). Arguably, inclusion of nicotine dependence in a manual of psychiatric diagnoses was the turning point in recognition of addiction as a disease. On successive iterations of the DSM, the American Psychiatric Association (APA) disagreed on terminology related to addiction. For example, in the DSM-IV (SAMHSA 2004), drug dependence was defined as, "a maladaptive pattern of substance use, leading to clinically significant impairment or distress, as manifested by three (or more) [criteria] occurring at any time in the same 12-month period." These criteria included tolerance, withdrawal, taking larger amounts [of the drug] or over a longer period than intended, persistent desire or unsuccessful efforts to cut down or control drug use, time spent on activities needed to obtain the drug, giving up recreational, social, or occupational activities because of the substance, and continued use of drug despite knowledge of consequences. If any three of these subjective criteria were met, dependence was diagnosed.

Drug abuse, on the other hand, required meeting only one criterion over a 12-month period. The four manifestations of abuse include: recurrent substance use resulting in a failure to fulfill major obligations, recurrent substance use in hazardous situations, recurrent substance-related legal problems, and continued drug use despite recurrent problems. In other words, drug abuse required a lower threshold of drug-related problems for diagnosis compared to dependency.

In the DSM-5, substance abuse and dependence were combined into "substance use disorders" with variable levels of severity. A list of 11 symptoms (similar to those used for abuse and dependence) is used to distinguish between mild, moderate, or severe disorders. No criteria for drug "addiction" are present in any edition of the DSM. Addiction has been broadly defined as, "a chronic, relapsing brain disease that is characterized by compulsive drug seeking and use, despite harmful consequences" (National Institute on Drug Abuse 2014). Although this definition loosely corresponds to the APA's definition of substance use disorder, addiction is a broad concept that incorporates multiple levels of disease from the brain to a person's lived environment.

The distinction between drug use and drug addiction is akin to the distinction between an acute and chronic disease. To illustrate this point, let us consider the case of a ten-year veteran construction worker, Joe. While working on a roofing job, Joe fell from a ten-foot ladder and acutely injured his back. After filing a workers' compensation claim, Joe went to an approved urgent care center for assessment and treatment. After a brief examination and x-ray, Joe was prescribed two weeks of bed rest and pain medication. Joe cannot afford to take unpaid sick time and no light duty assignments are available from his employer. As a result, he continues to work each day, relying on the prescribed painkillers to manage his back pain. Six months later, Joe has not sought treatment and his back pain has gradually worsened. He feels pain even when he has taken his medication. At this point, Joe's back pain has transitioned from acute to chronic. Had Joe followed his doctor's orders and terminated the activity that led to his pain (e.g., work), the acute pain would likely have resolved.

Although Joe is a fictional character, Joe's case is not unusual. In fact, a study published in the journal *Spine* found that 24 % of people who filed workers' compensation claims for lower-back pain were still receiving compensation payments three months later (Fransen et al. 2002). Although this case study is about back pain, the transition from acute drug use to chronic use (or addiction) follows a similar trajectory. In Joe's situation, he continued to work despite his pain, leading to development of further back problems and chronic pain. For a drug user, repeated exposure to substance(s) can alter brain chemistry to result in addiction, a phenomenon now conceptualized as a chronic disease (Volkow and Li 2004; Volkow et al. 2013).

Our treatments for lower back pain and addiction are fairly limited and often, they have a very small long-term effect. Similarly, behavioral programs for addiction, such as Alcoholics Anonymous (AA), have not been updated since they became broadly implemented in the 1980s (McKellar et al. 2003; Tonigan et al. 1996). Although some studies suggest that AA and related 12-step programs effectively elicit long-term change in substance use (Morgenstern et al. 1997), a debate remains in the literature on the effectiveness of these programs (Tonigan et al. 1996). Results from a meta-analysis of experimental studies even suggested that AA meeting attendance resulted in *worse* outcomes than no treatment at all (Kownacki and Shadish 1999). Given the scientific advances in the neurology of addiction, promising treatments in addiction pharmacotherapy are emerging that may have a long-term impact on addiction directly and criminal behavior indirectly.

How Prevalent is Drug Use?

Alcohol is by far the most prevalent, normative, and commonly used substance across the US, and only a small proportion of American adults have *never* used alcohol (lifetime abstainers; 11.1 % according to the NESARC III (Dawson et al. 2015), 17.9 % according the NSDUH) and about two-thirds (67–73 %) reported drinking alcohol at some point during the previous year. A quarter (23 %) report recent binge drinking and an additional 6.2 % report binge drinking frequently (Center for Behavioral Health Statistics and Quality 2015). Nearly half of all Americans (49.2 %) report having tried an illicit substance at least one time in their lifetime, with an average age of drug use initiation of just was 20 years in 2014 (Center for Behavioral Health Statistics and Quality 2015).

The second most commonly used illicit drug category—including 2.5 % of the population aged 12 years and older or an estimated 6.5 million Americans—is the non-medical use of prescription drugs, such as opioid medications, sedatives, tranquilizers, and stimulants (Center for Behavioral Health Statistics and Quality 2015; McCabe et al. 2008). Of these psychotherapeutics, opiates are most commonly used (4 % used opiates non-medically in their lifetime; 1.3 % in the past month) (Center for Behavioral Health Statistics and Quality 2015). Although the usage rates of prescription medications appear to have been in decline in recent years (Vaughn et al. 2016), the proportion of adolescents using prescription drugs non-medically increased from 2.2 % to 2.6 % between 2013 and 2014—a significantly higher usage rate (Center for Behavioral Health Statistics and Quality 2015).

Among adolescents, substance use is even more common. Data from the National Survey on Drug Use and Health (NSDUH) suggest that roughly 27 million Americans, or approximately 10 % of the total US population age 12 years or older, currently use illicit drugs (Center for Behavioral Health Statistics and Quality 2015). Compared to usage rates documented in 2012, this represents an increase of 4 to 5 million adolescents and adults reporting past-month illicit drug use. As expected, this estimate was driven largely by use of marijuana (22.2 million or 82 % of illicit drug users). Among alcohol users, earlier onset ages have been consistently associated with deviant, criminal, and violent behavior (Zhang et al. 1997).

Although drugs like marijuana have been used consistently for decades, prescription drug use is an emerging problem of public health and criminological importance. To illustrate the problem, prescription drug theft was largely blamed for the increase in crime (specifically, homicides) in

Baltimore, Maryland, after the 2015 civil unrest (Schaffer 2015). This purported relationship lacked empirical support, and homicide rates in Baltimore continued to exceed expected rates long after prescription drug circulation returned to baseline levels. Although studies in other settings support the notion that non-medical use of prescription drugs (e.g., use without a physician's prescription) is associated with crime and delinquency, non-prescription drugs are more strongly predictive of criminal behavior (Ford 2008; MacCoun et al. 2003).

Drug Use and Antisocial Behavior

An Introductory Illustration

As an illustration, let us consider a study of the intersections between alcohol use, illicit drug use, and criminal behavior among young adults in the London area (Richardson and Budd 2003). Almost all participants (97 %) used alcohol at some point in their lifetime, and 95 % used alcohol in the year prior to being interviewed. Two-thirds drank alcohol at least once in the last week, and 39 % were binge drinkers. Therefore, alcohol use in this sample largely exceeds the volume consumed among similarly aged populations in the US. Among binge drinkers, 59 % reported taking illegal drugs, and alcohol use while under the influence of illicit drugs was common. These binge drinkers were four times as likely to fight and five times as likely to have caused property damage compared to (non-binge) drinkers. This strong relationship between substance use and criminal behavior is not limited to London or even Europe, in fact, some studies have found evidence a similarly strong relationship between drug use and criminal behavior in the United States.

The Prevalence of Drug-Related Arrests

The magnitude of the drug problem in the United States is reflected in our arrest rates. According to the Federal Bureau of Investigation's Uniform Crime Reports (UCR), 11.2 million arrests were made in

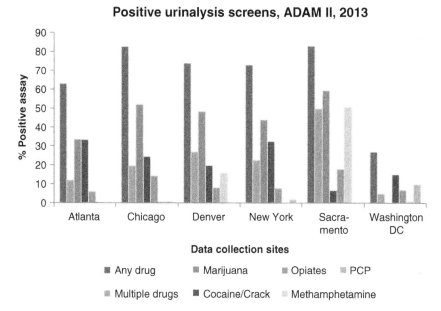

Fig. 1.1 Positive urinalysis screens from The Arrestee Drug Abuse Monitoring (ADAM) survey

2014 (US Department of Justice, 2015). Of these, 1.56 million were for drug-use violations. As expected, the vast majority of these arrests were for marijuana possession (40 %), followed by "other dangerous nonnarcotic drug" possession (18.7 % of total arrests, US Department of Justice, 2015). Possession of illicit drugs drove greatest proportion of drug arrests in 2012 (22 %). Interestingly, more arrests were made for heroin and cocaine sale or manufacturing (5.8 % of all drug arrests) than marijuana (5.2 %). These findings that heroin drives a large proportion of arrests supports historical research that some drugs, like "street" heroin, are more strongly associated with criminal behavior than drugs such as marijuana (Gropper 1985).

To further illustrate how pervasive substance use is among those involved in the criminal justice system, let's consider data from the Arrestee Drug Abuse Monitoring (ADAM II) survey (see Fig. 1.1). ADAM includes urinalysis results collected from males within 48 hours of arrest, thus shedding light on the prevalence of recent drug use among arrestees (Office of National Drug Control Policy 2014). These data suggest that drug use is pervasive among arrestees: as many as 83 % tested positive for at least one drug, and 50 % tested positive for more than one drug (Office of National Drug Control Policy 2014). Given the high usage rate of marijuana discussed earlier, it is less than surprising to find that marijuana was the most common drug present in positive screens (34–59 % of arrestees tested positive for marijuana). The average age of arrestees is higher than ever, and analysts suggest that this trend may be attributable to the aging population of cocaine and crack users. Between 2000 and 2003, the mean age of arrest centered around 35 years, but in 2010–2013, the mean age exceeds 40 years in many cities.

ADAM II data also tell us that cocaine (and crack) use has been declining, but use of heroin and other opiates has been on the rise. Given the recent upswing in heroin and other opiate use, it is not surprising that the rate of positive drug screens for heroin and opiates generally has increased in the arrestee population. At most study sites, the rate of positive heroin and opiate screens doubled between 2007 and 2013. For instance, in Sacramento, only 3 % of arrestees tested positive for opiates in 2000; but by 2007, this rate doubled to 6 %. In 2013, 18 % of arrestees tested positive for heroin or other opiates. Similarly, in Denver, 8 % tested positive in 2013—doubling since 2000 (4 %). In Chicago and New York, however, the trend in opiate use is in rapid decline (New York: 20 % in 2000 to 8 % in 2013; Chicago: 36 % in 2000 to 14 % in 2013). These discordant trends suggest tremendous regional differences in opiate use and possible ceiling effects observed in some large cities (e.g., New York and Chicago) in the early 2000s. Interestingly, non-medical use of opiate painkillers in the past three days ranged from 4 % to 9 % across ADAM data-collection sites. In comparison, use of amphetamines, such as Adderall, without a prescription ranged from less than 1 % in some cities to a high of 14 % in Atlanta. Given recent policy restrictions targeting pain clinics, physicians and pharmacies (Keast et al. 2015), it is possible that opiates like heroin are more easily accessible in 2016 than prescription drugs like oxycodone.

In some cities, particularly, Sacramento, polysubstance use (or the use of multiple drugs at the same time) is common. In Sacramento, 51 % of men tested positive for methamphetamine, a drug rarely used by the general population. The use of multiple substances is not surprising and has even been documented among US college students (Thombs et al. 2009) and young people in the United Kingdom. In the words of one drug user, "I only use speed [amphetamines] in like dire emergencies when I like really feel like doing some drugs and there's nothing around (18-year old female)" (Boys et al. 1999).

Positive drug screens do not necessarily reflect alcohol or other drug impairment during commission of the offense that led to arrest. According to a survey of prisoners, 32 % of state and 26 % of federal prisoners reported having committed the offense that led to their incarceration while they were under the influence of drugs (Mumola and Karberg 2006). Among state prisoners, drug offenders (44 %) and property offenders (39 %) reported the highest incidence of drug use at the time of the offense. Among federal prisoners, drug offenders (32 %) and violent offenders (24 %) were the most likely to report drug use at the time of their crimes. Among persons held in jails, 29 % of convicted inmates self-reported having used at least one illegal drug at the time they committed the offense (Karberg and James 2005). As expected, marijuana (14 %) and cocaine or crack (11 %) were the most commonly used drugs convicted inmates said they had used (Karberg and James 2005).

Drugs and Recidivism

If the relationship between drug use and crime was robust and substance use was truly responsible for criminal behavior, we would observe variation in re-arrest rates for drug offenders. In other words, persons arrested for drug crimes would be generalists and would be re-arrested for property crimes or violent crimes just as often as they are re-arrested for drug crimes. But among former drug offenders, more than half (51.2 %) were re-arrested for a drug offense. Nearly one-fourth (24.8 %) were arrested for a violent offense, 33.1 % for a property offense, and 56.1 % for a public order offense (prisoners may be arrested for more than one new offense; therefore, percentages exceed 100 %) (Karberg and James 2005). This distribution of re-arrest rates is very different from the patterns of recidivism generally. Most (58 %) released prisoners are re-arrested for public order offenses, but only 39 % are re-arrested for drug offenses, 38 % for property offenses, and 29 % for violent offenses (Karberg and James 2005).

Recidivism, or re-arrest, rates are lower than expected among persons originally arrested for drug offenses compared to those who were convicted of property crimes. Using data from a cohort of prisoners released in 1994, 44 % of former drug offenders were re-arrested within one year of release and two-thirds were arrested for a new crime within three years. In comparison, for persons convicted of burglary, larceny, motor vehicle theft, or other property crimes, half were re-arrested within one year and 74 % were re-arrested within a three-year period (Langan and Levin 2002). Data collected from a second cohort of prisoners released in 2005 confirmed these high recidivism rates among property offenders. Specifically, 82 % of property offenders, 77 % of drug offenders, and 71 % of violent offenders were arrested for a new crime over the next five years (Durose et al. 2014).

For the most part, former prisoners who were re-arrested were most likely to be re-arrested for the same offense. Former prisoners convicted of a violent offense were a notable exception, as one-third were re-arrested for a new violent offense, 30 % were arrested for a property crime, and 28.2 % were arrested for a drug offense. However, more than half of previous violent offenders were re-arrested for a new public order offense (55.3 %). Among former property and public order offenders, 38.5 % and 30 % were arrested for new drug offenses, respectively.

Adding to the Complexity of the Drug–Crime Problem: Mental Health

The relationship between drug use and crime is clearly complex, and there is little doubt that mental health is intertwined with substance use, abuse, dependence, addiction, and criminal behavior. Violence in general has been linked with mental illness (Blumstein and Cork 1996; Swanson et al. 1990; Swartz et al. 1998), but there is no consensus that specific mental health disorders are the reason for this link. Instead, there may be an intrinsic, non-directional co-morbidity consistently observed between mental health conditions and substance use and associated disorders. As evidence of this comorbidity, three-quarters of state prisoners who had a mental health problem and 56 % of those without a mental health problem were dependent on or abused alcohol or drugs (James and Glaze 2006). By specific type of substance, inmates who had a mental health problem had higher rates of dependence or abuse of drugs than alcohol (James and Glaze 2006). Among state prisoners who had a mental health problem, 62 % were dependent on or abused drugs and 51 % alcohol (James and Glaze 2006). Over a third (37 %) of state prisoners who had a mental health problem said they had used drugs at the time of the offense, compared to over a quarter (26 %) of state prisoners without a mental health problem (James and Glaze 2006).

Although unlikely, it is possible that the relationship between drugs and crime is spurious and the relationship is actually attributable to a third common variable, such as psychosis or schizophrenia (or some other mental health condition) or age. Recidivism rates decline with incrementally with age, and within five years of release from incarceration, 84 % of inmates 24-years old or younger at release were arrested for a new offense. When age increases to 25–39 years at release, recidivism rates decline to 79 %, and 69 % of those age 40 or older return to jail. Correspondingly, drug use is most prevalent among young adults (Center for Behavioral Health Statistics and Quality 2015), with the exception of crack users who are generally older. Interestingly, ADAM data show that male arrestees with positive drug tests were significantly *less* likely to be charged with a violent offense than a drug-related offense. This reflects the notion that most arrestees who tested positive for drugs were charged with drug-related, rather than violent, crimes (Galoub et al. 2012). Given the data presented above, it is possible that drug use is so pervasive among all offenders that other mechanisms are driving the well-documented drug–crime relationship.

Drugs and Victimization

A well-documented link between criminal behavior and victimization has been established (Jennings et al. 2012), thus allowing for the possibility that victim drug-use patterns may shed light on the relationship between drug use and crime. NESARC results suggest that 4.1 % of the general adult population were victims of criminal behavior in the previous year (Vaughn et al. 2010), and persons reporting violent and nonviolent antisocial behavior also were more likely to be victims of crime. Victims had higher rates of alcohol, cocaine, and opioid use disorders; paranoid personality disorder, major depressive disorder, and a family history of antisocial behavior compared to those that were not victimized in the previous year. Results from this study also suggest that those who participated in various violent behaviors (such as bullying, property destruction, rape, fighting, and so on) were significantly more likely to self-report victimization (Vaughn et al. 2010). This highlights the well-established victim–offender overlap, or the notion that many victims of crime are also criminal offenders (and vice-versa; Jennings et al. 2012; Reingle and Maldonado-Molina 2012).

The victim–offender overlap is also observed in the most serious of violent crimes: homicides. For example, a study of homicide victims in New Mexico conducted by Broidy et al. (2006), reported that 57 % of offenders and 50 % of homicide victims had a prior arrest. Similarly, Dobrin (2001) found that homicide victims were between four and ten times more likely to have been previously arrested for property crimes, violent crimes, and drug-related arrests, than non-victims. Similarly, marijuana users and binge drinkers are at elevated risk for being both perpetrators *and* victims of intimate partner violence (Moore et al. 2008; Reingle et al. 2012; Smith et al. 2012).

Popular Views of the Drugs–Crime Nexus

At least four explanations have been proposed to explain the relationship between alcohol and violence: a) reciprocal and psychopharmacological, meaning that the intoxicating effects of alcohol encourage violence to gain resources to support their drug/alcohol use (Goldstein 1985); b) the relationship is correlational, in that alcohol use increases violence because aggressive people self-select into situations that encourage alcohol consumption (Johnston et al. 1978); c) the relationship is bidirectional, and the arrow between alcohol use and violence may point in either or both directions (White et al. 1999); or d) the relationship is spurious, as problem behaviors cluster as part of a more general problem-behavior syndrome (Donovan et al. 1991).

A prevailing theory used to explain the relationship between drug use and crime suggests that drug-related violence is largely a function of pharmacological (drug craving), economic (pursuit of money), or systemic (protection of distribution networks) reasons (Goldstein and Brownstein 1987). This theory partially explains drug use among offenders, but psychosocial factors that drive drug use are left unexplained under this paradigm (Goldstein and Brownstein 1987; Huebner and Cobbina 2007). In fact, the notion of self-medication of physical health conditions has been absent from theories that attempt to explain drug use and the role of drug use in its relationship with criminal behavior (Abram and Teplin 1990; Haggard-Grann et al. 2006; Maldonado-Molina et al. 2010; White and Gorman 2000). By using the theory of self-medication to expand our understanding of the drug–crime nexus, we might infer that the relationship between drugs and crime might be better explained by assessing the role of psychosocial functioning, physical health, and self-medication as they relate to drug use (and as a result, re-arrest). The findings coincide with a large literature base that has evaluated the relationship between drug treatment and recidivism (for a comprehensive review, see Taxman 1998). Among offenders in the community, access to *any* treatment for a substance-use disorder reduced recidivism rates, longer time to arrest, and substance use, general illegal activity, and improved employment status (Hubbard et al. 2003; Taxman and Spinner 1997).

Given the psychopharmacological effects of alcohol, alcohol expectancies, and behavioral inhibitory control, we have reason to believe that alcohol and drug impairment during a violent event may influence one's decision to carry (Chen and Wu 2016) or use a weapon (for a review, see Ito et al. 1996) due to the pharmacological properties of the drug itself. Another particularly relevant theoretical explanation for the documented drug–crime relationship is the anxiolytic-disinhibition model, which posits that the influence of alcohol or drugs during a violent event may reduce the anxiety that would inhibit a violent response (Pihl et al. 1993). When alcohol or other drugs are used, social anxiety is suppressed, and an individual may act more aggressively, and by extension, use weapons.

The pharmacological effects of drugs and alcohol on behavior have been well- documented in intimate partner violence (IPV) research. Caetano et al. (2001) surveyed 1635 married couples throughout the United States and found that 30–40 % of the men and 27–34 % of the women perpetrated partner violence while under the influence of alcohol. Other studies have also found that alcohol was involved in 31 % of IPV episodes (Caetano et al. 2001; Reingle et al. 2014), that IPV perpetrators are more likely than victims to use alcohol (Ernst et al. 2008), and that IPV is more common retrospectively on days that heavy drinking occurred (Fals-Stewart 2003).

Is the Relationship Between Drug Use and Crime Causal, or Simply Correlational?

As alluded to in the introduction, research has been lagging in our understanding of the broad-scale temporality of the drug–crime problem. Does one become dependent on a substance, such as alcohol, which leads them to participate in violent or other criminal behavior? Or, does one cope with their criminal behavior and its consequences through alcohol use? Or, do each of these situations apply in different scenarios?

Few longitudinal studies have attempted to address the directionality of the alcohol–drug use–violence relationship, and the findings have been mixed. Dembo et al. (1990) conducted a cohort study of detained juvenile delinquents and found that alcohol use predicted violent behavior, and violence was a significant predictor of drug use (e.g., cocaine, marijuana) at the 10- to 15-month follow-up. Similarly, Ellickson et al. (2003) followed a cohort of seventh graders in California and Oregon through age 23 to evaluate the effects of early alcohol use. They found that early alcohol users were more likely to be delinquent and use other drugs in middle and high school compared to nondrinkers in seventh grade. At age 23, early alcohol users were at an increased risk for substance misuse, violence, and criminality (Ellickson et al. 2003). Another longitudinal study conducted using the first two follow-up surveys of the National Longitudinal Study of Adolescent Health found that alcohol use was a significant predictor of physical violence two years later (Resnick et al. 2004).

Despite the well-documented relationship between alcohol consumption as a predictor of violent behavior, another body of literature suggests that the violence predicts alcohol and drug use (e.g., the relationship is in the opposing direction as originally expected). For example, Windle (1990) used National Longitudinal Youth Survey data to assess the impact of various antisocial behaviors at ages 14–15 on other delinquent behaviors four years later. The results suggested that general delinquency (a function of the frequency of non-substance-related delinquent behavior) was a significant predictor of alcohol consumption. Similarly, a study of adolescents aged 12 to 18 evaluated the effects of early alcohol use among a sample of 218 males and 213 females (White et al. 1993). White et al. (1993) found that early aggression in males predicted alcohol consumption and alcohol-related aggressive behavior. In this study, more specific levels of alcohol use were not significantly associated with later aggression. In support of these findings, data from the same study were reanalyzed to evaluate the complex relationships between alcohol use, aggression, and alcohol-related aggression over time (White and Hansell 1996). They found that early initiation of alcohol use predicted physically aggressive behavior.

Several studies also provide support for a third theoretical explanation for the association between violence and alcohol use, that a bidirectional relationship exists. First, D'Amico et al. (2008) conducted a study of high-risk juveniles in the Los Angeles juvenile probation system between the ages of 13 and 17. They found that substance use predicted delinquency (a scale of drug-related crime, property crime, and interpersonal violent crime) and delinquency predicted substance use. In an eight-year study of high-school-aged African Americans in Michigan, Xue et al. (2009) tested the bidirectionality of alcohol use and violent behavior. Their results indicated that early violence (e.g., group fighting, hitting a teacher or supervisor, using a knife or gun to get something from a person) significantly predicted later alcohol use, and early alcohol use predicted future violent behavior. Among 15- to 19-year-old urban Mexican Americans and European Americans selected from a large health maintenance organization, Brady et al. (2008) noted reciprocal relationships between alcohol use and violence when adolescents were older. For example, perpetration of violence at age 18 significantly predicted alcohol use at age 19; however, violence at 15 did not predict alcohol use at age 19. Similarly, alcohol use at age 15 did not predict violent behavior at age 19, whereas alcohol use at age 18 significantly predicted perpetration of violence. Although these studies have consistent findings within ethnic groups, the limited external validity from single-site and incarcerated populations of juveniles must be considered when applying findings to these groups at the population-level.

In keeping with our IPV example, there is evidence that alcohol and marijuana use generally precede IPV (Lipsky et al. 2005; Reingle et al. 2012); however, given the highly sensitive nature of this topic and recall bias associated with reporting alcohol-impaired events, our knowledge about the true direction of this relationship is limited. Do couples use alcohol or other drugs to cope with partner violence? Or, does IPV emerge due to intoxication? These questions have yet to be definitively addressed in the literature.

Evidence in Support of a Spurious Relationship Between Drug Use and Crime

The evidence is clear that individual- and family-level factors increase the risk for violent behavior. For example, neurological deficiencies and cognitive impairments (Moffitt 1993), low IQ, hyperactivity, difficulty concentrating at school, beliefs and attitudes favorable to violence, antisocial behavior, and impulsivity have been consistently associated with violent behavior. At the family level, parental criminal behavior, child maltreatment, low levels of parental involvement, parental attitudes favorable to violence and drug/alcohol use, and separation of the parent and child have been identified as risk factors in a recent meta-analysis of longitudinal studies of risk factors for violence (Hawkins et al. 2000). Evidence suggests that adolescents who engage in delinquent behavior are more likely to engage in other high-risk activities (e.g., alcohol and other drug use, dropping out of school, gun ownership, gang membership, risky sexual activity and familial independence) (Huizinga et al. 1995) and increase their risk of health-related consequences (including serious injury and death) (Conseur et al. 1997). Each of these factors has been consistently associated with violence and delinquency, independent of alcohol or drug use.

Specificity of the Relationship Between Drug Use and Crime

As described in detail above, only 8 % to 10 % of the general population (Compton et al. 2007; Substance Abuse and Mental Health Services Administration [SAMHSA] 2012), but nearly half of all local (55 %), state (53 %), and federal (48 %) inmates have a diagnosed substance use disorder (Chandler et al. 2009). A wide variety of risk behaviors are associated with substance use and abuse including drug sales (White et al. 2008), violent and non-violent crime (Krug et al. 2002; White et al. 2002), intimate partner violence (Moore et al. 2008), prostitution (Yacoubian et al. 2001), gang involvement (Hill et al. 1999), and status offenses (Maynard et al. 2012). Notably, some studies have highlighted the fact that many individuals use illicit drugs without ever being involved in criminal activity (Vaughn et al. 2011). Contrary, some very serious offenders report little or no substance use (Vaughn et al. 2011). The overwhelming body of evidence clearly indicates that the use of illicit substances is strongly associated with a host of criminal behaviors ranging from shoplifting to armed robbery (Bennett et al. 2008); however, this relationship lacks specificity in some studies. In other words, if the relationship between drug use and crime was causal, we would expect all offenders to use drugs, and all drug users to be offenders. Because this is not the case, the hypothetical door is open to new possibilities, albeit biological, biosocial, or behavioral, that explain the inconsistencies in the specificity of the relationship between drug use and crime.

Conclusion

Alcohol and illicit drug use, oftentimes in concert, are prevalent among Americans generally and criminal offenders specifically. The research documenting the relationship between alcohol, drug use, and criminal behavior is robust. However, new scientific methods are needed to expand our knowledge in this domain, as current methods have inherently limited our ability to establish causality. Further, only recently has progress been made in bridging disciplines to understand (with the goal of long-term prevention) the interplay of biologic impacts of drug use and addiction with social behavior. This biobehavioral interaction has great potential to inform future criminological theories; however, our understanding of these relationships is in its infancy. This ever-emerging field of biobehavioral research in epidemiological criminology is likely to have a long-term impact on how we conceptualize the relationship between drug use and crime, which for decades researchers concluded to be solely a behavioral phenomenon.

References

Abram, K.M. & Teplin, L.A. (1990). Drug disorder, mental illness, and violence. *NIDA Research Monograph*, *103*, 222–238.

Barry, C.L., McGinty, E.E., Pescosolido, B.A., & Goldman, H.H. (2014). Stigma, discrimination, treatment effectiveness, and policy: Public views about drug addiction and mental illness. *Psychiatric Services*, *65*(10), 1269–1272.

Beaver, K.M., Vaughn, M.G., DeLisi, M., & Higgins, G.E. (2009). The biosocial correlates of neuropsychological deficits: Results from the National Longitudinal. *International Journal of Offender Therapy and Comparative Criminology*, *54*(8), 878–894.

Becker, G.S. & Murphy, J.M. (1988). A theory of rational addiction. *The Journal of Political Economy*, *96*(4), 675–700.

Bennett, T., Holloway, K., & Farrington, D. (2008). The statistical association between drug misuse and crime: A meta-analysis. *Aggression and Violent Behavior*, *13*, 107–118.

Blumstein, A., & Cork, D. (1996). Linking gun availability to youth gun violence. *Law and Contemporary Problems*, *59*(1), 5–24.

Boys, A., Marsden, J., Fountain, J., Griffiths, P., Stillwell, G., & Strang, J. (1999). What influences young people's use of drugs? A qualitative study of decision-making. *Drugs: Education, prevention and policy*, *6*(3), 373–387.

Brady, S.S., Tschann, J.M., Pasch, L.A., Flores, E., & Ozer, E.J. (2008). Violence involvement, substance use, and sexual activity among Mexican-American and European-American adolescents. *Journal of Adolescent Health*, *43*(3), 285–295. doi:10.1016/j.jadohealth.2008.02.007.

Broidy, L.M., Daday, J.K., Crandall, C.S., Sklar, D.P., & Jost, P.F. (2006). Exploring demographic, structural, and behavioral overlap among homicide offenders and victims. *Homicide Studies*, *10*(3), 155–180.

Brownstein, H.H. (2015). *The handbook of drugs and society.* Oxford, UK: Wiley Blackwell.

Caetano, R., Schafer, J., & Cunradi, C.B. (2001). Alcohol-related intimate partner violence among white, black, and Hispanic couples in the United States. [11496968]. *Alcohol Research and Health, 25*(1), 58–65.

Center for Behavioral Health Statistics and Quality (2015). *Behavioral health trends in the United States: Results from the 2014 National Survey on Drug Use and Health.* Retrieved from Rockville, MD: Center for Behavioral Health Statistics and Quality. www.samhsa.gov/data/sites/default/files/NSDUH . . . 2014/NSDUH-FRR1-2014.pdf.

Chandler, R.K., Fletcher, B.W., & Volkow, N.D. (2009). Treating drug abuse and addiction in the criminal justice system: Improving public health and safety. *Journal of the American Medical Association, 301*(2), 183–190.

Chen, D. & Wu, L.T. (2016). Association between substance use and gun-related behaviors. *Epidemiologic Reviews, 38*(1), 46–61.

Compton, W.M., Thomas, Y.F., Stinson, F.S., & Grant, B.F. (2007). Prevalence, correlates, disability, and comorbidity of DSM-IV drug abuse and dependence in the United States. *Archives of General Psychiatry, 64*, 566–578.

Conseur, A., Rivara, F.P., & Emanuel, I. (1997). Juvenile delinquency and adolescent trauma: How strong is the connection?. *Pediatrics, 99*(3), E5.

Crews, F., He, J., & Hodge, C. (2007). Adolescent cortical development: A critical period of vulnerability for addiction. *Pharmacology Biochemistry and Behavior, 86*(2), 189–199.

D'Amico, E.J., Edelen, M.O., Miles, J.N.V., & Morral, A.R. (2008). The longitudinal association between substance use and delinquency among high risk youth. *Drug and Alcohol Dependence, 93*, 85–92.

Danaei, G., Ding, E.L., Mozaffarian, D., Taylor, B., Rehm, J., Murray, C.J.L., et al. (2009). The preventable causes of death in the United States: Comparative risk assessment of dietary, lifestyle, and metabolic risk factors. *PLoS Medicine, 6*(4), e1000058.

Dawson, D.A., Goldstein, R.B., Saha, T.D., & Grant, B.F. (2015). Changes in alcohol consumption: United States, 2001–2002 to 2012–2013. *Drug Alcohol Depend, 148*, 56–61. doi:10.1016/j.drugalcdep.2014.12.016.

Dembo, R., Williams, L., La Voie, L., Getreu, A., Berry, E., Genung, L., Kern, J. (1990). A longitudinal study of the relationships among alcohol use, marijuana/hashish use, cocaine use, and emotional/psychological functioning problems in a cohort of high-risk youths. *International Journal of the Addictions, 25*(11), 1341–1382.

Dobrin, A. (2001). The risk of offending on homicide victimization: A case control study. *Journal of Research in Crime and Delinquency, 38*(2), 154–173.

Donovan, J.E., Jessor, R., & Costa, F.M. (1991). Adolescent health behavior and conventionality-unconventionality: An extension of problem-behavior therapy. *Health Psychology, 10*(1), 52.

Durose, M.R., Cooper, A.D., & Snyder, H.N. (2014). *Recidivism of prisoners released in 30 states in 2005: Patterns from 2005 to 2010*. Retrieved from Washington, DC: Bureau of Justice Statistics. www.bjs.gov/content/pub/pdf/rprts05p0510.pdf.

Ellickson, P.L., Tucker, J.S., & Klein, D.J. (2003). Ten-year prospective study of public health problems associated with early drinking. *Pediatrics, 111*(5 Pt 1), 949–955.

Ernst, A.A., Weiss, S.J., Enright-Smith, S., Hilton, E., & Byrd, E.C. (2008). Perpetrators of intimate partner violence use significantly more methamphetamine, cocaine, and alcohol than victims: A report by victims. *The American Journal of Emergency Medicine, 26*(5), 592–596.

Fals-Stewart, W. (2003). The occurrence of partner physical aggression on days of alcohol consumption: A longitudinal diary study. *Journal of Consulting and Clinical Psychology, 71*(1), 41.

Ford, J.A. (2008). Nonmedical prescription drug use and delinquency: An analysis with a national sample. *Journal of Drug Issues, 38*(2), 493–516.

Fransen, M., Woodward, M., Norton, R., Coggan, C., Dawe, M., & Sheridan, N. (2002). Risk factors associated with the transition from acute to chronic occupational back pain. *Spine, 27*(1), 92–98.

Galoub, A., Brownstein, H., & Dunlap, E. (2012). Monitoring drug epidemics and the markets that sustain them using ADAM II: Final technical report. Retrieved 12 August 2016 from www.ncjrs.gov/pdffiles1/nij/grants/239906.pdf.

Goldstein, P.J. (1985). The drugs/violence nexus: A tripartite conceptual framework. *Journal of Drug Issues, 15*, 493–506.

Goldstein, P.J., & Brownstein, H. (1987). *Drug related crime analysis—homicide*. New York: Narcotic & Drug Research Incorporated.

Gropper, B.A. (1985). *Probing the links between drugs and crime*. Retrieved 12 August 2016 from Washington, DC: National Criminal Justice ReferenceService. www.ncjrs.gov/App/Publications/abstract.aspx?ID=96668.

Haggard-Grann, U., Hallqvist, J., Langstrom, N., & Moller, J. (2006). The role of alcohol and drugs in triggering criminal violence: A case-crossover study. *Addiction, 101*(1), 100–108. doi:10.1111/j.1360-0443.2005.01293.x.

Hawkins, J.D., Herrenkohl, T.I., Farrington, D.P., Brewer, D., Catalano, R.F., Harachi, T.W., & Cothern, L. (2000, April). Predictors of youth violence. *Juvenile Justice Bulletin.*

Hill, K.G., Howell, J.C., Hawkins, J.D., & Battin-Pearson, S.R. (1999). Childhood risk factors for adolescent gang membership: Results from the Seattle Social Development Project. *Journal of Research in Crime and Delinquency, 36,* 300–322.

Hubbard, R.L., Craddock, S.G., & Anderson, J. (2003). Overview of 5-year followup outcomes in the drug abuse treatment outcome studies (DATOS). *Journal of Substance Abuse Treatment, 25*(3), 125–134.

Huebner, B.M. & Cobbina, J. (2007). The effect of drug use, drug treatment participation, and treatment completion on probationer recidivism. *Journal of Drug Issues, 37*(3), 619–641.

Huizinga, D., Loeber, R., & Thornberry, T.P. (1995). *Recent findings from the program of research on the causes and correlates of delinquency.* Retrieved from the Office of Juvenile Justice and Delinquency Prevention, U.S. Department of Justice, Washington, DC. www.ncjrs.gov/pdffiles1/Digitization/159042NCJRS.pdf.

Ito, T.A., Miller, N., & Pollock, V.E. (1996). Alcohol and aggression: A meta-analysis on the moderating effects of inhibitory cues, triggering events, and self-focused attention. *Psychological Bulletin, 120*(1), 60.

James, D.J., & Glaze, L.E. (2006). *Mental health problems of prison and jail inmates.* Washington, DC: US Department of Justice, Office of Justice Programs, Bureau of Justice Statistics.

Jennings, W.G., Piquero, A.R., & Reingle, J.M. (2012). On the overlap between victimization and offending: A review of the literature. *Aggression and Violent Behavior, 17*(1), 16–26. doi:10.1016/j.avb.2011.09.003.

Johnston, L.D., O'Malley, P.M., & Eveland, L.K. (1978). *Drugs and delinquency: A search for causal connections.* Chapel Hill: Hemisphere.

Kalivas, P.W. & Volkow, N.D. (2005). The neural basis of addiction: A pathology of motivation and choice. *American Journal of Psychiatry, 162*(8), 1403–1413.

Karberg, J.C. & James, D.J. (2005). *Substance dependence, abuse, and treatment of jail inmates, 2002.* Washington, DC: US Department of Justice, Office of Justice Programs, Bureau of Justice Statistics.

Keast, S.L., Nesser, N., & Farmer, K. (2015). Strategies aimed at controlling misuse and abuse of opioid prescription medications in a state Medicaid program: A policymaker's perspective. *The American Journal of Drug and Alcohol Abuse, 41,* 1–6.

Kownacki, R.J. & Shadish, W.R. (1999). Does Alcoholics Anonymous work? The results from a meta-analysis of controlled experiments. *Substance Use and Misuse, 34*(13), 1897–1916.

Krug, E.G., Mercy, J.A., Dahlberg, L.L., & Zwi, A.B. (2002). A world report on violence and health. *Lancet, 360,* 1083–1088.

Langan, P.A. & Levin, D.J. (2002). *Recidivism of prisoners released in 1994.* Retrieved from Washington, DC: Bureau of Justice Statistics. www.bjs.gov/content/pub/pdf/rpr94.pdf.

Lipsky, S., Caetano, R., Field, C.A., & Larkin, G.L. (2005). Psychosocial and substance-use risk factors for intimate partner violence. *Drug and Alcohol Dependence, 78*(1), 39–47.

MacCoun, R., Kilmer, B., & Reuter, P. (2003). Research on drugs-crime linkages: The next generation. *Toward a drugs and crime research agenda for the 21st century.* Washington, DC: U.S. Department of Justice, Office of Justice Programs, 65–95.

Maldonado-Molina, M.M., Reingle, J.M., & Jennings, W.G. (2010). Does alcohol use predict violent behaviors? The relationship between alcohol use and violence in a nationally representative longitudinal sample. *Youth Violence and Juvenile Justice, 9*(2), 99–111. doi:10.1177/1541204010384492.

Maynard, B.R., Salas-Wright, C.P., Vaughn, M.G., & Peters, K.E. (2012). Who are truant youth? Examining distinctive profiles of truant youth using latent profile analysis. *Journal of Youth and Adolescence, 41*(12), 1671–1684.

McCabe, S.E., Cranford, J.A., & West, B.T. (2008). Trends in prescription drug abuse and dependence, co-occurrence with other substance use disorders, and the treatment utilization: Results from two national surveys. *Addictive Behaviors, 33,* 1297–1305.

McKellar, J., Stewart, E., & Humphreys, K. (2003). Alcoholics Anonymous involvement and positive alcohol-related outcomes: Cause, consequence, or just a correlate? A prospective 2-year study of 2,319 alcohol-dependent men. *Journal of Consulting and Clinical Psychology, 71*(2), 302–308.

Moffitt, T.E. (1993). Adolescence-limited and life-course-persistent antisocial behavior: A developmental taxonomy. *Psychological Review, 100*(4), 674–701.

Moore, T.M., Stuart, G.L., Meehan, J.C., Rhatigan, D.L., Helmuth, J.C., & Keen, S.M. (2008). Drug abuse and aggression between intimate partners: A meta-analytic review. *Clinical Psychology Review, 28,* 247–274.

Morgenstern, J., Labouvie, E., McCrady, B.S., Kahler, C.W., & Frey, R.M. (1997). Affiliation with Alcoholics Anonymous after treatment: A study of its therapeutic effects and mechanisms of action. *Journal of Consulting and Clinical Psychology*, *65*(5), 768–777.

Mumola, C.J. & Karberg, J.C. (2006). *Drug use and dependence, state and federal prisoners, 2004*. Washington, DC: US Department of Justice, Office of Justice Programs, Bureau of Justice Statistics.

National Institute on Drug Abuse. (2014). The science of drug abuse and addiction: The basics. National Institute on Drug Abuse. Retrieved 12 August 2016 from www.drugabuse.gov/publications/media-guide/science-drug-abuse-addiction-basics.

Office of National Drug Control Policy. (2014). *2014 Annual Report, Arrestee Drug Abuse Monitoring Program II*. Retrieved 12 August 2016 from Washington, DC: Office of National Drug Control Policy. www.white house.gov/sites/default/files/ondcp/policy-and-research/adam_ii_2013_annual_report.pdf.

Pihl, R.O., Peterson, J.B., & Lau, M.A. (1993). A biosocial model of the alcohol–aggression relationship. *Journal of Studies on Alcohol*, *11*, 128–139.

Rehm, J., Taylor, B., & Room, R. (2006). Global burden of disease from alcohol, illicit drugs and tobacco. *Drug and Alcohol Review*, *25*, 503–513.

Reingle, J.M., Jennings, W.G., Connell, N.M., Businelle, M.S., & Chartier, K. (2014). On the pervasiveness of event-specific alcohol use, general substance use, and mental health problems as risk factors for intimate partner violence. *Journal of Interpersonal Violence*, *29*(16), 2951–2970.

Reingle, J.M. & Maldonado-Molina, M.M. (2012). Victimization and violent offending: An assessment of the victim–offender overlap among Native American adolescents and young adults. *International Criminal Justice Review*, *22*(2), 123–138. doi:10.1177/1057567712443966.

Reingle, J.M., Staras, S.A., Jennings, W.G., Branchini, J., & Maldonado-Molina, M.M. (2012). The relationship between marijuana use and intimate partner violence in a nationally representative, longitudinal sample. *Journal of Interpersonal Violence*, *27*(8), 1562–1578. doi:10.1177/0886260511425787.

Resnick, M.D., Ireland, M., & Borowsky, I. (2004). Youth violence perpetration: What protects? What predicts? Findings from the National Longitudinal Study of Adolescent Health. *Journal of Adolescent Health*, *35*(5), 424.e421-410. doi:10.1016/j.jadohealth.2004.01.011.

Richardson, A., & Budd, T. (2003). *Alcohol, crime and disorder: A study of young adults*. London: Home Office. Research, Development and Statistics Directorate.

SAMHSA. (2004). Appendix C: DSM-IV TR material: Criteria for substance dependence. Retrieved 12 August 2016 from www.ncbi.nlm.nih.gov/books/NBK64247/.

Schaffer, C. (June 4, 2015). Baltimore police commissioner: Drugs stolen during riots fueling increase in violent crime. Retrieved 12 August 2016 from www.abc2news.com/news/crime-checker/baltimore-city-crime/baltimore-police-commissioner-drugs-stolen-during-riots-fueling-increase-in-violent-crime.

Smith, P.H., Homish, G.G., Leonard, K.E., & Cornelius, J.R. (2012). Intimate partner violence and specific substance use disorders: Findings from the National Epidemiologic Survey on Alcohol and Related Conditions. *Psychology of Addictive Behaviors, 26*(2), 236–245. doi:10.1037/a0024855.

Substance Abuse and Mental Health Services Administration [SAMHSA]. (2012). *Results from the 2011 National Survey on Drug Use and Health: Summary of National Findings.* (NSDUH Series H-44, HHS Publication No. (SMA) 12-4713). Rockville, MD: US Department of Health and Human Services. Retrieved 12 August 2016 from www.samhsa.gov/data/NSDUH/2k11Results/NSDUHresults2011.htm.

Swanson, J.W., Holzer, C.E., 3rd, Ganju, V.K., & Jono, R.T. (1990). Violence and psychiatric disorder in the community: Evidence from the Epidemiologic Catchment Area Surveys. *Hospital and Community Psychiatry, 41*(7), 761–770.

Swartz, M.S., Swanson, J.W., Hiday, V.A., Borum, R., Wagner, H.R., & Burns, B.J. (1998). Violence and severe mental illness: The effects of substance abuse and nonadherence to medication. *American Journal of Psychiatry, 155*(2), 226–231. doi:10.1176/ajp.155.2.226.

Taxman, F. & Spinner, D. (1997). *Jail Addiction Services (JAS) Demonstration project in Montgomery County, MD.* Jail and community-based substance abuse treatment program model. University of Maryland, Tech. Rep.

Taxman, F.S. (1998). *Reducing recidivism through a seamless system of care: Components of effective treatment, supervision, and transition services in the community.* Washington, DC: Bureau of Governmental Research.

Thombs, D.L., O'Mara, R., Dodd, V.J., Merves, M.L., Weiler, R.M., Goldberger, B.A., et al. (2009). Event-specific analyses of poly-drug abuse and concomitant risk behavior in a college bar district in Florida. *Journal of American College Health, 57*(6), 575–586.

Tonigan, J.S., Toscova, R., & Miller, W.R. (1996). Meta-analysis of the literature on Alcoholics Anonymous: Sample and study characteristics moderate findings. *Journal of Studies on Alcohol & Drugs, 57*(1), 65–72.

US Department of Justice, F.B.o.I. (2015). Crime in the United States, 2014. Retrieved 12 August 2016 from Washington, DC: US Department of Justice, F.B.o.I. www.fbi.gov/about-us/cjis/ucr/crime-in-the-u.s/2014/crime-in-the-u.s.-2014/persons-arrested/main.

Vaughn, M.G., Beaver, K.M., & DeLisi, M. (2009). A general biosocial paradigm of antisocial behavior: A preliminary test in a sample of adolescents. *Youth Violence and Juvenile Justice, 7*(4), 279–298.

Vaughn, M.G., DeLisi, M., Gunter, T., Fu, Q., Beaver, K.M., Perron, B.E., et al. (2011). The severe 5 %: A latent class analysis of the externalizing spectrum in the United States. *Journal of Criminal Justice, 39*, 75–80.

Vaughn, M.G., Fu, Q., Delisi, M., Beaver, K.M., Perron, B.E., & Howard, M.O. (2010). Criminal victimization and comorbid substance use and psychiatric disorders in the United States: Results from the NESARC. *Annals of Epidemiology, 20*(4), 281–288. doi: http://dx.doi.org/10.1016/j.annepidem.2009.11.011.

Vaughn, M.G., Nelson, E.J., Salas-Wright, C.P., Qian, Z., & Schootman, M. (2016). Racial and ethnic trends and correlates of non-medical use of prescription opioids among adolescents in the United States 2004–2013. Journal of *Psychiatric Research, 73*, 17–24.

Volkow, N.D. & Li, T.K. (2004). Drug addiction: The neurobiology of behaviour gone awry. *Nature Reviews Neuroscience, 5*(12), 963–970.

Volkow, N.D., Wang, G.J., Tomasi, D., & Baler, R.D. (2013). Obesity and addiction: Neurobiological overlaps. *Obesity Reviews, 14*(1), 2–18.

Wassenberg, K. (2007). *Deutsches Archiv für Temperenz- und Abstinenz Literatur*. Retrieved 12 August 2016 from www.sgw.hs-magdeburg.de.

White, H.R., Brick, J., & Hansell, S. (1993). A longitudinal investigation of alcohol use and aggression in adolescence. *Journal of Studies on Alcohol. Supplement, 11*, 62–77.

White, H.R. & Gorman, D.M. (2000). Dynamics of the drug–crime relationship. *Criminal Justice, 1*(15), 1–218.

White, H.R. & Hansell, S. (1996). The moderating effects of gender and hostility on the alcohol–aggression relationship. *Journal of Research in Crime and Delinquency, 33*(4), 450–470.

White, H.R., Loeber, R., & Farrington, D.P. (2008). Substance use, drug dealing, gang membership, and the gun carrying and their predictive associations with serious violence and serious theft. In R. Loeber, D. P. Farrington, M. Stouthamer-Loeber, & H. R. White (Eds.), *Violence and serious theft: Development and prediction from childhood to adulthood* (137–166). New York: Routledge.

White, H.R., Loeber, R., Stouthamer-Loeber, M., & Farrington, D.P. (1999). Developmental associations between substance use and violence. *Development and Psychopathology, 11*(4), 785–803.

White, H.R., Tice, P., Loeber, R., & Stouthamer-Loeber, M. (2002). Illegal acts committed by adolescents under the influence of alcohol and drugs. *Journal of Research in Crime and Delinquency, 39*, 131–152.

Windle, M. (1990). A longitudinal study of antisocial behaviors in early adolescence as predictors of late adolescent substance use: Gender and ethnic group differences. *Journal of Abnormal Psychology, 99*(1), 86.

Xue, Y., Zimmerman, M.A., & Cunningham, R. (2009). Relationship between alcohol use and violent behavior among urban African American youths from adolescence to emerging adulthood: A longitudinal study. *American Journal of Public Health, 99*(11), 2041–2048. doi:10.2105/ajph.2008.147827.

Yacoubian, G.S., Urbach, B.J., Larsen, K.L., Johnson, R.J., & Peters, R.J. (2001). A comparison of drug use between prostitutes and other female arrestees. *Journal of Alcohol and Drug Education, 46*(2), 12–26.

Zhang, L., Wieczorek, W.F., & Welte, J.W. (1997). The impact of age of onset of substance use on delinquency. *Journal of Research in Crime and Delinquency, 34*(2), 253–268.

2

Prevailing Conceptions of Drug Abuse and Addiction

Introduction

Recent decades have witnessed tremendous change in the ways that we think about drug abuse and addiction. Rigorous scientific research has helped us to appreciate drug abuse and addiction as complex and multifaceted phenomena that influence—and are influenced by—our biology, psychological makeup, cultural factors, and the social and political environments that we inhabit. In subsequent chapters, we will consider the ways in which cutting-edge, biosocial research can help us to make sense of both drug abuse and antisocial behavior. However, in this chapter we will focus only on drug abuse and addiction, laying out the prevailing conceptual frameworks that have emerged as researchers have become increasingly sophisticated in understanding the nature of drug use initiation, drug abuse and dependence, and recovery. We will pay particular attention to the ways in which the addictions research and theory have evolved to quite naturally integrate the insights from biological research (most notably, neurobiology and genetics) with psychological, behavioral, and social science research to arrive at a highly promising, transdisciplinary understanding of drug abuse and addiction.

© The Author(s) 2016
C.P. Salas-Wright et al., *Drug Abuse and Antisocial Behavior*,
Palgrave's Frontiers in Criminology Theory,
DOI 10.1057/978-1-137-55817-6_2

Prevailing Conceptualizations

There is no shortage of theories aimed at making sense of drug abuse and addiction. Robert West's (2001) often-cited editorial in the leading journal, *Addiction*, entitled "Theories of Addiction" references literally dozens and dozens of theories. Some aim to provide insight into the nature and processes of addiction; others delineate the effects of addictive stimuli, individual susceptibility, and environmental factors; and still others focus on the nature of recovery and relapse. Since 2001, we have seen even more articles, chapters, and books written to try to describe and explain the ways in which alcohol and drug abuse can powerfully take over our lives (West and Brown 2013). This is all to say that we have no illusions about exhaustively summarizing in a single chapter all that has been written on the theories of drug abuse and addiction. However, we can lay the foundation for the two most important ways of understanding drug abuse and addiction; namely, we will briefly delve into the *moral model of addiction* and provide a detailed overview of the *brain disease model of addiction*, as well as present two frameworks that nicely complement the understanding of addiction as a socially and environmentally contextualized brain disorder.

The Moral Model of Addiction

Historically, there have been numerous movements designed to stamp out immoral behavior; the temperance movement is perhaps chief among these. One of the primary objectives of these initiatives was to characterize alcoholism as a moral failure and act upon this belief. Conventional wisdom has long been rooted in the belief that drug abuse and addiction are fundamentally moral issues. Predicated on the fact that *trying* alcohol and other drugs is typically a voluntary behavior,[1]

---

[1] The understanding of drug use initiation as a voluntary behavior is arguably more complex than at first glance. In subsequent chapters we will discuss the ways that biological and psychosocial factors profoundly influence the likelihood that young people will have access to drugs and, when presented with the opportunity, will elect to try them. While it is accurate to view drug use

proponents of the moral model of addiction conclude that *continued use* is best understood to be deliberate as well (Schaler 2000). That is, individuals who regularly use substances—particularly those who do so despite experiencing substance-related physical, interpersonal, or occupational problems—are seen as fully choosing to do so and as fundamentally unwilling to make good decisions, consider consequences, and put their lives in order. Within this framework, substance abuse is best understood a willful behavior and the term "addiction" simply serves to describe the comportment of individuals who consistently elect to use alcohol and other drugs and lack the strength of character to suspend use when it becomes problematic (Pescosolido et al. 2010). Simply put, the moral model posits that addiction is not a health or a medical issue, but rather drug use is always a free choice and thereby rooted firmly in the domains of character and ethical decision-making.

There is a certain appeal of the clarity and simplicity of the moral model. It is neat and tidy and makes for straightforward categorizations and interpretations. If addiction is best understood as a failure of the will and a function of poor decision-making, then recovery becomes about simply changing one's mind and making good decisions. Taken at face value, such thinking aligns nicely with Western ideals of self-reliance, steadfastness, and determination. Moral-model advocates offer a clear message: the solution is in your hands—if you have a problem with alcohol or other drugs, grab a hold of yourself and make the decision to find other ways to spend your time. To be sure, this sort of mindset seems to undergird the powerful experiences of a substantial number of people who have managed to curb or eliminate the consumption of alcohol and other drugs (Lewis 2013). Moreover, the moral model ostensibly coheres with evidence from epidemiological studies suggesting that a substantial proportion of people who experience alcohol or drug

---

initiation as a voluntary behavior, the likelihood of being exposed to drugs and, in turn, *choosing* to try alcohol and other drugs is by no means the same for all people. That is, it can be argued that drug use initiation is more voluntary for some than for others.

use problems are able at some point in their lives to discontinue use, often without any professional or medical assistance (Heyman 2013; Lopez-Quintero et al. 2011; Sobell 2007).

To be clear, while the moral model of addiction undoubtedly persists in the public imagination, this framework is—at best—a straw man within the realm of academic research on drug abuse and addiction. Although there are certainly a few voices that continue to highlight the virtues of the moral model, the overwhelming majority of scholars agree that this framework falls short in the face of an expansive body of clinical, epidemiological, and neurobiological research. Indeed, scholarly critics of the brain disease model of addiction are invariably careful to note that a critique of the disease model is by no means an endorsement of the simplistic logic of the moral model of addiction (see Hall et al. 2015; Hammer et al. 2013). This does not mean that most scholars embrace a deterministic view of addiction or consider motivation, choice, decision-making, and self-control to be unimportant. On the contrary, these constructs are vital to a full understanding of addiction and recovery,[2] but they cannot be understood independent of our emerging understanding of neurobiology, social ecology, and public health. Finally, there is also concern that a rigidly moral framing of addiction can lead to serious issues in terms of the stigmatization of addiction and the marginalization of persons struggling with alcohol and drug abuse (Barry et al. 2014). Indeed, if addiction is primarily rooted in an unwillingness to make good decisions and recovery is ultimately about an individual's character and moral fiber, then it makes perfect sense to lay a hefty dose of judgment on those who persist in the use of alcohol and other drugs despite negative consequences.

---

[2] Substantial research has examined these constructs in a very sophisticated and nuanced fashion. For instance, the transtheoretical model of behavior change has examined drug abuse and recovery and is dedicated entirely to understanding the complexities of motivation, willingness to change, and maintaining behavior change (DiClemente & Prochaska, 1998). Similarly, relapse prevention and other cognitive behavioral approaches to recovery are focused in large measure on the science of decision-making in the face of the biosocial challenges that addiction and recovery present (Marlatt & Donovan, 2005). Finally, the neurocognitive complexities of self-control have been studied in depth and will be examined repeatedly throughout this and other chapters.

The Brain Disease Model of Addiction

Building upon several decades of scientific research, the brain disease model of addiction comes at the issue of drug abuse from a different position altogether. Rather than situate drug abuse and addiction within the charged logic of moral behavior, the brain disease model conceptualizes compulsive drug-seeking and use within the more dispassionate language of health, illness, and recovery. Addiction is not viewed as an issue of moral decision-making or character, but rather it is framed as a complex medical condition influenced—just like other serious conditions such as heart disease, diabetes, chronic pain, and lung cancer—by biological, behavioral, and psychosocial factors. Notably, the brain disease model is not simply an alternative to the moral model; it has emerged as the predominant framework in addiction science and is increasingly coming into view as a powerful construct in popular culture.

Evidence of the brain disease's ascendancy is all around us. In terms of science, it is fair to say that the brain disease model of addiction is *the* predominant model promoted by the extraordinarily influential National Institute on Drug Abuse (NIDA) as well as the National Institute on Alcohol Abuse and Alcoholism (NIAAA). In fact, if you go online to look at NIDA's "Drug Facts" page dedicated to "Understanding Drug Abuse and Addiction," you will find brain disease language front and center:

> It is often mistakenly assumed that drug abusers lack moral principles or willpower and that they could stop using drugs simply by choosing to change their behavior. In reality, *drug addiction is a complex disease* [emphasis added], and quitting takes more than good intentions or a strong will. In fact, because *drugs change the brain in ways that foster compulsive drug abuse* [emphasis added], quitting is difficult, even for those who are ready to do so. (NIDA, 2016)

Beyond the academy, a Google search for the complete phrase "Addiction is a disease" yields more than 300,000 results while searching for "addiction AND disease" generates 115 million results. At present, the White House's webpage on *Drug Policy for the 21st Century* features the word "disease" five times on its front page, including references to the similarities between addiction and other chronic diseases such as diabetes, asthma, and hypertension. Simply put, the brain disease model of addiction has made a massive impact on how researchers and the public think and talk about drug abuse.

But what exactly do we mean by the disease model of addiction? This phrasing is now so widely used that often times its original—and quite specific—meaning can be lost. Perhaps the clearest articulation of the brain disease model of addiction is that of the former director of the NIDA, Alan Leshner, published in the leading journal *Science*, entitled: "Addiction Is a Brain Disease, and It Matters." In the article—which has been cited nearly 1200 times according to Google Scholar—Leshner lays out several principles that have come to encapsulate the prevailing understanding of addiction within the brain disease framework. Leshner's principles provide an ideal template for understanding the disease model of addiction and serve as a springboard for other theorizing that has been built upon and alongside the brain disease model. Let's take an in-depth look at what Leshner and other influential voices have to say.

Addiction is a Brain Disease

Leshner's first principle is that "Addiction is a Brain Disease." While perhaps straightforward, this principle is critical inasmuch as it makes the unequivocal claim that the disease understanding of addiction is to be situated primarily *within the brain*. Given that we focus an entire chapter on the neuroscience of addiction and antisocial behavior (see Chap. 4, "Neurobiological Contributions"), we will not go into too much detail as to the neurological underpinnings of addiction. However, here we'll make three overarching points that underscore the central importance of the brain in terms of a disease model of addiction.

First, it has now been demonstrated quite clearly that an essential characteristic of all drugs of abuse is that they powerfully turn on parts of our brain associated with enjoyment and behaviors we would like to repeat (Koob and Simon 2009). The activation of this "reward pathway" of the brain is a critical component of what makes drugs of abuse appealing and is one of the primary reasons why people often want to use drugs again and again. Second, not only do drugs of abuse *stimulate* the brain in important ways, but the repeated use of alcohol and other drugs can lead to a "hijacking" of the neural systems related to reward (Heyman 2013; Volkow and Li 2005). That is, the repeated use of psychoactive substances can lead our brains to prioritize drug use over other essential or "natural" rewards such as hunger, thirst, or sex. It is in this way that NIDA Director Nora Volkow has come to reference the fundamental nature of addiction as a brain disease that, in effect, interferes with our capacity to exercise free will (Volkow 2015). Finally, the chronic use of a variety of drugs of abuse has been shown to actually impact brain structure in important ways (Goldstein and Volkow 2011; Koob and Simon 2009). Specifically, neuroimaging research has now demonstrated that regular substance abuse can lead to damage in the regions of the brain crucial to self-control and decision-making. As a result, it becomes part of a vicious cycle: drugs change the brain and, in turn, such changes can weaken a person's capacity to resist and control powerful impulses to use alcohol and other drugs and so use continues and continues (Volkow 2015).

We will circle back to these points in far greater detail later in Chap. 4 ("Neurobiological Contributions"), but the takeaway here should be clear: the chronic use of alcohol and other drugs of abuse impacts the brain in profound ways. In this way, addiction is a phenomenon that we can understand as residing primarily—but certainly not exclusively—in the brain. This is what we mean when we speak of addiction as a brain disease. The brain is where much of the action is and the brain is where critical components of addiction play out. The scientific evidence around this point is quite compelling. In the same breath, however, we should note that there is nothing simple about the neuroscience of addiction. The brain is extraordinarily complex and addiction is a multi-faceted phenomenon. Situating our understanding of addiction within the framework of the brain has proved to advance our understanding immeasurably. It is reasonable to think that the technical tools that allow us to study addiction and the brain may lead to the development of powerful biosocial treatments for drug abuse and addiction. And yet, to borrow a recent quote from a commentary by Nora Volkow and NIAAA Director George Koob (2015), "Addiction is a complex disease of a complex brain" (p. 678). That is to say, there is much that we now know about addiction as a brain disease, but there remains much for us to continue to learn well on into the future. Both optimism and a degree of caution are warranted.

Addiction is a Chronic, Relapsing Brain Disorder

Addiction is not only a brain disease, but it is a brain disease that tends to manifest as a chronic, relapsing condition that requires treatment approaches consistent with other chronic conditions such as diabetes, hypertension, and asthma. What is the case for conceptualizing addiction as a chronic, relapsing disorder? First, drug abuse and addiction are typically not conditions that immediately go away with treatment. In fact, it is relatively uncommon for people—particularly those with a severe addiction—who seek treatment for a substance use disorder to achieve a lasting recovery after only a single treatment episode (Friedmann 2013). Evidence from state-of-the-art treatment studies consistently indicates that a minority of people seeking first-time treatment for alcohol or other drug-use disorders ceases use and remains completely abstinent for a sustained period of time (Cacciola et al. 2005; Flynn et al. 2003; Miller et al. 2001; Simpson and Sells 1990). The second point builds upon the first: Individuals who seek out addictions treatment and are able to achieve a period of abstinence are, regretfully, at substantial risk for relapse.[3] In fact, as pointed out by Thomas McLellan—former Deputy Director of the White House Office of National Drug Control Policy—in a highly

---

[3] The use of alcohol and other drugs at some point after drug abuse treatment is such the norm that influential voices in addiction treatment research have even called for "retiring" the construct of relapse altogether (Miller, 2015). The argument here is that, in conceptualizing recovery as the absolute maintenance of abstinence and viewing relapse as a critical violation of recovery, we are missing something very important about the nature of addiction and recovery. That is, the prevailing understanding of relapse is viewed as running contrary to the chronic disease understanding of addiction. As we will argue below, recovery may be better viewed as a long-term pattern of treatment adherence, even if that includes an occasional "relapse".

influential commentary, only 40–60 % of individuals who complete drug-abuse treatment remain abstinent one year after discharge (McLellan et al. 2000). Interestingly enough, this is roughly equivalent to the proportion of adults who experience relapse with other chronic health conditions such as diabetes (30–50 %), hypertension (50–70 %), and asthma (50–70 %).

The framing of addiction as a chronic, relapsing disorder might seem a bit discouraging. And, indeed, this conceptualization has recently faced a number of compelling critiques, in part, on the grounds of being viewed as unnecessarily pessimistic (Hall et al. 2015; Flynn and Brown 2015). However, our take is that the chronic disease conceptualization, although certainly not imperfect in its design, provides a valuable template that matches up with epidemiological data and offers a number of very important and positive implications. For one, framing addiction as a chronic—rather than acute—disorder informs the nature of drug-abuse and addictions treatment. The treatment of chronic disorders calls for not only short-term and intensive interventions (such as detoxification and inpatient treatment) but also the provision of ongoing services such as therapeutic case management, regular attendance of a support group or group therapy sessions, regular appointments with a healthcare provider or psychiatrist to discuss medication adherence, and booster sessions designed to provide follow-up to the initial inpatient rehabilitation interventions. In the words of Dackis and O'Brien (2005), "Treatment for this chronic disorder is labor-intensive, requiring a comprehensive assessment by qualified practitioners, as well as ongoing individual, group and family interventions" (p. 1436). Risk of relapse is an issue in the treatment of addiction, but approaching the treatment of addiction from a chronic-disease perspective leads to outcomes that are far superior to short-term, one-time approaches that frame addiction is an acute condition (McLellan et al. 2005).

Additionally, the *assessment* of successful treatment outcomes for a chronic condition is markedly distinct from that of an acute condition. The way in which success is measured for the treatment of a first-degree burn or food poisoning is categorically distinct from the ways in which a physician would measure success in the treatment of chronic conditions like diabetes or asthma. Namely, success is defined not by a complete and irrevocable reduction in symptoms, but rather by sustained treatment adherence and the reduction of symptoms associated with the condition. Framing addictions treatment within the logic of chronic-disease management has the power to transform the way that relapse is to be viewed by individuals in recovery and by treatment professionals (Miller 2015). Rather than conceptualizing a single episode of relapse as a failure, the chronic-disease-management model emphasizes the importance of taking a broader view of recovery. For instance, a relapse episode can be used as "grist for the mill" that can foster learning about the components of addiction (e.g., triggers, craving, etc.) that can present challenges to long-term recovery. Along the same lines, success is not limited to cases in which individuals achieve a sustained and unwavering period of abstinence, but rather it also includes the experiences of individuals who occasionally experience relapse as part of a long-term pattern of recovery and treatment adherence.

In much the same way, the chronic-disease model of addiction has important implications for stigma. Stigma, the mark of shame and discredit associated with addiction, serves to impede those who need help from seeking professional assistance, undermines the long-term efforts to manage and prevent relapse, and even has the potential to get in the way of good health policy related to the treatment of alcohol and drug abuse. Fundamentally, the chronic-disease conceptualization not only matches up with epidemiological and clinical data, but it offers a framework that can short-circuit stigma and, in doing so, foster help seeking and desirable treatment outcomes.

One final implication of the chronic brain disease model is that it points to the importance of alcohol and drug abuse prevention. Recognizing addiction as a chronic, relapsing brain disease is vital for the treatment and assessment of alcohol and drug use disorders, as well as for reducing stigma. However, the fact that drug abuse and addiction are less akin to acute conditions than they are to chronic conditions also means that treatment is often challenging, intensive, and requires a long-term treatment strategy (Dackis and O'Brien 2005). As such, while substantial time and money has been dedicated to developing evidence-based drug-abuse treatment protocols, scientists and health professionals have become increasingly interested in learning how to effectively prevent young people from initiating substance use and circumvent the development of addiction among those who have begun to misuse alcohol and other drugs (Hawkins et al. 1992). Earlier we discussed the Obama administration's use of the language of "disease" on the White House webpage on *Drug Policy for the 21st Century*. If we go back to that webpage, we see clear evidence that the Executive Branch of the United States federal government draws a clear connection between the disease conceptualization and the vital importance of prevention. In particular, we see statements regarding the importance of "emphasizing prevention over incarceration" and "training health-care professionals to intervene early before addiction develops." In a word, the chronic disease framework underscores the importance of preventing addiction before it starts.[4]

Addiction is a Brain Disease with Context

Most of the time, our brains are not floating in jars. Uri Bronfenbrenner and a host of ecological-systems theorists might note that our brains—drug addicted or not—are invariably situated within our bodies which, in turn, are typically situated within families and within social networks that are influenced by the conditions of the neighborhoods we reside in, the schools where we learn, and the environments where we work and spend our days. So far, we have highlighted the importance of paying attention to the ways in which addiction is a disease that in large part plays out in the brain. However, just as a failure to appreciate the importance of the neurological aspects of addiction profoundly limits our understanding, so too are we hamstrung if we fail to capture the ways in which addiction is also a disease that resides within a context that stretches far beyond the brain and the body.

Our research—and that of countless other scholars—has helped to highlight the ways in which a variety of social and environmental factors influence risk for alcohol and drug use and the development of

---

[4] Here we aim to simply highlight the connection between the disease conceptualization and the importance of prevention. However, we circle back to the importance of this insight in far greater detail in our discussion of "Prevention and Treatment" later on in the text (see Chap. 8).

substance-use disorders. For instance, we have looked at the ways in which exposure to stressful experiences like child abuse and parental suicidal behavior profoundly increases the likelihood of struggling with an alcohol or drug use disorder later on in life (O'Brien et al. 2015; Vaughn et al. 2015b). Similarly, we have looked at the ways in which school-related factors such as motivation and connectedness with teachers, truancy and dropout, and even homeschool status shed light on our understanding of drug abuse during adolescence and beyond (Maynard et al. 2015; Reingle Gonzalez et al. 2016; Salas-Wright et al. 2015d; Vaughn et al. 2013, 2015a). We have studied refugees and immigrants across multiple generations to understand how factors like place of birth, culture, and acculturation impact drug use and drug addiction (Salas-Wright et al. 2014, 2015a, b; Salas-Wright and Vaughn 2014). The list goes on and on as we have observed the manifold ways that social factors of all sorts help us make sense of who is and isn't at heightened risk of addiction. Beyond the specifics, the takeaway here is that, while neurobiology is indispensable to a state-of-the-art understanding of addiction, there is simply no getting around the fact that drug abuse and addiction are phenomena that are also profoundly social in nature.

Above we mentioned that some thinkers would likely suggest we situate our understanding of addicted brains within a broader social context. We should note that such thinking is not unique to ecological-systems theorists, but rather is an assertion that is also made by the leading proponents of the brain disease model of addiction. Leshner (1997) notes quite clearly in his seminal piece on addiction as a brain disease that "Addiction is not just a brain disease. It is a brain disease for which the social contexts in which it has both developed and is expressed are critically important" (p. 46). Similarly, McLellan et al. (2000), in their original article casting addiction as a chronic medical illness, unequivocally underscore the critical importance of factors such as socioeconomic status and social supports in the successful treatment of addiction and other chronic illnesses. Along the same lines, even a cursory review of the neurobiological model proposed by Volkow and Baler (2014) points to the foundational impact of factors in the economic, social, and built environment in influencing risk for drug use disorders. Simply, since its inception, leading theorists have continually recognized that the genetic and neurobiological understanding of addiction must be situated within a social, economic, and environmental context. In the words of Carter and Hall (2012),

> A major challenge for addiction policy and ethics will be finding ways to educate the public about the neurobiological basis of addiction in ways that recognize that drug use and addiction involves changes in the brain, but can still nevertheless be affected by individual and social choices, and the social environment (p. 249).

Ecological Systems and Biological Integration

While situating drug abuse and addiction within a broader context is by no means unique to ecological-systems theory, ecosystems theorists undoubtedly have made an important contribution. Ecodevelopmental theory, in particular, has helped to provide an increasingly sophisticated understanding of the ways in which multiple levels of intrapersonal (including neurobiological factors), interpersonal, and broader social and ecological factors influence the etiology, prevention, and treatment of addictions (Szapocznik and Coatsworth 1999; Szapocznik et al. 2007). Although much has been written about the ways in which ecological-systems theory contributes to an understanding of addictions, for the purposes of this chapter, we will simply highlight three overarching conceptual contributions that are of particular salience.

First, ecological-systems theory provides a useful heuristic model for understanding the ways in which individuals (and their brains!) are situated within social environments that are, in the words of Bronfenbrenner (1994), nested within one another "like a set of Russian dolls" (p. 39). Bronfenbrenner and others describe the ways in which individuals are rooted within *microsystems* (such as families, schools, peer groups, neighborhoods) that, taken as a constellation of interconnected systems of influence, can be understood as *mesosystems*. Microsystems can contribute positively or negatively to the well-being of individuals in the sense that, for example, a person's peer group can be primarily prosocial and adaptive or can tend to go the other way. Our own research with high-risk youth has highlighted the importance of peer microsystems as a robust predictor drug abuse and other health-risk behaviors during adolescence and young adulthood (Salas-Wright et al. 2013a, b). With respect to mesosystems, ecosystems theory is concerned with both the strength of the connection between microsystems and the degree to which such systems complement one another (Szapocznik and Coatsworth 1999). For instance, a school-neighborhood mesosystem in which both school administrators and community leaders are committed to drug-abuse prevention and work actively together to this end is more likely to lead to positive outcomes than a more fragmented mesosystem.

The ecological system extends beyond the level of microsystem and mesosystem. Namely, mesosystems are situated within progressively more distal systems—*exosystems* and *macrosystems*—that influence the development of individuals by means of larger social, cultural, political, and structural mechanisms. Exosystems refers to factors that indirectly shape microsystems, such as the ways in which workplace conditions and social networks influence how well family microsystems function. For instance, a highly stressful and demanding work environment can influence a parent's well-being which, in turn, can lead to stress and strain and associated marital, parenting, or family-system problems. Macrosystems are the broadest domain within the ecosystems framework, referring to the "overarching institutional and ideological patterns of the culture or subculture" in a given ecosystem (Bronfenbrenner 1977, p. 527). Macrosystemic influences are far-reaching and—in reference to alcohol and drug abuse—can be understood to include everything from drug policy to social and cultural norms related to the use of alcohol, marijuana, and other illicit drugs (Szapocznik and Coatsworth 1999; Szapocznik et al. 2007). While there are many specifics here, the overall takeaway is relatively straightforward: Individuals reside within a social environment and the problems we face (e.g., drug abuse and addiction) are influenced by interrelated factors ranging from proximal influences such as family and friends to distal influences such as sociocultural norms, social welfare programs, and criminal justice policy.

A second important (and perhaps less overly general) conceptual contribution of ecological systems theory relates to the importance of understanding drug abuse and addiction within a developmental framework. Indeed, the nested structures of the ecosystems framework (e.g., microsystem, mesosystem, etc.) are by no means intended to be understood as static. To the contrary, from beginning to end, the ecosystems framework is explicitly designed to delve into the ways in which enduring patterns of interaction shape an individual's well-being and dysfunction over time (Bronfenbrenner 1979). As summed up by Szapocznik et al. (2007), ecosystems thinking fundamentally strives to "take into consideration the complex set of contexts, their interaction, and *the developmental trajectory of these processes over time* [emphasis added] as they reciprocally influence each other and behavior" (p. 81). So, when ecosystems theorists examine addiction, the framework is one in which drug use initiation and drug abuse are understood from a life course perspective (Elder 1979). To this end, ecosystems theory speaks of *chronosystems* which stretch our understanding of ecological systems beyond the static social environment to include the dimension of time (Bronfebrenner 1994). An analysis that considers chronosystems is concerned not only with patterns of stability and change in the life of a particular individual, but also larger changes to the ecosystems that individuals inhabit (Bronfenbrenner 1988; Elder 1994). Such changes may be as "micro" as variations in family or neighborhood structure or they may be changes that are fundamentally "macro" as in the vicissitudes currently observed with respect to the perception, use, and distribution of marijuana in the United States and elsewhere (Salas-Wright et al. 2015c). Whatever the specifics, the core insight here is that *time matters* when it comes to conceptualizing addiction within an ecological systems framework.

Finally, one important advance within ecological systems theory is that it has come to increasingly recognize the importance of a biosocial perspective (Rosa and Tudge 2013). As noted by Szapocznik and Williams (2000), central to ecological theory is the understanding that intra-personal characteristics such as genetic, neurological, and other biological influences are "nested within the individual who is nested in the family, peer group, school; and all of these, in turn, might be nested within the neighborhood and larger social processes such as cultures and political processes" (p. 127). Such thinking is evident not only in ecological—or bioecological—systems thinking in general, but also in ecologically based theories that have been developed with a specific focus on drug abuse (Szapocznik and Coatsworth 1999; Szapocznik et al. 2012). Again, beyond any specifics, the important point to highlight is the fact that social ecological theories evolved to emphasize the salience of situating biological factors within the broader understanding of social, cultural, and historical influences.

While useful as a general orientation to systems thinking, the ecological-systems approach does have its shortcomings. One major criticism is that the framework is so general that it lacks practicality for generating any specific scientific theories or testable hypotheses. Moreover, ecological-systems theory does not seem to prioritize any specific aspect of the system and comes across at times as vague, unnecessarily cumbersome, and too distal. As such, ecological-systems theory is not directly testable but instead serves to provide a way to think abstractly about phenomena across multiple levels of influence. Finally, because the ecological systems perspective has historically not included genetic factors, it is quite possible that many of the factors attributed to ecological systems may very well be confounded by genetics (more on this in Chap. 3, "Genetic Underpinnings").

A Public Health Framework

One of the real advances of the brain disease model of addiction is that it facilitates the framing of drug abuse and addiction with in the language of public health. The World Health Organization (2016) defines public health as referring to organized efforts to "prevent disease, promote health, and prolong life among the population as a whole. Its activities aim to provide the conditions in which people can be healthy and focus on entire populations, not on individual patients or diseases." Along the same lines, the American Public Health Association (APHA) (2016) notes that while the task of physicians and other health professionals has traditionally been the treatment of those experiencing illness or disease, the task of public health is to "prevent people from getting sick or injured in the first place . . . [and to] promote wellness by encouraging healthy behaviors."

Fundamentally, public health efforts are oriented around the surveillance of health conditions, the design and implementation of public policies intended to address health concerns, and ensuring access to preventive, health promotion, and treatment services.

Applying the logic and language of public health to drug abuse and addiction has a number of important implications. First, situating drug abuse and addiction within the conceptual framework of public health means that we are often less likely to talk about addiction primarily within the framework of crime and criminal justice. Indeed, a recent American Public Health Association (2013) policy statement entitled, "Defining and Implementing a Public Health Response to Drug Use and Misuse" identified the movement to shift away from the criminalization of drug possession and use as a core component of a public health approach. Specifically, the APHA statement highlights the ways in which ushering drug users into the criminal justice system has made treatment more difficult, created other public health problems, and—not inconsequentially—contributed to the problem of mass incarceration in the United States. Along the same lines, others have noted that incarceration alone is often an abysmal approach to addressing the struggles faced by individuals living with an addiction. Chandler et al. (2009) note that "Punishment alone is a futile and ineffective response to drug abuse" and argue for the importance of integrating evidence-based drug abuse treatment opportunities into criminal justice settings (p. 189).

Understanding addiction within the framework of public health is also important because it can allow us to leverage the strengths of epidemiology and public health practice and policy to address the challenges of drug abuse and addiction. For instance, situating drug abuse and addiction within the framework of public health, we have seen exciting advances in the epidemiology of substance use. The subdiscipline of genetic epidemiology is beginning to profoundly enhance our capacity to understand, prevent, and treat drug abuse and addiction (Kendler et al. 2012; Merikangas and McClair 2012). Social epidemiology has helped us to appreciate the way which social and contextual factors—such as family and social network norms, neighborhood characteristics and community violence, discrimination and segregation—influence risk for substance abuse and addiction (Galea et al. 2004; Winstanley et al. 2008). Beyond epidemiology, a public health approach to drug abuse and addictions opens up exciting possibilities with respect to large-scale health promotion efforts designed to prevent drug abuse before it starts, increase treatment access, and reduce drug-related health consequences among active users.

Of course, framing addiction as a public health issue is not a particularly new idea. In 1914, Charles E. Terry published a commentary in the *American Journal of Public Health* in which he states unequivocally, "I believe that few... [challenges] confronting us affect more seriously the public health than this of drug addictions. It directly and indirectly increases the death rate and... closely resembles, in its dissemination, contact infection of disease" (p. 47). While a public health framework for conceptualizing addiction may not be new, it is certainly powerful. It constitutes, in part, a potential alternative to models rooted primarily in a criminal justice framework and offers many tools that are helpful for the prevention and treatment of drug abuse and addiction.

Conclusion

In this chapter we have examined two of the prevailing frameworks for understanding drug abuse and addiction. We began by discussing the *moral model of addiction* in which drug abuse is understood fundamentally as a matter of choice and drug addiction is situated firmly within the realm of character. Within the moral model, there is very little—if any—room for considering the ways in which drugs of abuse influence our biology or potentially compromise our capacity for choice and behavior change. The *brain disease model of addiction* turns the moral model on its head by emphasizing the ways in which addiction influences our brain and, particularly in its more severe forms, closely resembles chronic medical conditions such as diabetes, hypertension, and asthma. Looking at the brain disease model, we examined the ways in which framing addiction within the language of health contributes to a richer understanding of the etiology, prevention, and treatment of addiction.

You may have noted that—in a text that is dedicated to theorizing around both addiction and antisocial behavior—this chapter barely mentions violence, crime, or antisocial behavior. Guilty as charged. We took this approach for two reasons. First, in a text that is written primarily for criminological audiences, our assessment was that an in-depth review of the prevailing frameworks of drug abuse and addiction might be helpful to many readers. In laying out a biosocial approach to drug abuse and antisocial behavior, it is critical that we create a foundation that includes a solid understanding of the core theoretical components of addiction. The second reason is that emerging theorizing related to drug abuse and addiction is fascinating and powerful and possesses relevance to perspectives on crime that readers will readily find apparent. Indeed, a close look at the brain disease model of addiction reveals a robust, transdisciplinary theoretical conversation that has been underway for several decades. Addictions research is a field in which empirical and theoretical contributions not only have the freedom to incorporate a biosocial perspective, but it is a field in which a biosocial approach is simply to be expected.

By no means are all arguments settled when it comes to biosocial theory and addiction. Leading scholarly proponents of the brain disease model of addiction are quick to observe that addiction is a profoundly complex disorder of a profoundly complex brain (not to mention a highly complex social environment), and no serious scholars are pretending that all questions are answered. As with any biosocial approach, both optimism and caution are warranted. At the same time, however, leading voices in fields such as psychology and psychiatry have firmly underscored the importance of integrating transdisciplinary and biosocial insights into our understanding of behavior, health, and well-being (Caspi and Moffitt 2006; Schwartz et al. 2016). Addictions research has done this well for several decades, and we see no reason why twenty-first-century theorizing around addiction and antisocial behavior should be any different.

References

American Public Health Association (APHA) (2016). What is public health? Retrieved 29 January 2016 from www.apha.org/what-is-public-health.

Barry, C.L., McGinty, E.E., Pescosolido, B.A., & Goldman, H.H. (2014). Stigma, discrimination, treatment effectiveness, and policy: Public views about drug addiction and mental illness. *Psychiatric Services*, 65(10), 1269–1272.

Bronfenbrenner, U. (1977). Toward an experimental ecology of human development. *American psychologist, 32*(7), 513–531.

Bronfenbrenner, U. (1979). *The ecology of human development.* Cambridge, MA: Harvard University Press.

Bronfenbrenner, U. (1988). Interacting systems in human development. Research paradigms: Present and future. In N. Bolger, A. Caspi, G. Downey, & M. Moorehouse (Eds.), *Persons in contexts: Developmental processes* (pp. 25–49). Cambridge, UK: Cambridge University Press.

Bronfenbrenner, U., & Ceci, S. J. (1994). Nature-nuture reconceptualized in developmental perspective: A bioecological model. *Psychological Review, 101*(4), 568–586.

Cacciola, J.S., Dugosh, K., Foltz, C., Leahy, P., & Stevens, R. (2005). Treatment outcomes: First time versus treatment-experienced clients. *Journal of Substance Abuse Treatment, 28*(2), S13–S22.

Dackis, C. & O'Brien, C. (2005). Neurobiology of addiction: Treatment and public policy ramifications. *Nature Neuroscience, 8*(11), 1431–1436.

DiClemente, C.C. & Prochaska, J.O. (1998). *Toward a comprehensive, transtheoretical model of change: Stages of change and addictive behaviors.* New York: Plenum Press.

Carter, A., & Hall, W. (2012). *Addiction neuroethics: The promises and perils of neuroscience research on addiction.* New York: Cambridge University Press.

Caspi, A. & Moffitt, T. E. (2006). Gene–environment interactions in psychiatry: joining forces with neuroscience. *Nature Reviews Neuroscience, 7*(7), 583–590.

Chandler, R. K., Fletcher, B. W., & Volkow, N. D. (2009). Treating drug abuse and addiction in the criminal justice system: improving public health and safety. *JAMA, 301*(2), 183–190.

Elder Jr, G.H. (1994). Time, human agency, and social change: Perspectives on the life course. *Social Psychology Quarterly, 57*(1), 4–15.

Elder, G.H. & Rockwell, R.C. (1979). The life-course and human development: An ecological perspective. *International Journal of Behavioral Development, 2*(1), 1–21.

Flynn, P.M. & Brown, B.S. (2015). Misrepresenting the accomplishments of treatment. *Substance Use & Misuse, 50*(8–9), 978–980.

Flynn, P.M., Joe, G.W., Broome, K.M., Simpson, D.D., & Brown, B.S. (2003). Looking back on cocaine dependence: Reasons for recovery. *The American Journal on Addictions, 12*(5), 398–411.

Friedmann, P.D. (2013). Alcohol use in adults. *New England Journal of Medicine, 368*(4), 365–373.

Galea, S., Nandi, A., & Vlahov, D. (2004). The social epidemiology of substance use. *Epidemiologic Reviews, 26*(1), 36–52.

Goldstein, R.Z. & Volkow, N.D. (2011) Dysfunction of the prefrontal cortex in addiction: neuroimaging findings and clinical implications. *Nature Reviews. Neuroscience, 12*(11), 652–669. doi: 10.1038/nrn3119.

Hall, W.G., Gartner, C., & Forlini, C. (2015) Ethical issues raised by a ban on the sale of electronic nicotine devices. *Addiction, 110*(7), 1061–1067.

Hawkins, J.D., Catalano, R.F., & Miller, J.Y. (1992). Risk and protective factors for alcohol and other drug problems in adolescence and early adulthood: Implications for substance abuse prevention. *Psychological Bulletin, 112*(1), 64–105.

Hammer, R., Dingel, M., Ostergren, J., Partridge, B., McCormick, J., & Koenig, B. A. (2013). Addiction: Current criticism of the brain disease paradigm. *AJOB Neuroscience, 4*(3), 27–32.

Heyman, G.M. (2013). Addiction and choice: Theory and new data. *Frontiers in Psychiatry, 4*(31), 1–5.

Kendler, K.S., Chen, X., Dick, D., Maes, H., Gillespie, N., Neale, M.C., et al. (2012). Recent advances in the genetic epidemiology and molecular genetics of substance use disorders. *Nature Neuroscience, 15*(2), 181–189.

Koob, G.F. & Simon, E.J. (2009). The neurobiology of addiction: Where we have been and where we are going. *Journal of Drug Issues, 39*(1), 115–132.

Leshner, A.I. (1997) Addiction is a brain disease, and it matters. Science. 3;278 (5335), 45–47.

Lewis, M. (2013). *Memoirs of an addicted brain: A neuroscientist examines his former life on drugs.* New York, NY: PublicAffairs.

Lopez-Quintero, C., Hasin, D.S., de Los Cobos, J.P., Pines, A., Wang, S., Grant, B.F., et al. (2011). Probability and predictors of remission from lifetime nicotine, alcohol, cannabis or cocaine dependence: Results from the national epidemiologic survey on alcohol and related conditions. *Addiction, 106*(3), 657–669.

Marlatt, G.A. & Donovan, D.M. (2005). *Relapse prevention: Maintenance strategies in the treatment of addictive behaviors.* New York, NY: Guilford Press.

Maynard, B.R., Salas-Wright, C.P., & Vaughn, M.G. (2015). High school dropouts in emerging adulthood: Substance use, mental health problems and crime. *Community Mental Health Journal, 51*(3), 289–299.

McLellan, A.T., Lewis, D.C., O'Brien, C.P., & Kleber, H.D. (2000). Drug dependence, a chronic medical illness: Implications for treatment, insurance, and outcomes evaluation. *Journal of the American Medical Association, 284*(13), 1689–1695.

McLellan, A.T., Weinstein, R.L., Shen, Q., Kendig, C., & Levine, M. (2005). Improving continuity of care in a public addiction treatment system with clinical case management. *American Journal on Addictions, 14*(5), 426–440.

Merikangas, K.R. & McClair, V.L. (2012). Epidemiology of substance use disorders. *Human Genetics, 131*(6), 779–789.

Miller, W.R. (2015). Retire the concept of "relapse." *Substance Use & Misuse, 50*, 976–977.

Miller, W.R., Walters, S.T., & Bennett, M.E. (2001). How effective is alcoholism treatment in the United States? *Journal of Studies on Alcohol, 62*(2), 211–220.

National Institute on Drug Abuse (2016). DrugFacts – Understanding drug use and addiction. Retrieved from: https://www.drugabuse.gov/publica tions/drugfacts/understanding-drug-use-addiction.

O'Brien, K., Salas-Wright, C.P., Vaughn, M.G., & LeCloux, M. (2015). Childhood exposure to a parental suicide attempt and risk for substance use disorders. *Addictive Behaviors, 46*, 70–76.

Pescosolido, B.A., Martin, J.K., Long, J.S., Medina. T.R., Phelan, J.C., & Link, B.G. (2010) A disease like any other? A decade of change in public reactions to schizophrenia, depression, and alcohol dependence. *American Journal of Psychiatry, 167*(11). 1321–1330. doi: 10.1176/appi.ajp.2010.09121743.

Reingle Gonzalez, J.M., Salas-Wright, C.P., Connell, N.M., Clipper, S.J., Kassarjian, K., & Businelle, M.S. (2016). The long-term effects of school dropout and GED attainment on substance use disorders. *Drug and Alcohol Dependence, 158*(1), 60–66.

Rosa, E.M. & Tudge, J. (2013) Urie Bronfenbrenner's theory of human development: Its evolution from ecology to bioecology, Journal of Family Theory & Review, 5(4),243–258.

Salas-Wright, C.P. & Vaughn, M.G. (2014). A refugee paradox for substance use disorders? *Drug and Alcohol Dependence, 142*, 345–349.

Salas-Wright, C.P., Olate, R., & Vaughn, M.G. (2013a). Religious coping, spirituality, and substance use and abuse among youth in high-risk communities in San Salvador, El Salvador. *Substance Use and Misuse, 48*(9), 769–783.

Salas-Wright, C.P., Olate, R., Vaughn, M.G., & Tran, T.V. (2013b). Direct and mediated associations between religious coping, spirituality, and youth violence in El Salvador. *Pan American Journal of Public Health, 34*(3), 183–189.

Salas-Wright, C.P., Vaughn, M.G., Clark, T.T., Terzis, L., & Córdova, D. (2014). Substance use disorders among first and second-generation immigrants in the USA: Evidence of an immigrant paradox? *Journal of Studies on Alcohol and Drugs, 75*(6), 958–967.

Salas-Wright, C.P., Clark, T.T., Vaughn, M.G., & Córdova, D. (2015a). Profiles of acculturation among Hispanics in the United States: Links with discrimination and substance use. *Social Psychiatry and Psychiatric Epidemiology, 50*, 39–49.

Salas-Wright, C.P., Robles, E.H., Vaughn, M.G., Córdova, D., & Figueroa, R. P. (2015b). Toward a typology of acculturative stress: Findings from a national sample of Hispanic immigrants. *Hispanic Journal of Behavioral Sciences, 37*(2), 223–242.

Salas-Wright, C.P., Vaughn, M.G., Todic, J., Córdova, D., & Perron, B.E. (2015c). Trends in the disapproval and use of marijuana among adolescents and young adults in the United States: 2002–2013. *The American Journal of Drug and Alcohol Abuse, 41*(5), 392–404.

Salas-Wright, C.P., Vaughn, M., Ugalde, J., & Todic, J. (2015d). Substance use and teen pregnancy in the United States: Evidence from the NSDUH 2002–2012. *Addictive Behaviors, 45*, 218–225.

Schaler, J.A. (2000). *Addiction is a choice.* Chicago: Open Court Publishing.

Schwartz, S.J., Lilienfeld, S.O., Meca, A., & Sauvigné, K.C. (2016). The role of neuroscience within psychology: A call for inclusiveness over exclusiveness. *The American Psychologist, 71*(1), 52–70.

Simpson, D.D. & Sells, S.B. (1990). *Opioid addiction and treatment: A 12-year follow-up.* Malabar: Krieger Publishing Co.

Sobell, L.C. (2007). The phenomenon of self-change: Overview and key issues. In H. Klingemann & L.C. Sobell (Eds.), *Promoting self-change from addictive behaviors* (pp. 1–30). New York: Springer.

Szapocznik, J. & Coatsworth, J.D. (1999). An ecodevelopmental framework for organizing the influences on drug abuse: A developmental model of risk and protection. In M. Glantz, & C.R. Hartel (Eds.), *Drug abuse: Origins and interventions* (pp. 331–366). Washington, DC: American Psychological Association Press.

Szapocznik, J., & Williams, R. A. (2000). Brief strategic family therapy: Twenty-five years of interplay among theory, research and practice in adolescent behavior problems and drug abuse. *Clinical child and family psychology review, 3*(2), 117–134.

Szapocznik, J., Prado, G., Burlew, A.K., Williams, R.A., & Santisteban, D.A. (2007). Drug abuse in African American and Hispanic adolescents: Culture, development, and behavior. *Annual Review of Clinical Psychology, 3*, 77–105.

Szapocznik, J., Schwartz, S.J., Muir, J.A., & Brown, C.H. (2012). Brief strategic family therapy: An intervention to reduce adolescent risk behavior. *Couple and Family Psychology: Research and Practice, 1*(2), 134–145.

Terry, C.E. (1914). Drug addictions, a public health problem. *American Journal of Public Health, 4*, 28–37.

Vaughn, M.G., Maynard, B.R., Salas-Wright, C.P., Perron, B.E., & Abdon, A. (2013). Prevalence and correlates of truancy in the U.S.: Results from a national sample. *Journal of Adolescence, 36*(4), 767–776.

Vaughn, M.G., Salas-Wright, C.P., Kremer, K.P., Maynard, B.R., Roberts, G., & Vaughn, S. (2015a). Are homeschooled adolescents less likely to use alcohol, tobacco, and other drugs? *Drug and Alcohol Dependence, 155*, 97–104.

Vaughn, M.G., Salas-Wright, C.P., Underwood, S., & Gochez-Kerr, T. (2015b). Subtypes of non-suicidal self-injury based on childhood adversity. *Psychiatric Quarterly, 86*(1), 137–151. Advance online publication.

Volkow, N. (2015) Dr. Nora Volkow on Addiction: A Disease of Free Will. Washington, DC: National Institute on Drug Abuse. www.drugabuse.gov/videos/dr-nora-volkow-addiction-disease-free-will

Volkow, N.D. & Baler, R. D. (2014) Addiction science: Uncovering neurobiological complexity. Neuropharmacology. *76* Pt B, 235–249. doi: 10.1016/j.neuropharm.2013.05.007.

Volkow, N.D. & Koob, G. (2015) Brain disease model of addiction: why is it so controversial? Lancet Psychiatry. *2*(8), 677–679. doi: 10.1016/S2215-0366(15)00236-9.

Volkow, N. & Li, T.K. (2005) The neuroscience of addiction. Nature Neuroscience. *8*(11), 1429–1430.

West, R. (2001). Theories of addiction. *Addiction, 96*(1), 3–13.

West, R. & Brown, J. (2013). *Theory of addiction* (2nd ed.). Hoboken, NJ: John Wiley & Sons.

Winstanley, E.L., Steinwachs, D.M., Ensminger, M.E., Latkin, C.A., Stitzer, M.L., & Olsen, Y. (2008). The association of self-reported neighborhood disorganization and social capital with adolescent alcohol and drug use, dependence, and access to treatment. *Drug and Alcohol Dependence, 92*(1), 173–182.

World Health Organization (2016). Public health. Retrieved 5 February 2016 from www.who.int/trade/glossary/story076/en/.

3

Genetic Underpinnings

Introduction

Why do some individuals appear to be more prone to addiction than others? And why do some addicted persons engage in antisocial acts while other addicted persons do not? While previous chapters have focused on the epidemiology of addiction and antisocial behavior and conceptualizations of addiction, the present chapter directs our attention to answering the aforementioned questions by examining the genetic underpinnings of the addiction–crime phenomenon. Although criminologists have only begun to recognize the importance of genes, the addiction sciences have been searching and uncovering the genetic basis of addictive disorders for many years. It is taken as a given in both addiction science and in criminological science that substance dependence and offending runs in families; however, the former science accepts that genes drive this result, while the latter has been slower to acknowledge the genetic basis for intergenerational transmission. Because genetics comprise a major component of the biosocial perspective of addiction and antisocial behavior, in this chapter we review the existing literature published on genes and

C.P. Salas-Wright et al., *Drug Abuse and Antisocial Behavior*,
Palgrave's Frontiers in Criminology Theory,
DOI 10.1057/978-1-137-55817-6_3

addiction. We also highlight the avenues by which genetics give rise to addiction-related antisocial behavior.

Understanding the genetic etiology of addiction and by extension, antisocial behavior, is important for several reasons. Perhaps the most important reason is that knowing the underlying causes of addiction allows us to target those causes for amelioration through policy, prevention, and treatment. Criminal justice practitioners and policymakers can benefit from knowledge of the genetics of addiction by treating their clients in a more scientifically informed and humane way. Despite the utility of this information, many people still hold erroneous views related to addiction. For example, some continue to see addiction as a character flaw, while others believe that recovery from addiction is as straightforward as putting one's mind to becoming (and remaining) abstinent. These negative biases, among many others, become attenuated through sound scientific elucidation of the complex causes of addiction.

The Evolutionary Context

In 1859, Charles Darwin published, *On the Origin of Species by Means of Natural Selection, or the Preservation of Favoured Races in the Struggle of Life* (in 1872, the sixth edition was simply titled *The Origin of Species*). In this text, Darwin advanced his theory of evolution as the unified scientific explanation for adaptation and survival over thousands of generations. Very few would dispute that Darwin's theory of evolution is on the short-list of the most influential contributions in the history of science. At its core, Darwin's theory of natural selection is rather simple (or elegant), essentially stating that characteristics that facilitate the survival and reproductive success of an organism persist, whereas characteristics that do not tend to desist. This process of natural selection sculpts traits over time.

But must there always be an adaptive advantage for a trait to occur in a population? Importantly, evidence seems to suggest that the answer is no. For instance, Motoo Kimura (1968), in a landmark study of study of evolutionary processes at the molecular level, calculated the rate of evolution of nucleotide substitutions and found that it was so high that many of the mutations occurred neutrally and not as the result of some adaptive advantage during the process of natural selection. In essence, this means that a substantial degree of genetic evolution is random. This idea is commonly referred to as genetic drift. Subsequent geneticists have supported Kimura's theory that a significant portion of genetic evolution is simply based in chance. Over time, this random chance smooths in a direction favorable to the survival of the organism. In other words, natural selection is powerful, but there is little doubt that random mutations are also at work.

Given the 20,000 to 25,000 genes in the human body, it is surprising that a single mutation can have a big impact on the development of an organism. Take, for example, diseases that are caused by a single gene inherited from the mother or the father. These are often termed Mendelian disorders, named after Gregor Mendel (1822–1884) who was famous for his experiments with pea plants. It is important to point out at this juncture that addiction is not a simple Mendelian disorder. There is no single gene or set of genes that cause addiction. Rather, antisocial and addictive behaviors are said to be polygenic in as much as they are influenced in complex ways by many genes. Since over half of the genes in the human genome relate to brain functions (Carey 2003), neuro-genetic sites are obvious targets for gene hunting expeditions. From this point of view, it is easy to see why behavioral genetics and neuroscience are natural allies (Caspi and Moffitt 2006). Addiction, like antisocial behavior, may be a complex multifactorial behavioral phenotype. The level of complexity researchers are confronting is aptly stated by Volkow and Muenke (2012):

In the case of substance use disorders, the powerful modulatory role played by complex environmental factors on brain processes which further muddle the picture, is particularly relevant. This is because, in the absence of drug exposure, itself an environmental factor, the specific addiction phenotype would remain hidden, even in the presence of an overwhelming genetic load. On the other hand, brain development and architecture, which are partly determined by genetic factors, can be affected by exposure to drugs. These two way interactions highlight the importance of genes involved in human brain development and function in the subsequent emergence of personality styles and emotional behavior reactivities. (p. 773)

And yet, despite the enormous complexity, critical advances have been made in uncovering clues about the genetics of these multifactorial phenotypes.

Genetics, Addiction, and Antisocial Behavior

The Genetic Framework for Studying Addiction

Studying the genetic architecture of addiction requires a unique and powerful set of interrelated techniques and methods. These techniques include heritability estimates, molecular genetics, and gene–environment interplay (which include studies of gene–environment interaction as well correlation studies). Each offers a unique contribution to our understanding of the inter-relationships between genetics and addiction, as well as antisocial behavior. As expected of almost any technique, each method faces a number of important limitations. It is worthwhile here to take a look the fundamental method and contribution of each of the major approaches used in studying the influence of genetic factors in addiction, antisocial behavior, and human behavior in general.

Heritability Estimates

Behavioral geneticists usually organize the variance in addiction (and other behaviors as well) along three quantitative dimensions. One of these three dimensions is heritability (h^2) which, of course, reflects the contribution of genetics to addiction. The remaining two dimensions are environmental in nature. One is known as the shared environment (c^2) and the other the nonshared environment (e^2). These are often difficult to explain, but—if you think of a study of adoptive and nonadoptive siblings—one can think of the shared influence of family, household, and community factors (e.g., family stress, the number of books in the home, or exposure to community violence) to be the *shared* environment. The *nonshared* environment refers to factors outside of the family, household, or community (e.g., the influence of nonshared peers, different teachers or schools, and other nonshared experiences).

Heritability (h^2) is a population statistic, or correlation, that ranges from 0.0 (no correlation) to 1.0 (identical genetic profiles). As just alluded to, the usual estimation method involves twins. The genetic correlation between identical (i.e., monozygotic) twins is a perfect 1.0, while for fraternal (i.e., dyzogtic) twins the correlation is 0.50. Surprisingly perhaps, to the general public and social scientists alike, most of the variance found in studies of behavioral phenotypes involves mostly genes and the nonshared environment. In fact, it is not unusual in a twin study estimating heritability for the variance in the shared environment to be zero. However, heritability estimates vary depending on environmental conditions and at different points in the life course (e.g., childhood or adulthood). In a major study published in the prestigious journal *Nature,* Polderman et al. (2015) meta-analyzed the results of 50 years of studies examining thousands of complex human traits among more than 14 million twin pairs. These traits were far-reaching and diverse, including characteristics such as metabolic function, height, mental and substance use disorders, brain function, cognitive function, and even the structure of the eyeball. Quite remarkably, they found that about half (49 %) of the variance in complex human traits may be attributed to heritability. Clearly, evidence from twin studies makes a strong case that genes matter.

Similar to the findings of this meta-analysis, twin studies of the heritability of addiction indicate that approximately 50 % of the variance in addiction specifically is due to genetic factors (Demers et al. 2014). Notably, these results are not largely impacted by the addictive substance used. What is impacted, however, is that heritability estimates change depending on the particular period of life course that is being studied. To illustrate this point, consider that the importance of genetic factors increases from early adolescence to adulthood, suggesting that early substance use may be more a function of environmental factors such as family or social risk than heritability (Kendler et al. 2008). Of course, this also suggests that addiction is more preventable through environmental interventions initiated earlier in the life course. Although heritability studies are useful, arguably it is more important to identify and study the genes that make an individual more or less susceptible to addiction, and to study the interplay between specific genes and modifiable environment risk factors, to have the greatest long-term impact on addiction through prevention.

Molecular Genetics

The working assumption behind molecular genetic studies of addiction is that there are important genes that underlie key systems in the brain that are linked to addiction susceptibility. Several of these genes (reviewed in greater detail later) can be found in such systems as the dopaminergic, serotonergic, or adrenergic systems and other major receptor sites involving critical neurotransmitters. Molecular genetic studies are typically associational; meaning, they test whether there is a statistically significant association between a specific genotype (or gene) and a specific trait, or phenotype. The genes related to addiction are polymorphic; indicating that there is more than one form (allele) of the specific gene that is associated with increased or decreased risk.

The reason why studies of genetic polymorphisms have important implications for addiction is that these polymorphisms provide biomarker-like clues that may shed light on individual vulnerability to addiction. Further, these polymorphisms are linked to systems that can be targeted for treatment using various medications. For example, some medications used to treat addiction block the pleasurable or craving effects of addictive substances, and thereby attenuate the rewarding "high" that typically follows drug administration. This simple brain receptor blockage makes drug use less rewarding by removing of pleasurable effects of the drug. Sometimes these polymorphisms interact with environmental events or cues that increase the likelihood of developing an addiction. Importantly, these environmental cues have been identified as driving the tremendous difficulty associated with maintaining abstinence. From this standpoint, an individual may either be more vulnerable or resilient to particular environmental exposures (e.g., early trauma or repeated exposure to

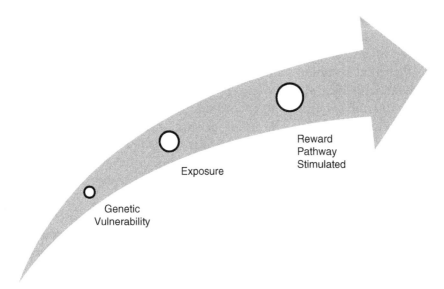

Fig. 3.1 The rise of addiction based on genetic vulnerability

drug using peers) based upon whether they possess a specific genetic polymorphism. Figure 3.1 depicts the rise of addiction based on genetic vulnerability, exposure (whether by substance-seeking or peer initiation), and subsequent stimulation of the reward pathway in the brain.

Gene–Environment Interplay

Another important concept is that of gene–environment correlation and interaction—this is where things get really interesting for the biosocial perspective. Traditionally in the social sciences, we tend to think of the environment as something that is poured into us over time and makes us what we are. But in gene–environment correlation research, a person's genetic makeup (genotype) actually influences his or her environmental exposure.

There are three major types of gene–environment correlations: active, evocative, and passive. The active type of correlation manifests itself when individuals seek out environments that are compatible with their own genotype. For example, children who are good at singing might join a choir or band. In the case of addiction, persons may seek out venues or peers where psychoactive substances are available or, in the case of pathological gambling, seek out locations where gambling is more pronounced, such as Las Vegas. The environment then acts as a reinforcer to the original genetic attribute. An evocative form of gene–environment correlation is where genetic attributes cause others to behave towards the person in particular ways. For instance, children with difficult temperaments may provoke certain behavioral responses (e.g., anger, disgust, derision) from parents and caregivers that would not ordinarily occur in the presence of non-challenging children. These points illustrate how genetically based attributes set a series of environmental responses in motion. In the past, however, we believed that this could only occur the other way around (e.g., the environment impacts the behavior of a person).

Passive gene–environment correlations occur when the environment is molded or modified in some way by parents who share genes with the recipient of the particular environmental setting. For addiction, this could mean that parents who have histories of addiction or antisocial behavior are more likely to create environments conducive to substance use in which a child is exposed to opportunities to learn substance-using behavior. At the same time, however, these environmental stage-setting effects are confounded through heritability, as parents are passing on their genetic susceptibility to the child.

As one might conclude, the highly intertwined nature of genes and environment is extremely complex. As mentioned, between 20,000 and 25,000 genes exist in the human genome, and sorting through those that are important for addiction and antisocial behavior using large enough samples to detect significant effects (without forging a hypothetical fishing expedition) is a daunting and difficult task. However, one can readily see that the range of genetic influences in producing behavior is impossible to ignore. Any theory of addiction and antisocial behavior that purports to be biosocial must include these important genetic elements—not as an end to themselves, but to understand its complex multilevel etiology.

Susceptibility Genes

Popular-culture explanations of gene-related disorders often incorrectly suggest that there exists a causal relationship between a specific gene and some behavioral outcome in a straightforward and direct manner. However, as previously mentioned, addictive disorders and antisocial behavior are not inherited in a direct Mendelian way (i.e., there is a single gene *for* addiction or crime). In general, complex behaviorally-oriented phenotypes like addiction and antisocial behavior manifest indirectly and involve a cascade of mechanisms. Several highly influential scholarly works make this abundantly clear (Chakravarti and Little 2003; Meyer-Lindenberg and Weinberger 2006; Rutter et al. 2006). Nevertheless, a number of genes have been consistently identified as playing an important role in addiction manifestations, and many of these genes overlap with externalizing and antisocial behavior. For example, research findings from the Collaborative Study on the Genetics of Alcoholism suggest that GABRA2, which is expressed more strongly in men and codes for proteins in a major inhibitory neurotransmitter region, is associated with dependence on alcohol (Edenberg et al. 2004) but may also be related to general externalizing behavior (Dick et al. 2009). Because replication in "gene hunting" studies is of critical importance (as with science in general), it is noteworthy to point out that several well-conceived investigations have replicated the alcohol dependence finding (Agrawal et al. 2006; Covault et al. 2004; Fehr et al. 2006; Soyka et al. 2008) but not antisocial behavior per se. This cycle of replication across studies gives us confidence that progress is being made to advance our understanding of the genetic underpinnings of addiction.

In addition to GABRA2, genes in the endogenous opioid system have been identified as potentially being linked to addiction. The endogenous opioid system is the system that creates molecules in the body resembling morphine and other pain-relieving compounds that naturally occur within the body. As such, this system appears to be good terrain for possible gene discoveries involving addiction. Findings suggest that one particular gene in that system, OPRM1, is associated with an increased sensitivity to alcohol (Ray and Hutchison 2004); however, the preponderance of the research on OPRM1 and addiction to other drugs have turned up empty (Dick and Agrawal 2008). Other genes in the endogenous opioid system such as OPRK1 and OPRD1 have been implicated with mixed results (see Dick and Agrawal 2008). Meanwhile, a gene in the excitatory cholinergic system, CHRM2, has been associated with alcohol and drug dependence and this finding has been replicated in multiple samples (see Dick and Agrawal 2008).

One of the most extensively studied and more interesting genes in the pursuit of a genetic basis to antisocial behavior is the low-activity alleles of the monoamine oxidase A (MAOA), which is sometime referred to as the "warrior" gene due to its effects found in males. MAOA appears to confer an increased risk of developing a range of antisocial behaviors, including substance dependence (Guo et al. 2007). In a clinical sample of 488 German males including 59 alcoholics with antisocial personality disorder, Samochowiec et al. (1999) that the frequency of the low-activity 3-repeat allele was significantly higher among the 59 antisocial alcoholics compared with 185 controls (51 % vs. 35 %, $p < .05$). Beaver et al. (2010) found that individuals possessing the low MAOA activity alleles were more likely to join a gang and while in the gang more likely to fight and use weapons. The hypothesized mechanism by which low-activity MAOA functions is increased emotional arousal and diminished regulation in the prefrontal cortex.

Key Neurotransmitters

Neurotransmitters are chemicals that transmit signals to allow for communication between neurons in the brain. Neurotransmitters are commonly organized as amino acids, monoamines, and peptides. They are usually classified according to their functions as either excitatory (e.g., "go" responses) and inhibitory (e.g., "stop" responses). Because they are so fundamentally related to addiction, neurotransmitters have received a fair amount of attention among researchers. Although there are numerous neurotransmitters, we discuss two of the more important neurotransmitters, dopamine and serotonin, below.

Perhaps the most important neurotransmitter related to addiction is dopamine, which has been referred to as nature's reward circuit. In fact, dopamine ensures our basic survival through its reinforcing mechanistic effects. Dopamine facilitates increased communication between receptors in the brain that are associated with heightened states of pleasure. As such, the reinforcing effects of dopamine are present when we eat, drink, and engage in sex. Numerous substances "hijack" this dopamine system and provide powerful, pleasurable rewards that we wish to experience and replicate over and over. The use of amphetamines, cocaine, opiates, nicotine, alcohol, and cannabis involve the release of dopamine in the nucleus accumbens. Not surprisingly, dopamine receptor genes (e.g., DRD2) have been consistently associated with heightened risk for addiction (Noble 2000). Another dopamine gene, DRD4, has been explored due to its linkage with this system and its association with novelty-seeking behavior. Novelty seeking can be defined as a disposition to exploratory behavior and excitement in response to new things in a given environment (see Cloninger 1987). Results from a study by Vaughn et al. (2009) suggest that DRD4 is associated with binge drinking among other "novelty-seeking" behaviors.

Serotonin, another important neurotransmitter, plays an important role in mood regulation and as such has been of keen interest to addiction and violence researchers. In general, decreases in serotonin are linked with alcohol use and aggressive behavior (Nelson and Chiavegatto 2001). One genetic polymorphism that has undergone intense study is the low activity short allele (5-HTTLPR). A wide array of diverse studies has implicated this gene in depression and in a more limited capacity, in alcohol dependence. Many of these studies have produced interactions effects suggesting that this area of the brain may be particularly sensitive to environmental stressors. However, it is important to point out that not all studies have corroborated these findings. For example, Positron Emission Tomography examinations, known as PET scans, among patients being treated for alcohol dependence found no evidence of differences in the serotonin transporter gene (5-HTT) between aggressive or non-aggressive individuals (Brown et al. 2007).

Gene–Environment Interactions

Gene–environment interactions represent exciting possibilities because they reveal how, and to what extent, an environmental factor can moderate the underlying genetic risk. The past decade has witnessed the search for these interactions. Although promising, one of the major hurdles and gene–environment interaction research is the lack of replicability across samples. Many of the genes previously mentioned, such as DRD2, DRD4, and MAOA, have been subject to scrutiny in this domain. For example, in a systematic review of 53 published gene–environment interaction studies of externalizing behavior focusing on major candidate genes (MAOA, DRD2, DRD4, DAT1, 5-HTTLR, and COMT), Weeland et al. (2015) found that findings are heterogeneous and do not unanimously support the role of a single gene in corresponding addiction-related behaviors. Specifically, large differences were identified across samples in how the gene–environment interaction is conceptualized, and in the power to detect significant statistical interactions. The environmental factor in most of these studies was a form of family adversity. The overarching conclusion of the review was that this body of literature cannot be synthesized quantitatively given the tremendous variation in methodologies used. The solution to this problem, according to these researchers, is to develop theory-driven hypotheses with respect to the underlying mechanisms of action driving the observed relationships. Three predominant mechanisms purported to explain findings from this literature base include emotional reactivity, reward sensitivity and punishment sensitivity. The rationale for these mechanisms is that they represent vulnerabilities to environmental events. Still, it is not clear how the mechanisms functions across the many levels that are necessary to produce an addictive phenotype. Despite the heterogeneity observed across the literature, it is important to note that the most studied of these genetic polymorphisms, MAOA, has indeed been found to interact with family adversity to produce externalizing behavior in 16 of the 31 published studies on MAOA. It is also worth noting that numerous environmental pathogens may interact with these genetic polymorphisms singularly or in combination (polygenic risk scores) that have not been tested. One of the more obvious environmental pathogens germane to addiction and antisocial behavior include deviant peers. Also worth noting is that there are apparent sex differences with respect to sensitivity to environmental exposure (sometimes opposite effects are reported) and how this plays out differentially for boys and girls remains largely unknown. One possibility is that gender differences in sex hormone levels, like testosterone, could modulate the diathesis–stress reaction. It is also important to point out that gene–environment interactions can occur during gestation, infancy, adolescence, and adulthood. Research in this area remains in its infancy, as we have yet to learn how these interactions vary over the life course.

In a unique study designed to articulate the underlying genetic vulnerability to externalizing disorders (substance use and antisocial behavior), Hicks et al. (2009) found that six environmental risk factors each interacted with genetic indicators of risk to produce externalizing. These environmental factors included academic achievement and engagement, deviant and prosocial peer affiliations, relationship problems experienced as a child with mother and/or father, and stressful life events. Findings also revealed that when adversity comprised a part of the environmental milieu, genetic vulnerability was more strongly predictive in the development of externalizing behaviors. Although replication is needed, this study provides support for biosocial theory and suggests that genetic influences are not constant across all segments of the population.

Another form of gene–environment interplay that can provide insight into the study of addiction and antisocial behavior are twin discordant research designs. The logic behind twin discordant studies is that studying monozygotic (MZ) twins who share 100 % of their DNA isolates only environmental effects. For example, if you find that one MZ twin uses cocaine and the other does not, then you have isolated an environmental effect that can be targeted. A powerful illustration of this effect was reported by Nelson et al. (2006), who observed that when one MZ twin experienced abuse and the other did not, the twin who experienced abuse was more likely to experience addiction. To our knowledge, twin discordant studies in criminology are rare and part of the challenge in these studies is to have large enough samples of MZ twins to be able to identify discordance and to have the analytic power to study environmental differences.

Proximal Environmental Pathogens and Their Distal Context

The topic of gene–environment interactions raises the issue of distance or proximity of an environmental exposure on a genetically vulnerable phenotype, or modifiable behavior. Yet the specific environmental pathogen is itself conditioned within a larger environmental context. As such, a discussion of distal and proximal environmental factors is necessary.

Proximal environmental pathogens represent variables such as deviant peers, family adversity, and environmental cues that individuals have direct contact with. These factors are so crucial and interact with genes because they are involved with the development, maintenance, and desistance from addiction. Often these pathogens are conceptualized as risk factors. While having some practical utility, risk factors do not constitute theory (although they may inform it). As Glantz (2010, p. 63) has elegantly stated, "identifying risk factors is not the equivalent of a comprehensive characterization of vulnerability or etiology.... vulnerability is not just the degree of accumulation of risk factors."

Numerous studies have identified peer effects as being correlated with substance use and addiction (e.g., Gunning et al. 2009; Scholte et al. 2007). Yet, why some youth have contact with deviant peers and others do not, or how that contact actually translates into misbehavior among some but not others are fundamental questions, the answers to which likely involve gene–environmental interactions or correlations. As discussed above, these influences may be further complicated by bi-directional or reciprocal interactions between the person and their environment. Proximal environmental factors can be thought of as a disease vector or contagion in which vulnerable youth come in contact. But the question of how such youth come in contact with these vectors in the first place remains. Genes may play a substantial role in this initial interaction, as youth predisposed to seek out novelty or sensation-seeking (moderately heritable phenotypes) may look for these opportunities to engage in substance use or antisocial behavior. In this case, we have the reciprocal state of environments acting on individuals, while individuals are simultaneously seeking out these types of environments.

But aren't peers nested within families, and families nested within neighborhoods? The answer to this question is yes, and while there is a long line of research in criminology investigating the role of neighborhoods and crime, less research has been conducted on the role of neighborhoods as related to addiction specifically. We do know that concentrated disadvantage is associated with a range of unhealthy outcomes, including drug abuse (Lambert et al. 2004); however, the causal status of neighborhoods on addiction is unclear and seemingly the effect would be indirect or perhaps misspecified. It is also possible that neighborhoods act as incubators that make their inhabitants more susceptible to addiction. In this case, the neighborhoods themselves might play a spurious role in actually causing addiction. One important direction for future research is to include assessments of biological vulnerability either by collecting genetic samples or stress-panel hormones such as cortisol over time to attempt to disentangle the effects of neighborhoods on addiction phenotypes. A guiding hypothesis in this line of research would be that living in distressed neighborhoods increases resident stress levels, which in turn increases the need to self-medicate. Those who self-medicate and who are more likely to be vulnerable to addiction would more likely become substance-dependent. Given the difficulties and stresses associated with living in distressed areas, individuals may turn to criminal acts to obtain substances necessary for self-medication. We would expect to observe a dose–response relationship—those who have been living in the area the longest and those with highest cortisol levels have the greatest risk of addiction. But what about the distal environment, like policies criminalizing marijuana use, that conditions the proximal environmental pathogens? Research of this kind would provide important insight into the role of neighborhoods for addiction scientists.

While seemingly far removed from the everyday life of an addicted person, there are distal environmental factors that are critical to informing a comprehensive etiologic understanding of addiction. Examples of these distal factors include climate, soils, and vegetation, transportation routes, political economy, and ideology. On the supply side, many drugs of abuse such as cocaine, heroin, and marijuana are plants and depend on proper soils and climate. In short, they tend to thrive in certain locales but not in others. It is also important to understand that many substances of abuse, like alcohol and tobacco, are explicitly marketed to the general population through television and billboard advertisements. Product placements in movies and music (cocaine or cannabis) indirectly advertise these consumer products. There is also a political economy surrounding the processing and distribution of substances that is quite lucrative. The proceeds from alcohol and drug sales, whether legal or illegal, provide capital that can be used to influence laws and law enforcement. In many countries where these plants are grown and harvested, they are a powerful and strategic resource. As a result, opium poppies or coca can be a major force in the underground economies of these and other nations that consume these goods or depend upon the funds generated from drug-related revenue streams. With a minor modification of a distal factors (e.g., through pollutants that make land uninhabitable), an individual simply could not become dependent on these substances because they would be unavailable (or in very limited supply if grown under artificial conditions). For example, let's say an individual who is predisposed genetically to become addicted lives alone on a deserted island where there are no psychoactive substances. This individual could attempt to manufacture some type of chemical from plants, become obsessed with a particular type of food, or compulsively seek out certain activities that would stimulate the reward center. But even under these conditions, this person simply does not have the same capacity to become addicted as a person living outside of this isolated island.

Pulling all of this information together (see Fig. 3.2), the role of genetic vulnerability to addiction and antisocial behavior also necessarily involves the distal environment, proximal environmental pathogens, key neural substrates (more about this in the next chapter), and of course behavioral activation and conscious decision-making.

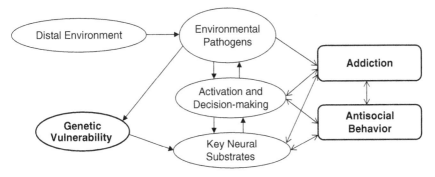

Fig. 3.2 Role of genetic vulnerability in addiction and antisocial behavior

Conclusion

Revealing the genetic architecture to addiction and antisocial behavior is an exciting quest. Despite the promise, major challenges remain in elucidating the genetic influences on these phenotypes. One major barrier is there are few criminologists involved in this research endeavor. Most of the research is taking place on the biomedical side of campuses and most criminology programs are housed at campuses that do not have a medical school or infrastructure for biomedical research. Another practical barrier is the lack of data stemming from low funding of criminological research. There is relatively little money set aside by federal and foundation sources to fund research on the genetic influences on crime—admittedly a controversial topic. The good news is there is a growing recognition that collecting genetic data can help reveal environmental clues that can be targeted for prevention. A more fundamental barrier is the inherent complexity of fully understanding the multilevel dynamism across the biosocial spectrum. This research requires long-term planning and funding. Although no breakthroughs have emerged, it is clear that progress has been made. Briefly, we conclude that genes matter. Our biosocial perspective seeks to integrate genetics into existing behavioral research and theory to contribute to the direction of future criminological studies and inform public policy.

References

Agrawal, A., Edenberg, H.J., Foroud, T., Bierut, L.J., Dunne, G., Hinrichs, A.L., et al. (2006). Association of *GABRA2* with drug dependence in the collaborative study of the genetics of alcoholism sample. *Behavioral Genetics, 36*(5), 640–650.

Beaver, K.M., DeLisi, M., & Vaughn, M.G. (2010). MAOA genotype is associated with gang membership and weapon use. *Comprehensive Psychiatry, 51*(2), 130–134.

Brown, A.K., George, D.T., Masahiro, F., Jeih-San, L., Masanori, I., Hibbeln, J., et al. (2007). PET [11C] DASB imaging of serotonin transporters in patients with alcoholism. *Alcoholism: Clinical and Experimental Research, 31*(1), 28–32.

Carey, G. (2003). *Human genetics for the social sciences*. Thousand Oaks, CA: Sage.

Caspi, A. & Moffitt, T.E. (2006). Gene–environment interactions in psychiatry: Joining forces with neuroscience. *Nature Reviews Neuroscience, 7*(7), 583–590.

Chakravarti, A. & Little, P. (2003). Nature, nurture and human disease. *Nature, 421*, 412–414.

Childress, A.R. (2006). What can human brain imaging tell us about vulnerability to addiction and to relapse? In W. R. Miller & K. M. Carroll (Eds.), *Rethinking substance abuse: What the science shows, and what we should do about it* (pp.46–60). New York: Guilford Press.

Cloninger, C. R. (1987). A systematic method for clinical description and classification of personality variants. *Archives of General Psychiatry, 44*, 573–588.

Covault, J., Gelernter, J., Hesselbrock, V., Nellissery, M., & Kranzler, H.R. (2004). Allelic and haplotypic association of GABRA2 with alcohol dependence. *American Journal of Medical Genetics Part B: Neuropsychiatric Genetics, 129B*(1), 104–109.

Darwin, C. (1859). *On the origin of species by means of natural selection, or the preservation of favoured races in the struggle for life.* London: John Murray.

Demers, C.H., Bogdan, R., & Agrawal, A. (2014). The genetics, neurogenetics and pharmacogenetics of addiction. *Current Behavioral Neuroscience Reports, 1*(1), 33–44.

Dick, D.M. & Agrawal, A. (2008). Genetics of alcohol and other drug dependence. *Alcohol Research and Health, 31*(2), 111–118.

Dick, D.M., Latendresse, S.J., Lansford, J.E., Budde, J.P., Goate, A., Dodge, K.A., et al. (2009). Role of GABRA2 in trajectories of externalizing behavior across development and evidence of moderation by parental monitoring. *Archives of General Psychiatry, 66*(6), 649–657.

Edenberg, H.J., Dick, D.M, Xuei, X., Tian, H., Almasy, L., Bauer, L.O., et al. (2004). Variations in GABRA2, encoding the alpha 2 subunit of the GABA(A) receptor, are associated with alcohol dependence and with brain oscillations. *American Journal of Human Genetics, 74*(4), 705–714.

Fehr, C., Sander, T., Tadic, A., Lenzen, K.P., Anghelescu, I., Klawe, C., et al. (2006). Confirmation of association of the *GABRA2* gene with alcohol dependence by subtype-specific analysis. *Psychiatric Genetics, 16*(1), 9–17.

Glantz, M.D. (2010). Theories of substance dependence etiology. In L.M. Scheier (Ed.), *Handbook of drug use etiology: Theory, methods, and empirical findings.* Washington, DC: American Psychological Association Press.

Gunning, M., Sussman, S., Rohrbach, L.A., Kniazev, V., & Masagutov, R. (2009). Concurrent predictors of cigarette and alcohol use among U.S. and Russian adolescents. *Journal of Drug Education, 39*(4), 385–400.

Guo, G., Wilhelmsen, K., & Hamilton, N. (2007). Gene-lifecourse interaction for alcohol consumption in adolescence and young adulthood: Five monoamine genes. *American Journal of Medical Genetics Part B (Neuropsychiatric Genetics), 144B*(4), 417–423.

Hicks, B.M., South, S.C., DiRago, A.C., Iacono, W.G., & McGue, M. (2009). Environmental adversity and increasing genetic risk for externalizing disorders. *Archives of General Psychiatry, 66*(6), 640–648.

Kendler, K.S., Schmitt, E., Aggen, S.H., & Prescott, C.A. (2008). Genetic and environmental influences on alcohol, caffeine, cannabis, and nicotine use from early adolescence to middle adulthood. *Archives of General Psychiatry, 65*(6), 674–682.

Kimura, M. (1968). Evolutionary rate at the molecular level. *Nature, 217,* 624–626.

Lambert, S.F., Brown, T.L., Phillips, C.M., & Ialongo, N.S. (2004). The relationship between perceptions of neighborhood characteristics and substance use among urban African American adolescents. *American Journal of Community Psychology, 34,* 205–218.

Meyer-Lindenberg, A. & Weinberger, D.R. (2006). Intermediate phenotypes and genetic mechanisms of psychiatric disorders. *Nature Reviews Neuroscience, 7*(10), 818–827.

Nelson, E.C., Heath, A.C., Lynskey, M.T., Bucholz, K.K., Madden, P.A.F., Statham, D.J., et al. (2006). Childhood sexual abuse and risks for licit and illicit drug-related outcomes: A twin study. *Psychological Medicine, 36,* 1473–1483.

Nelson, R.J. & Chiavegatto, S. (2001). Molecular basis of aggression. *Trends in Neuroscience, 24*(12), 713–719.

Noble, E.P. (2000). Addiction and its reward process through polymorphisms of the D2 dopamine receptor gene: A review. *European Psychiatry, 15*(2), 7–89.

Polderman, T.J.C., Benyamin, B., de Leeuw, C., Sullivan, P.F., van Bochoven, A., Visscher, P.M., et al. (2015). Meta-analysis of the heritability of human traits based on fifty years of twin studies. *Nature Genetics, 47*(7), 702–709. doi:10.1038/ng.3285.

Ray, L.A. & Hutchison, K.E. (2004). A polymorphism of the μ-opioid receptor gene (*oprm1*) and sensitivity to the effects of alcohol in humans. *Alcohol: Clinical and Experimental Research, 28*(12), 1789–1795.

Rutter, M., Moffitt, T.E., & Caspi, A. (2006). Gene–environment interplay and psychopathology: Multiple varieties but real effects. *Journal of Child Psychology and Psychiatry, 47*(3–4), 226–261.

Samochowiec, J., Lesch, K.P., Rottman, M., Smolka, M., Syagailo, Y.V., Okladnova, O., et al. (1999). Association of a regulatory polymorphism in the promoter region of the MAOA gene with antisocial alcoholism. *Psychiatry Research, 86*(1), 67–72.

Scholte, R.H., Poelen, E.A., Willemsen, G., Boomsmsa, D.I., & Engels, R.C. (2007). Relative risks of adolescent and young adult alcohol use: The role of drinking fathers, mothers, siblings, and friends. *Addictive Behaviors, 33*(1), 1–14.

Soyka, M., Preuss, U.W., Hesselbrock, V., Zill, P., Koller, G., & Bondy, B. (2008). GABA-A2 receptor subunit gene (*GABRA2*) polymorphisms and risk for alcohol dependence. *Journal of Psychiatric Research, 42*(3), 184–191.

Vaughn, M.G., Beaver, K.M., DeLisi, M. Howard, M.O., & Perron, B.E. (2009). Dopamine D4 receptor gene exon III polymorphism associated with binge drinking attitudinal phenotype. *Alcohol, 43,* 179–184.

Volkow, N.D., & Muenke, M. (2012). The genetics of addiction. *Human Genetics, 131*(6), 773–777.

Weeland, J., Overbeek, G., de Castro, B. O., & Matthys, W. (2015). Underlying mechanisms of gene–environment interactions in externalizing behavior: A systematic review and search for theoretical mechanisms. *Clinical Child and Family Psychology Review, 18*(4), 413–442.

4

Neurobiological Contributions

Introduction

Although many offenders have initiated their criminal careers prior to their substance-abuse careers and most are not crime committing "dope fiends" (as often depicted in cultural mediums), there is little doubt that drug abuse plays an important role in violent and non-violent crime. We recognize that it is difficult to overcome the many stereotypes that the general public, policymakers, and even researchers have of drug abuse and crime. Beyond these entrenched cultural narratives, there is little doubt that views on the drugs–crime connection are conditioned by trends in popular culture. For example, some powerful movies have had these consuming life challenges at the very heart of their plots, highlighting behaviors such as compulsive substance-seeking. Classic films such as *The Lost Weekend* (1945) starring Ray Milland, *Days of Wine and Roses* (1962) with Jack Lemmon, and more recently *Leaving Las Vegas* (1995) with Nicholas Cage, as well as lesser known films such as *Drugstore Cowboy* (1989), comprise the notable standouts in this genre. Almost everyone in the Unites States can name a famous musical

© The Author(s) 2016   **73**
C.P. Salas-Wright et al., *Drug Abuse and Antisocial Behavior*,
Palgrave's Frontiers in Criminology Theory,
DOI 10.1057/978-1-137-55817-6_4

artist who died of a drug overdose. Considering this, addiction seems almost baked into popular culture DNA.

Although not without challenge, the application of neuroscience to the study of addiction and crime is appealing and provocative. Findings on the neural substrates of addiction and of antisocial behavior are being reported with regular frequency in both biomedical and behavioral journals. A crude Google Scholar search using the terms "neuroscience" and "addiction" turn up thousands of scientific publications. A growing cadre of criminologists has recognized these developments and has begun to incorporate neuroscience findings into their work, thus casting new light on traditional criminological focal concerns. Despite the promise of integrating neuroscience into criminology, the many aspects of the brain have yet to be understood by scientists. Although it is unclear how the lower-level parts of the brain operate and how these brain functions influence behavior, we do know that the brain is funda-mental to human behavior, 20 % of the body's energy (Kandel et al. 2000; Swaminathan 2008). Billions of neurons communicate with one another via synapses in the brain (Kandel et al. 2000). Gathered from external stimuli, sensory neurons send information to the brain and motor neurons send information from the brain to the spinal cord and from there, to muscles and organs. Humans have developed substantial frontal regions of the brain that facilitate executive functioning and high-level cognitive tasks. The areas of the brain most relevant to the study of addiction and antisocial behavior (and all human behavior) are those related to reward processing, motivation, emotion, and behavioral inhibition.

The basic functions of reward, motivation, emotion, and behavior inhibition are universally observed. As a result, we presume that these functions are hard-wired. From an evolutionary standpoint, emotional centers of the brain otherwise known as the limbic system (to be discussed in detail later in the chapter) preceded the development of the prefrontal cortex (critical for executive functioning) in evolutionary time. As noted by MacLean (1990) in his triune brain theory, there are many more connections running from the emotional circuits to the frontal areas than vice versa, suggesting that emotions are quite capable of overwhelming our ability to inhibit powerful emotions. Of course,

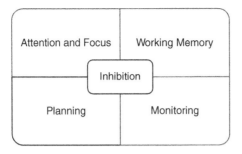

Fig. 4.1 Key executive functions related to addiction

there is individual variation on the emotion side and the executive governance side. Clearly, reward-seeking behavior taxes our self-control resources.

The taxing of self-control resources is tied to executive functions. Executive functions regulate or "govern" behavioral and emotional responses to the environment by way of attention, monitoring, planning, problem solving, memory, and judgment and decision-making (see Fig. 4.1). The prefrontal cortex is the home of these executive functions. As one might readily surmise, there is some give and take between the emotional and executive centers of the brain. Basic living is dependent on the governance that occurs in these areas. As Vaughn et al. (2013, p. 86) note, "The phrase 'check your tongue' is instructive. Some people have difficulty inhibiting their true thoughts about particular topics or other people, and thus state aloud what they are thinking. Many times, this unfiltered behavior creates controversy, hurts other people's feelings, or creates social conflict. An individual who is able to 'check themselves' and refrain from making inappropriate comments embodies the executive functions, and the vital ways in which they contribute to self-regulation." Executive functions are important for a wide swath of human behavior including personality (Unsworth et al. 2009), wealth accumulation and eminence (Rindermann and Thompson 2011), and work performance (Parasuraman 2011), and of course addiction and antisocial behavior (Berkman et al. 2011). Addiction and related problem behaviors simply cannot be properly understood without attention to executive functioning, and substantial research has documented a relationship between impairment in the frontal regions and antisocial and risky behavior (Brower and Price 2001).

Although the basis of executive functioning is largely genetic, there is substantial plasticity in the developing brain that is highly sensitive to environmental stimuli. This is because there is an enormous amount of new connections being rapidly formed related to memory, attention to novel stimuli, fine-motor skills, and goal-driven behavior (Barkley 2012). The roots of problem behavior can be observed during early childhood, as some children have a very difficult time controlling their impulses in socially adaptive ways. Not surprisingly, this apparent lack of effortful control makes them more likely to be rejected by other children. Later, deficits in executive functions begin to play out in harmful ways with increases in risk-taking behaviors. Several well-designed studies have shown that early problems (as early as age 3) in executive function is tied to a host of problems in adulthood including a greater probability of addiction and offending (Fergusson et al. 2007; Moffitt et al. 2011; Tarter et al. 2004). Combining these executive governance deficits with harmful environments seems particularly deleterious. Theoretically, children who reside in riskier environments and who possess lower levels of effortful control seemingly have less "margin for error" for behavioral problems than similar youth that reside in more enriched environments comprised of greater protective mechanisms.

How Do We "Map" Addiction and Offending in the Brain?

Much has been written and accepted about addiction as a brain disease. In contrast, there is very little acceptance that offending is a brain disease. Criminology has been largely situated as a sub-domain of the social sciences (in particular, sociology), whereas addiction science has largely evolved in a biomedical context. Much of the knowledge about brain disease conceptualization stems from scientists' ability to image the brain.

There are five major neuroimaging technologies that have been employed to delineate the structure and function of addiction processes including structural magnetic resonance imaging, functional magnetic resonance imaging, positron emission tomography, single photon emission computed tomography, and magnetic resonance spectroscopy (see Fowler et al. 2007). Each technology possesses strengths and limitations. Chief among the advantages is the ability to make direct comparisons between persons who are at different stages of abuse and dependence with non-substance-using controls. Additional controls such as age, race, gender, socioeconomic status, and behavioral histories serve to further isolate the differences that may be attributable to substance use. Simply, these technologies allow investigators to peer into the addicted brain. Findings from brain imaging studies clearly point to structural, functional, and metabolic processes in the brain that influence or are influenced by substances of abuse. These results also point to areas of the brain that subserve key components of addiction such as decision-making, planning, and craving. While brain imaging studies are invaluable in expanding our understanding of addiction, they do have their drawbacks. Notably, they are very expensive and cumbersome, and are therefore confined to small sample sizes. This limits the statistical power of these studies to detect small differences in addition to generalizability.

The Key to Addiction: The Reward Pathway

As previously mentioned in Chap. 2, Alan Leshner, former director of the National Institute on Drug Abuse, famously declared in 1997 that "Addiction is a Brain Disease, and it Matters." Leshner argued that accumulated research has shown convincingly that addiction is a special type of brain disease involving key neural circuits. We use the term "special type" because addiction is a disease that occurs within a social environment. That is, addiction is a brain disease that is context-contingent. This is because humans and their brains are nested in a context of social relations. The social context plays a role in the genesis, maintenance, and recovery from addiction.

The major neural circuit that Leshner (and many other addiction scientists) invoke is known in common terms as the reward pathway. At some point, any etiological theory or perspective of addiction and antisocial behavior needs to include the reward pathway as a central feature. As such, we include a fairly detailed rendering of this critical circuit below. To contextualize the importance of the reward pathway, also known as the mesolimbic reward system, it is deemed necessary for survival. The reward pathway has evolved to provide the positive reinforcement needed to ensure that humans eat, drink, have sex, and sustain other basic functions for survival. Specifically, the nucleus accumbens within the reward pathway is the pleasure center that is stimulated when rewarding behaviors occur. Because eating, drinking, and sex are behaviors necessary for survival, chemicals such as dopamine are released to reinforce these behaviors when we engage in them. However, when we ingest psychoactive substances of abuse, supernormal amounts of dopamine are released. In fact, so much dopamine is triggered through use of psychoactive drugs that addiction researchers refer to this process as the "hijacking" of a neural circuit. Once hijacked, compulsive drug-seeking and craving often follow; this represents one of the chief pathways to crime.

Now, let us add to the discussion a few technical details about the reward pathway. The areas of the brain that constitute the mesolimbic reward pathway are composed of the ventral tegmental area (VTA), the amygdala, and the nucleus accumbens (NAc). The VTA is the beginning of the reward pathway and is located beneath a substantial number of the brain's opiate receptors. Opiate-receptor stimulation occurs either by use of opiate-based substances (morphine, heroin, or pain-relieving pharmaceuticals such as Oxycontin) or by the release of natural endorphins (e.g., "runner's high") which then signals the VTA to release a flood of dopamine that streams to the amygdala.

The amygdala is home to the "fight or flight" response that is crucial for detecting and evaluating threats. The amygdala passes information on to higher levels of the brain for processing. As a result of drug use, the amygdala receives a substantial amount of dopamine that initiates a series of neurotransmissions to the NAc.

The NAc is the final home for the dopamine cascade. In this brain region, long-lasting changes in levels of reinforcement via dopamine levels are recorded in one's memory. As such, the NAc is directly involved in the reward expectation response, commonly referred to as "cravings." With drug abuse, the NAc becomes conditioned to regular and large amounts of dopamine. The NAc learns that this behavior is desirable and continues to record these levels of dopamine. As a result, physical addiction is born and the need to maintain these recorded homeostatic dopamine level becomes of primary concern. Once trained, the NAc in effect has become permanently altered and returning to lower levels becomes difficult to achieve. Craving is a common symptom in addiction and its hallmark feature is memory of the pleasurable aspects of drug ingestion. These memories typically occur when one is experiencing a negative emotional state (Koob and LeMoal 2008; Markou et al. 1998).

The hypothalamus-pituitary-adrenal (HPA) axis is also central to the fight-or-flight response. The fight-or-flight response is achieved by the secretion of cortisol-releasing factor (CRF), dynorphin, and norepinephrine, which leads to the eventual production of adrenaline and cortisol. When levels of dopamine are depleted or are in low supply, cortisol, dynorphin, and norepinephrine act to produce feelings of discomfort, distress, unease, and agitation. This state of discomfort continues until the brain is able to replenish adequate supplies of dopamine and thereby reestablish homeostasis. In short, the new homeostatic normal of physical addiction is demanding, and the expectation of reward that results is pernicious.

At this point, an important question needs to be raised: If the reward pathway is so powerfully stimulated by drugs of abuse, then why doesn't everyone who uses become addicted? First, as established in the previous chapter on genetics, there is substantial individual vulnerability to addiction. As stated by Belsky and Pluess (2009), people have *differential susceptibility* to developing problem behaviors. Second, the counterweight to the "go" system of compulsive drug-seeking is strong "brakes" in the form of the ability to exercise inhibitory control. Childress (2006) suggests that this "stop" and "go" analogy provides a simple heuristic for understanding not only the basic proves of drug seeking but also its

	High Risk	Low Risk
Attenuated Risk	High Go	High Stop
Attenuated Risk	Low Stop	Low Go

Fig. 4.2   Risk categories based on the neural "go" and "stop" systems

variation and risk categorization (see Fig. 4.2). In keeping with our analogy, the ancient reward pathway is parallel to the gas pedal of an automobile and the executive centers are the brakes. Not only is their individual-level variation (e.g., high go-low stop or high go-high stop) but also developmental heterogeneity in these systems over the life course.

As with all drives for pleasure-seeking, some people with stronger self-regulation capacity are able to resist or redirect the urges to use substances. The inability to resist should not be interpreted as weakness given our data on the genetic and neurobiological underpinnings of impulse control. Some drugs of abuse, such as heroin, overwhelm our ability to implement effective executive governance. After repeated administrations of a drug, an individual reaches a stage known as tolerance, characterized by the need for larger doses of a drug to achieve the desired psychoactive effect. Commonly larger amounts of the drug are needed for a user to feel "normal," since the NAc has been hyper-stimulated to the point that even normal everyday pleasures provide very little positive reinforcement.

Although later chapters include substantially more discussion about life-course influences on addiction, it is important to note that developmental periods such as adolescence, where drug experimentation and antisocial behavior are often typical or normative (Moffitt 1993) is also a time period when executive functions are not fully developed and thus inhibitory control is diminished. This sets the stage for a scenario where a strong reward response is coupled with a weak "stop" system (Childress 2006). This basic relationship between reward and response inhibition is often regarded as a central feature of adolescent risk for addiction

(Steinberg 2007). Individual vulnerability is further compounded by peer networks, which serve as an additional source of reinforcement and opportunity to use substances.

The Role of Stressful Life Events

Early adversity may play a role in affecting brain development in ways that increase the vulnerability to both addiction and antisocial behavior. Although it is well understood that some stress is normal, and in fact needed in in order for the body to adapt physiologically for basic survival (Selye 1975), too much accumulated stress or severe stress can be damaging. Stress plays an important role in aggression and externalizing problems for children and adolescence (Campbell et al. 1996). Children under high levels of stress have altered neurofunctioning (Carrion and Wong 2012), which commonly results in lower capacity for impulse control. Moreover, in stressful situations, children may have impaired fear processing due to stunted hippocampus maturation which can result in an over- or underreaction to threats. In fact, studies published more than 30 years ago suggested that children raised in adverse conditions, such as abuse exposure, react with heightened threat sensitivity. For example, a day-care study by Main and George (1985) found that non-abused toddlers responded to the distress of other toddlers with concern and empathy while abused toddlers reacted in hostile ways to their distress. While there are certainly potential confounds in the study, it does illustrate that even early non-imaging studies found differential behavioral effects that are consistent with threat perception.

It is no surprise that the brain is sensitive to stress during early developmental periods as it undergoes rapid and important changes. Stress triggers the release of glucocorticoids via signals from hypothalamus–pituitary–adrenal (HPA) axis to ready the body for fight or flight. However, glucocorticoid receptors are found throughout the brain, and the impact of these stress hormones at high or chronic levels is likely to be broad and deleterious. Studies of children whose mothers experienced psychological stress indicate pronounced changes to the brain. Maternal stress hormones can even be passed to the developing fetus in the womb

(Weinstock 2008). Maternal stress is associated with increased basal HPA axis activity in offspring across developmental periods ranging from six months and ten years. One pathway by which stress leads to substance use likelihood is via heightened activity of the HPA axis, which increases levels of glucocorticoids (McEwen 2007) which leads to a biochemical cascade that results in higher levels of dopamine which then activates a person's risk-taking capacity (Casey et al. 2008). Another route to increased risk can occur due to chronic stress that results in reduced dopaminergic functioning in the central nervous system. Under this scenario, impulse-control regions of the brain are hypoactive with respect to dopamine levels and sensation-seeking behaviors may follow (Mead et al. 2010).

There are also important sex differences in the way individuals experience stress. These differences are explained through biological and cultural avenues. Men display heightened HPA-axis reactivity to status and achievement-related tasks; high HPA reactivity for women is more likely to result from emotional disconnections, such as rejections from a social group or social disapproval (Del Giudice et al. 2011). Although both males and females will tend to respond in a hyper-vigilant manner when placed in an unpredictable environment, males are more likely to respond aggressively.

Neuropsychological Effects, Compulsive Drug-Seeking and Crime

Outside of systemic violence associated with the distribution of drugs and protection of drug markets, there are two notable avenues for drug abuse and crime that stem directly from the neuroscience of addiction. The first is antisocial behavior directly stemming from drug ingestion and the second is crime committed due to compulsive drug-seeking. The actual causal effect that drugs have on persons committing violence is difficult to measure without controlling for an individuals' pre-existing tendency to engage in violence. Psychoactive compounds tend to facilitate or amplify pre-existing aggressive tendencies, and some substances are better primed to have this effect than others. For example, the behavioral disinhibition effects of alcohol enhance aggressive tendencies more so than marijuana. Several studies show that alcohol-dependent persons are more likely to respond aggressively than non-alcohol-dependent controls (Kose et al. 2015). Numerous imaging studies have also revealed that there are inhibitory deficits and emotion dysregulation in alcohol dependent persons (Sullivan and Pfefferbaum 2005; Zhang et al. 2013). Again, these studies do not rule out the likely possibility that it is not the substance causing these reactions but pre-existing compromised regions of the brain that are original causes. For example, a meta-analytic review of thirteen imaging studies involving adolescents (ages 12–17) with conduct problems and substance-dependency problems revealed gray matter reductions in frontal regions and in the emotional processing areas (i.e., amygdala) (Rogers and De Brito 2016). This provides evidence in support of a relationship between conduct problems and brain structure that manifest in the form of substance use. Similarly, a substantial portion of people have overlapping alcohol dependence (and other drug-use disorders) and antisocial personality disorder (Sher and Trull 1994), a syndrome characterized by disregard for the rights of others suggesting convergent evidence of shared etiology.

As previously discussed, the reward pathway is greatly stimulated by drugs of abuse and seeking the "high" often becomes of upmost importance. Given the illegal nature and costs of most psychoactive substances, addictions can be quite expensive. Drug-abusing persons sometimes engage in theft, robberies, or other illegal activities in order to provide money to purchase substances to satisfy their cravings. For instance, a heroin-addicted person may sell available stock of heroin at a higher price or marijuana to someone they know in order to purchase larger quantities of their drug of choice. For example, in a study of juvenile offenders who sold drugs, a majority (approximately 70 %) kept more than half of the drugs for themselves (Shook et al. 2011). While this is considered low-level drug dealing, there is still risk of apprehension or conflict that could escalate. Studies of drug-selling youth and young adults in the general population reveal that there is substantial heterogeneity; that is, there are relatively unique subgroups that differ in important respects. These studies found that most of these drug sellers also use drugs (Vaughn et al. 2015).

Neurobiological Links to Social Cognition

Social cognition is tied to the neuroscience of addiction etiology (McCusker 2001; Scheier 2010). According to Volkow (2003, p. 3): "We are beginning to understand that drugs exert persistent neurobiological effects that extend beyond the midbrain centers of pleasure and reward to disrupt the brain's frontal cortex—the thinking region of the brain, where risks and benefits are weighed and decisions made." The poor decisions made by drug abusers and offenders alike suggest that some kind of cognitive remediation or restructuring is needed due to the repetitive thoughts and habitual behavioral patterns involved. The encoding of learned associations occur in the brain and are environmentally mediated through behavioral reinforcement and cues. In this way, social learning theory can be thought of as a biosocial theory. The pathology of motivating behavior that occurs in addiction and to a large extent in chronic offending suggests that motivational influences are important for change (e.g., Miller and Rollnick 2002). Cognitive processes are helpful to explain many of the self-defeating behaviors that are central to drug abuse and antisocial behavior even though their more ultimate etiology is rooted in biology.

Critiques of the Brain Disease Approach

Much of this chapter is built on the notion that addiction is a brain-centered illness. The overwhelming scientific consensus is supportive of the basic tenets of the brain disease model of addiction. The influential journal *Nature* published an editorial in 2014 in which the brain disease model of addiction was described and supported by a succinct summary of several decades of neurological research (*Nature* 2014). The editors punctuate their description of the basics of the neurobiology of addiction by noting unequivocally that there is nothing about the brain disease model of addiction "that is particularly controversial, at least among scientists" (p. 5). More recently, the *New England Journal of Medicine* published a major review article authored by the world's foremost advocates of the brain disease model of addiction (Volkow et al. 2016). In brief, the leading voices in the science of addiction are clear in their support for the framework that we have described in detail above.

Although we agree with the brain disease model position and also realize this is the official position taken by many scientists and scientific bodies, including the National Institutes on Drug Abuse, social scientists might find this position uncomfortable; more important to us, however, is to recognize there are indeed legitimate critiques. We would be remiss if we did not note that concerns among some scholars remain when it comes to the brain disease model. In particular, there is concern that the predominance of the brain disease model of addiction has led to a disproportionate investment in research focused on the brain and on the treatment of individuals with severe addiction (Hall et al. 2015a). It is argued that the focus on "the neurobiology of severe forms of addiction has been at the cost of research into the role of population-based policies" that have been demonstrated to reduce problems related to alcohol and drug abuse (Hall et al. 2015b, p. 867). A related critique focuses on the assertion that loss of control and compulsive behavior are the hallmarks of addiction. Citing the demonstrated effectiveness of contingency management interventions—that is, interventions that offer financial rewards to incentivize abstinence from alcohol and drug use—critics argue that addiction does not seem to fully extinguish self-control in all people (Prendergast et al. 2006).

Critics also charge that portraying addiction as a brain disease is not neutral and causes a shift in thinking among addicted persons, clinicians, and society at large that biases the portrayal of the drug-dependent as biologically defective and produces just as much stigma as labeling someone as weak in character (Hammer et al. 2013). While we agree that this is possible, history clearly shows that addicted persons were indeed thought of as flawed in character and scientific evidence is mounting that there is a scientific basis to addictive processes and they are not merely a social construction though they are, as most addiction scientists acknowledge, socially contingent or situated. In short, addiction is a biosocial process.

Perhaps a stronger criticism is that the biology of addiction will lead to pharmaceutical solutions that trade one pill for another. While one could argue that this trade results in ultimately less harm, it is still less than ideal. With respect to problem behavior there have been empirical studies of the classic tradeoff between heroin and methadone maintenance. Research on methadone maintenance suggests the benefits are indeed favorable. For example a meta-analysis conducted on the outcomes of opiate use, HIV transmission risk, and criminality found that methadone maintenance resulted in consistent statistically significant reduction in these behaviors (Marsch 1998).

Another criticism, made for example by Hall et al. (2015a), is that the brain disease model has yet to deliver on its potential or promises. One of their major criticisms is that the emphasis on brain-related technologies and costly treatment that stem from the brain disease model is simply not affordable or cost-effective for most addicted persons. Moreover, the scientific returns have been modest in advancing our understanding of addiction. The concern is that the bells and whistles of neuroscience have led to an inordinate focus on the brain and, more specifically, on the brains of severely addicted individuals, with little gained. Volkow and Koob (2015) disagree, suggesting that tremendous strides in understanding the neural basis of addiction have been made across animal and imaging models. There are two implications from these critiques that we think require separation. First, uncovering the neuroscientific basis of addiction is a worthy goal and we support and partially build our approach on continued basic research in this vein. We agree that there is a tendency to overemphasize the genetic and neurobiological understanding of addiction (not to mention research funding) without adequate integration of environmental and life-course factors. Second, it is true that many of the practical implications of a neurocentric model can be problematic. However, we see this as a classic case of a false dichotomy. In other words, pursuing a neural understanding of addiction can be accomplished within a wider multi-level framework of biology and environment. With respect to crime, a socially contextualized brain disease model might help to view offenders with co-occurring mental health and substance-use disorders as needing evidence-based therapies; providing these will ultimately aid in reintegration and reduced recidivism.

Conclusion

Findings on the neural substrates of addiction and of antisocial behavior are commonplace. Knowledge about the prominent roles that the brain's reward pathway, executive functions, and stress play in the pathogenesis of addiction is critically important when attempting to understand the nexus of drug abuse and crime. In the near term, criminologists should consider not only using standard drug-abuse measures but also incorporating neuropsychological assessments and physiological measures that tap such factors as deficits in executive governance and resting hear rate (see Cornet 2015). Doing so may necessitate that criminologists and other social scientists work in multidisciplinary research teams often utilizing resources of medical schools. Unfortunately, many doctoral-level and other criminology and criminal justice programs are located at universities that do not have medical schools. Despite these drawbacks, there are exciting possibilities for criminologists as neurobiological factors are highly integrateable with existing psychological and social theories of drug abuse and antisocial behavior.

References

Barkley, R.A. (2012). *Executive functions: What they are, how they work, and why they evolved.* New York: The Guilford Press.

Belsky, J. & Pluess, M. (2009). Beyond diathesis–stress: Differential susceptibility to environmental influence. *Psychological Bulletin, 135*(6), 885–908.

Berkman, E.T., Falk, E.B., & Lieberman, M.D. (2011). In the trenches of real-world self-control: Neural correlates and breaking the link between craving and smoking. *Psychological Science, 22*(Feb.), 498–506.

Brower, M.C. & Price, B.H. (2001). Neuropsychiatry of frontal lobe dysfunction in violent and criminal behavior: A critical review. *Journal of Neurology, Neurosurgery, and Psychiatry, 71*(6), 720–726.

Campbell, S.B., Pierce, E.W., Moore, G., Marakovitz, S., & Newby, K. (1996). Boys' externalizing problems at elementary school age: Pathways from early behavior problems, maternal control, and family stress. *Development and Psychopathology, 8*(4), 701–719.

Carrion, V.G. & Wong, S.S. (2012). Can traumatic stress alter the brain? Understanding the implications of early trauma on brain development and learning. *Journal of Adolescent Health, 51*(2Suppl.), S23–S28.

Casey, B.J., Jones, R.M., & Hare, T.A. (2008). The adolescent brain. *Annals of the New York Academy of Sciences, 1124*(Mar.), 111–126.

Childress, A.R. (2006). What can human brain imaging tell us about vulnerability to addiction and to relapse? In W. R. Miller, & K. M. Carroll (Eds.), *Rethinking substance abuse: What the science shows, and what we should do about it* (pp. 46–60). New York: Guilford Press.

Cornet, L.J.M. (2015). Using basic neurobiological measures in criminological research. *Crime Science, 4*(7). doi:10.1186/s40163-015-0018-5.

Del Giudice, M., Ellis, B.J., & Shirtcliff, E.A. (2011). The adaptive calibration model of stress reactivity. *Neuroscience and Biobehavioral Reviews, 35*(7), 1562–1592.

Fergusson, D.M., Horwood, L.J., & Ridder, E.M. (2007). Conduct and attentional problems in childhood and adolescence and later substance use, abuse and dependence: Results of a 25-year longitudinal study. *Drug and Alcohol Dependence, 88*(S1), S14–S26.

Fowler, J.S., Volkow, N.D., Kassed, C.A., & Chang, L. (2007). Imaging the addicted human brain. *NIDA Science and Practice Perspectives, 3*(2), 4–16.

Hall, W., Carter, A., & Forlini, C. (2015a). The brain disease model of addiction: Is it supported by the evidence and has it delivered on its promises? *The Lancet Psychiatry, 2*(1), 105–110.

Hall, W., Carter, A., & Forlini, C. (2015b). Brain disease model of addiction: Misplaced priorities? *The Lancet Psychiatry, 2*(10), 867.

Hammer, R., Dingel, M., Ostergren, J., Partridge, B., McCormick, J., & Koenig, B.A. (2013). Addiction: Current criticism of the brain disease paradigm. *AJOB Neuroscience, 4*(3), 27–32.

Kandel, E.R., Schwartz, J.H., & Jessel, T.M. (2000). *Principles of neural science.* New York: McGraw-Hill Professional.

Koob, G. & LeMoal, M. (2008). Addiction and the brain anti-reward system. *Annual Review of Psychology, 59*, 29–53.

Kose, S., Steinberg, J., Moeller, F., Gowin, J., Zuniga, E., Kamdar, Z., et al. (2015). Neural correlates of impulsive aggressive behavior in subjects with a history of alcohol dependence. *Behavioral Neuroscience, 129*(2), 183–196.

Leshner, A.I. (1997). Addiction is a brain disease, and it matters. *Science, 278* (5335), 45–47.

MacLean, P.D. (1990). *The triune brain in evolution: Role in paleocerebral functions.* New York: Plenum Press.

Main, M. & George, C. (1985). Responses of abused and disadvantaged toddlers to distress in agemates: A study in the day care setting. *Developmental Psychology, 21*(3), 407–412.

Markou, A., Kosten, T.R., & Koob, G.F. (1998). Neurobiological similarities in depression and drug dependence: A self-medication hypothesis. *Neuropsychopharmacology, 18*(3), 135–174.

Marsch, L.A. (1998). The efficacy of methadone maintenance interventions in reducing illicit opiate use, HIV risk behavior and criminality: A meta-analysis. *Addiction, 93*(4), 515–532.

McCusker, C.G. (2001). Cognitive biases and addiction: An evolution in theory and method. *Addiction, 96*(1), 47–56.

McEwen, B.S. (2007). Physiology and neurobiology of stress and adaptation: Central role of the brain. *Physiological Reviews, 87*(3), 874–904.

Mead, H.K., Beauchaine, T.P., & Shannon, K.E. (2010). Neurobiological adaptations to violence across development. *Development and Psychopathology, 22*(1), 1–22.

Miller, W.R. & Rollnick, S. (2002). *Motivational interviewing: Preparing people for change*, 2nd ed. New York: Guilford Press.

Moffitt, T.E. (1993). Life-course persistent and adolescence-limited antisocial behavior: A developmental taxonomy. *Psychological Review, 100*(4), 674–701.

Moffitt, T.E., Arseneault, L., Belsky, D., Dickson, N., Hancox, R.J., Harrington, H., et al. (2011). A gradient of childhood self-control predicts health, wealth, and public safety. *Proceedings of the National Academy of Sciences of the United States of America, 108*(7), 2693–2698.

Nature. (2014). Animal farm: Europe's policy-makers must not buy animal-rights activists' arguments that addiction is a social, rather than a medical, problem. www.nature.com/news/animal-farm-1.14660.

Parasuraman, R. (2011). Neuroergonomics: Brain, cognition, and performance at work. *Current Directions in Psychological Science, 20*(3), 181–186.

Prendergast, M., Podus, D., Finney, J., Greenwell, L., & Roll, J. (2006). Contingency management for treatment of substance use disorders: A meta-analysis. *Addiction, 101*(11), 1546–1560.

Rindermann, H. & Thompson, J. (2011). Cognitive capitalism: The effect of cognitive ability on wealth, as mediated through scientific achievement and economic freedom. *Psychological Science, 22*(6), 754–763.

Rogers, J.C. & De Brito, S.A. (2016). Cortical and subcortical gray matter volume in youths with conduct problems: A meta-analysis. *JAMA Psychiatry, 73*(3), 64–72.

Scheier, L.M. (2010). Social-cognitive models of drug use etiology. In L. M. Scheier (Ed.), *Handbook of drug use etiology: Theory, methods, and empirical findings*. Washington, DC: American Psychological Association Press.

Selye, H. (1975). *Stress without distress*. Philadelphia: J.B. Lippincott.

Sher, K.J. & Trull, T.J. (1994). Personality and disinhibitory psychopathology: Alcoholism and antisocial personality disorder. *Journal of Abnormal Psychology, 103*(1), 92–102.

Shook, J.J., Vaughn, M.G., Goodkind, S., & Johnson, H. (2011). An empirical portrait of youthful offenders who sell drugs. *Journal of Criminal Justice, 39* (3), 224–231.

Steinberg, L. (2007). Risk-taking in adolescence: New perspectives from brain and behavioral science. *Current Directions in Psychological Science, 16*(2), 55–59.

Sullivan, E.V. & Pfefferbaum, A. (2005). Neurocircuitry in alcoholism: A substrate of disruption and repair. *Psychopharmacology, 180*(4), 583–594.

Swaminathan, N. (2008). Why does the brain need so much power?. Scientific American, 29 April. www.scientificamerican.com/article.cfm?id=why-does-the-brain-need-s.

Tarter, R.E., Kirisci, L., Habeych, M., Reynolds, M., & Vanyukov, M. (2004). Neurobehavior disinhibition in childhood predisposes boys to substance use disorder by young adulthood: Direct and mediated etiologic pathways. *Drug and Alcohol Dependence, 73*(2), 121–132.

Unsworth, N., Miller, J.D., Lakey, C.E., Young, D.L., Meeks, J.T., Campbell, W.K., & Goodie, A.S. (2009). Exploring the relations among executive functions, fluid intelligence, and personality. *Journal of Individual Differences, 30*(4), 194–200.

Vaughn, M.G., DeLisi, M., & Matto, H. (2013). *Human behavior: A cell to society approach.* Hoboken: John Wiley and Sons.

Vaughn, M.G., Salas-Wright, C.P., DeLisi, M., Shook, J.J., & Terzis, L. (2015). A typology of drug selling among young adults in the United States. *Substance Use and Misuse, 50*(3), 403–413.

Volkow, N.D. (2003). The addicted brain: Why such poor decisions? *NIDA Notes, 18*(4), 1–15.

Volkow, N.D. & Koob, G. (2015). Brain disease model of addiction: Why is it so controversial? *Lancet Psychiatry, 2*(8), 677–679.

Volkow, N.D., Koob, G.F., & McLellan, A.T. (2016). Neurobiologic advances from the brain disease model of addiction. *New England Journal of Medicine, 374*, 363–371.

Weinstock, M. (2008). The long-term behavioural consequences of prenatal stress. *Neuroscience and Biobehavioral Reviews, 32*(6), 1073–1086.

Zhang, L., Kerich, M., Schwandt, M.L., Rawlings, R.R., McKellar, J.D., Momenan, R., et al. (2013). Smaller right amygdala in Caucasian alcohol-dependent male patients with a history of intimate partner violence: A volumetric imaging study. *Addiction Biology, 18*(3), 537–547.

5

Childhood Antecedents of Drug Abuse and Antisocial Behavior

Introduction

Now we are going to shift gears a bit. Namely, beginning with childhood, the focus of the next three chapters will move from a discussion of biosocial thinking in general to a specific focus on examining the role of biosocial factors from a life-course perspective. While biosocial factors are undoubtedly of vital importance to our understanding of drug abuse and antisocial behavior in general, much can be gleaned by delving into the unique importance and influence of such factors during key developmental moments. Invariably, salient intrapersonal and socioenvironmental factors change and evolve in important ways across the spectrum of childhood, adolescence, young adulthood, and beyond. For instance, in the previous chapter we pointed out that the brain is essential to a comprehensive understanding of both addiction and antisocial behavior. Importantly, however, research has made it quite clear that the brain is not static across the life course, but rather it looks and functions quite differently as we age and grow. This is but one example of how a biosocial approach to understanding addiction and antisocial behavior must be situated within a developmental, life-course perspective.

© The Author(s) 2016   **93**
C.P. Salas-Wright et al., *Drug Abuse and Antisocial Behavior*,
Palgrave's Frontiers in Criminology Theory,
DOI 10.1057/978-1-137-55817-6_5

In the current chapter, we will begin by providing a working definition of childhood and, in turn, examine what behavior problems look like at different stages in childhood. Next, we will take a close look at the life-course perspective and consider the developmental importance of behavior problems during the childhood years. In particular, we will consider what empirical research and theory tell us about the importance of early behavioral problems for understanding behavioral outcomes down the road. Beyond behavior, we will also examine several particularly salient intrapersonal and contextual factors that are helpful in terms of understanding the etiology of behavior problems in childhood as well as drug abuse and antisocial behavior at later developmental stages. Finally, we will conclude by discussing both the promises and perils of examining the childhood antecedents of addiction and antisocial behavior from a biosocial perspective.

Childhood and the Life Course

Defining Childhood

Let us begin by laying out a working understanding of what we mean when we talk about childhood. For starters, when does it begin and when does it end? The former is easier to determine than the latter. By and large, our discussion of childhood begins at birth. Once you are out of the womb and crying, you have officially entered into the developmental stage of childhood. We might, however, note two important caveats to that definition. First, while childhood begins at birth, we should be careful to note that biosocial factors (e.g., maternal nutrition, parental stress, drug exposure, etc.) begin shaping our development from the moment of conception.[1] The truth is that exposure to risky and adverse factors often begins well before a child is born. Second, when it comes to

---

[1] In fact, emerging evidence increasingly supports the notion that biosocial factors can actually influence our developmental outcomes across generations. For instance, transgenerational evidence indicates that malnutrition during fetal gestation impacts not only the developing fetus, but also the health and well-being of the offspring of the malnourished fetus (Veenendaal et al. 2013). In this way, we might say that some biosocial factors have the power to shape our development decades before conception.

behavior, it is fair to say that we—and most researchers focused on child behavior problems—are most concerned with children beginning with the toddlerhood stage (i.e., roughly 12 to 36 months). That being said, we will also see that there is much we can learn from carefully monitoring the ways that children respond, emotionally and behaviorally, to the world around them from very, very early on in life.

Determining the end of childhood is less cut and dried. Historically, the period of childhood as we understand it today really hasn't lasted very long. Indeed, the understanding of childhood as an extended period dedicated to learning, play, and psychosocial development is very new (Fass and Mason 2000). One need not go back very far in American history—the early part of the 20th century—to find children as young as five or six taking on responsibilities related to family economic status and well-being. In many developing countries, such practices continue to be the norm for many early on in life (Edmonds and Pavcnik 2005) and our research with immigrants suggests that those born outside of the United States are substantially more likely than the US-born to report having taken on adult tasks and responsibilities as children (Vaughn et al. 2015a). In a determined effort to push back against cultures and contexts in which the window of childhood is narrow, the United Nations General Assembly (1989) adopted the Convention on the Rights of the Child in which it was affirmed that childhood should stretch as far as 18 years of age. All this is to say, in sociopolitical and historical terms, the end of childhood is a contested topic.

For our purposes, we view the end of childhood—and, notably, the beginning of adolescence—as marked by the onset of puberty. In terms of average age, this definition places the conclusion of childhood around roughly age 12 for girls and age 13 for boys (Lee et al. 2001). The highly influential psychologist, Lawrence Steinberg (2014), aptly sums up the utility of relying on puberty as a marker:

> Experts use puberty to mark the beginning of adolescence because it's easy to measure, has obvious consequences (like sexual maturation), and is universal. In societies that have formal rites of passage, puberty has long been used to indicate when people are no longer children. (p. 46)

We should note, however, that using puberty as a marker of the end of childhood also has its challenges. For one, the onset of puberty is highly variable. That is to say, not everyone hits puberty at exactly the same age. Data on American children from the Health Behavior in School-Aged Children (2009–2010) study (Iannotti 2013) demonstrate this variability quite clearly. For instance, while 96 % of girls report having begun to menstruate by age 14, substantial proportions report having done so far earlier (e.g., 7 % of girls report having menstruated by age 10, 22 % by age 11, and 54 % by age 12). Evidence also points to clear differences in pubertal timing across gender and racial/ethnic groups with girls going through puberty well before boys[2] and African American girls beginning puberty earlier than their non-Hispanic white and Hispanic counterparts (Chumlea et al. 2003; Herman-Giddens et al. 1997). Data also seem to suggest that the age of average pubertal onset is getting earlier and earlier among youth in general (Euling et al. 2008) which—as we will discuss later in the text (see Chap. 6: "Adolescence")—may have important implications for adolescent psychosocial development and risk behavior.

Of course, childhood is not simply a period of years between birth and puberty. Rather, childhood is a critical and vast developmental stage in which we transition from lying flat on our backs as infants to exhibiting a wide range of verbal, psychological, physical, and interpersonal abilities well before the end of middle childhood (Qvortrup et al. 2009). Our experiences during childhood have the power to radically influence our health, well-being, and behavior across the life course (Braveman and Barclay 2009). It is well beyond the scope of this chapter to delve into the details of child development during the first decade of life. However, for our purposes we can clearly state that—beyond merely spanning a particular timeframe and reflecting socio-historical understandings of the needs and rights of children—childhood is a time of

---

[2] For instance, if we go back to the HBSC data, we see that only 7% of boys at age 10, 11% of boys at age 11, and 18% of boys at age 12 have "definitely" started to grow facial hair. By age 14, only 40% can definitely report having a little mustache or stubble (Iannotti 2013). Facial hair is by no means a perfect marker of pubertal maturation, but it does paint a picture that puberty clearly tends to come later among males.

profound biological, psychological, and social development (Calkins 2015; Olson and Sameroff 2009).

A Life-Course Perspective

We have now put together a working definition of childhood. However, a fuller conceptualization of childhood demands that we situate our understanding of this important life stage within a broader contextual and developmental framework. Indeed, childhood is not an entity or experience that exists independently, but rather our childhood experiences are profoundly influenced by our relationships with our parents, families, schools, and neighborhoods. Child development and experiences of childhood do not take place in the abstract or in anything even remotely akin to the controlled environment of the laboratory. For every individual, childhood plays out within a social and historical context and is rooted within ecological systems and structures. Moreover, our childhood experiences are related in important ways to our growth and development during later developmental stages. As we will discuss in more detail, childhood behavior—as well as childhood intrapersonal and contextual factors—have important implications for the first decade of life, but also can influence the shape of our life-course trajectories for decades.

The work of Glen Elder and other life-course scholars provides a very helpful framework for situating childhood and other developmental stages within a broader, biosocial, and contextual understanding. Elder (1974) describes the life course as defined by a series of interconnected trajectories that play out as individuals move from birth to death. Typically, these trajectories relate to education, work, and family (Elder Jr 1998), but increasingly scholars have come to examine trajectories related to other phenomena, including drug abuse and antisocial behavior (Hser et al. 2007; Piquero et al. 2012). Asserting that life is often not a straight path, the life-course perspective is concerned with patterns of stability as well as gradual and abrupt changes in trajectories. To this end, life-course theorists are particularly interested in life transitions and turning points. *Transitions* refer to changes in roles or status that are not as long-lasting as trajectories but are nevertheless often of substantial importance and long-term impact (Elder Jr 1985). Transitions typically refer to normative life changes, such as entry into kindergarten, beginning puberty, graduating high school, getting married, and having a child. However, they can also be conceptualized with respect to drug abuse or antisocial behavioral transitions like initiating alcohol/drug use or delinquent behavior, getting arrested and facing incarceration, seeking substance abuse treatment or achieving a lasting recovery. Notably, transitions are typically understood as being embedded within and giving shape to life trajectories and invariably bring with them a degree of stress and required adaptation. *Turning points* are major life events or transitions that mark a substantial change in one's life-course trajectory. For instance, Sampson and Laub (1996) found that, for some delinquent youth, compulsory military service in World War II functioned as a turning point in which young men's life trajectories were transformed for the better. Getting married has also been highlighted as an important life event that can lead to a turning away from addiction and crime (Laub and Sampson 2003). With respect to the marriage effect, it is interesting to note that it has been found to be partially due to genetic factors (Beaver et al. 2008).

The life-course perspective is rooted in several core principles (Elder Jr 1998), all of which have implications for our developmental understanding of addiction and antisocial behavior. First, the life-course perspective is unequivocal in affirming the importance of *historical time and place*. That is, our life trajectories take shape not within a vacuum, but rather in fluid social and historical contexts. For instance, alcohol and drug-use trajectories are embedded within the social contexts of families and neighborhoods as well as within particular historical periods with varying policies and views related to alcohol and drug use. Just think of how different alcohol use trajectories looked before, during, and after Prohibition, as well as today in an era of increased openness and access to marijuana.[3] A related principle is that of *linked lives*. This principle highlights the ways in which social and historical

---

[3] Evidence suggests that alcohol consumption in the United States dropped markedly during the early years of Prohibition before slowly increasing during Prohibition and, eventually, returning to pre-Prohibition levels in the decades after the repeal of the 18th Amendment (Miron & Zwiebel 1991; Dills et al. 2005). Along the same lines, our recent research examining trends in marijuana

factors influence the lives of individuals by impacting the lives of people in an individual's social network. For instance, an economic downturn might increase parental and family stress, which, in turn, might increase the likelihood of harsh parenting practices or corporal punishment (see Elder Jr et al. 1985). Regretfully, as we will see below, harsh parenting and corporal punishment seem to have important implications for the emergence and persistence of behavior problems during childhood.

The life-course perspective also pays particular attention to the *timing of lives*. More precisely, the sequence and timing of life events is understood as shaping the impact that life experiences have on our life-course trajectories. For instance, while consuming alcohol is a relatively normative behavior—data from the National Survey on Drug Use and Health (NSDUH) 2002–2013 suggest that roughly 90 % of young people in the United States have tried alcohol by age 21—the impact and implications of alcohol initiation is different among 12-year-olds (9 % have tried alcohol by age 12) than it is among youth later in adolescence or young adulthood. Elder and others have looked at the timing of other life events such as marriage or the birth of a first child and examined the ways in which early transitions can set in motion a cumulative sequence of advantageous or, often, disadvantageous events (e.g., early pregnancy can impact educational trajectories which, in turn, can impact earning potential and so on; Elder Jr 1998; Sampson and Laub 1997). The insight here is that timing matters not only in terms of the particular historical context that youth inhabit, but also in terms of the age at which particular normative and non-normative behaviors and events take place. Finally, the life-course perspective tends to affirm the notion of *human agency*. In this respect, Elder and others are careful to affirm that, while social and historical conditions undoubtedly shape life trajectories, the life-course perspective rejects notions of strict determinism (Laub and Sampson 1993, 2003).

---

perception found a marked decrease in marijuana disapproval among young adults between 2002 and 2013 (Salas-Wright et al. 2015).

The life-course perspective is a very powerful framework that offers many insights for a biosocial examination of addiction and antisocial behavior across childhood, adolescence, young adulthood, and beyond. As noted by Braveman and Barclay (2009),

> The life course perspective focuses on understanding how early life experiences can shape health across an entire lifetime, and potentially across generations; it systematically directs attention to the role of context, including social and physical context along with biological factors, over time. (p. S163)

It is a perspective that is designed to account not only for life-course continuity, but one that aims to explain and appreciate the twists and turns observed across many life trajectories. This type of an approach is very useful for thinking about the patterns of onset, escalation, and cessation that are often observed in lives marked by addiction and antisocial behavior (DiClemente 2006; Hser et al. 2007; Farrington 2003; Moffitt 1993; Piquero 2008; Sampson and Laub 1996; Teruya and Hser 2010). Throughout the remainder of this chapter, as well as the chapters on adolescence and adulthood, we will often return to consider the ways in which psychobiological, intrapersonal, and contextual changes in our lives shape life trajectories (Elder Jr 1998).

Behavior Problems in Childhood and Beyond

The developmental window of childhood is vast. The cognitive, psychological, linguistic, and gross motor differences between infants, toddlers, preschool children, and prepubescent school-aged boys and girls are monumental and have important implications for our understanding of what constitutes problem behavior at different childhood stages. Evidence from empirical studies indicates that behavior problems appear to manifest across the spectrum of childhood, but our understanding of such behavior must be contextualized within a developmental framework. Failure to do so can lead us to both overlook behavior problems

that should be recognized and to misinterpret developmentally normative behavior as pathological. In other words, we need to be particularly
mindful about the ways that we conceptualize and measure behavior
problems over the first to decade or so of life.

A Developmentally Specified Understanding of Childhood Behavior Problems

Infancy: Birth to 12 Months

So how early can we actually begin to speak meaningfully about
behavior problems in childhood? And what exactly do behavior problems look like very early on in life? Researchers have actually
attempted to identify externalizing behavior as early as infancy. By
and large, infant externalizing can be thought of as relating to noncompliant behavior, temper tantrums, and physically aggressive acts
such as hitting or biting. If you have a child or know any children, you
are most certainly familiar with one or more of these behaviors, likely
beginning somewhere around the child's first birthday. Parents of small
children know quite well that kids will sometimes scratch our faces,
whack us (unintentionally, intentionally, or in frustration) in the head,
and even bite. For a majority of parents, this is simply a part of the
experience of having small kids.

Beyond parental anecdotes, developmental researchers have examined
infant behavior problems systematically and over time. For instance, a
study by Van Zeijl et al. (2006)—artfully titled, "Terrible ones?"—
looked carefully at parental reports of oppositional, aggressive, and
overactive behavior among 12-month-old children in the Netherlands.
Using the Child Behavior Checklist (CBC; Achenbach and Rescorla
2000), the study found that substantial proportions of infants sometimes
or often destroy others' things (14 %), hit others (10 %), intentionally
hurt others (37 %), and exhibit disobedience (42 %). Moreover, a
minority of infants (10 %) were found to sometimes/often take part in
a wide range of oppositional, aggressive, and overactive behaviors. Most
notably, the externalizing behavior of 12-month-olds was found to be

significantly associated with intrapersonal (e.g., difficult temperament) and parental (e.g., family-related stress) factors known to be linked with externalizing at later developmental stages. Such findings are consistent with other studies that have looked at physical aggression among the one-year-old set (see Carter et al. 2003; Tremblay et al. 1999).

These types of studies are, of course, quite interesting. However, we might note two important caveats. First, the stability of behavior problems among 12-month-old children is markedly lower than that of 24- or 36-month-old children (Van Zeijl et al. 2006). In other words, it is less likely that oppositional, aggressive, or overactive behavior observed on one's first birthday will be observable one year later than it is that the problem behavior of two-year-olds or three-year-olds will persist over the course of a year. Second, while we can observe some degree of problem behaviors among 12-month-old children, the prevalence of such behavior is far lower at 12 months than it is at 24 or 36 months of age (Alink et al. 2006). That is to say, infants have certainly been found to exhibit problem behavior, but they tend to exhibit less of it than we commonly see among two- or three-year-old children.

The take away here is that something akin to problem behavior can be observed among children within the first year of life. Infants can be noncompliant, can begin to have temper tantrums, and can exhibit some physical aggression. However, what we would call externalizing behavior among infants is relatively rare and there isn't much continuity in such behavior among infants over the course of a year (particularly compared to what we see among toddlers and older children). Does this mean that nothing can be learned about future externalizing from taking a close look at infant children? Absolutely not. In fact, we will dedicate substantial attention later on in this chapter to looking at what research on childhood temperament during the first year has shown us about problem behavior across the life course. However, in terms of behavior problems, research seems to suggest that—while the more extreme forms of infant externalizing may be a flag for future issues—you shouldn't be surprised or particularly concerned if your infant son or daughter lands, during a moment of frustration or exhaustion, an occasional whack to the face or a well-placed kick.

Toddlerhood and the Preschool Years

There is no doubt that a tremendous amount happens during the first year of life, including changes that allow for the emergence of potentially troubling behaviors such as physical aggression. As impressive as infant development is, the normative developmental changes that take place during toddlerhood (ages one to three) and the preschool years (ages three to five) are equally—if not more—astounding. Here we see children transform from being, quite literally, shaky on their feet and very limited in terms of verbal communication as toddlers to being, by ages four or five, physically and verbally adroit and capable of a wide array of imaginative and tangible creations. While Wolfgang Amadeus Mozart was, of course, extraordinarily precocious in his ability to compose sophisticated musical arrangements by age five, many five-year-olds can do a variety of impressive and important things such as follow relatively complex directions, successfully interact with other children their age, manage transitions from one task to another, and follow rules and routines. By the time most children reach age four or five, we have witnessed great advances in their capacity to manage conflict and regulate reactions and emotions (Bronson 2000). During toddlerhood and the preschool years children grow by leaps and bounds in a process that is often enjoyable and impressive to watch.

Of course, not all kids are Mozart and many do not behave like little angels either. That is, during toddlerhood and the preschool years, we also see an important amount of—both developmentally normative and potentially developmentally disconcerting—behavior problems, including loss of temper, noncompliance, high activity level, difficulty regulating impulses, and physical aggression. One important point that we should underscore quite clearly here is that there is scholarly consensus that a degree of disruptive behavior is to be expected during these early stages (Campbell 2006; Tremblay 2000). Take, for example, physical aggression. Studies defining aggression as behaviors that could cause physical harm to people, animals, or objects (e.g., hitting, kicking, fighting) have found that early childhood aggressive behavior is astoundingly common. A well-cited study by Alink et al. (2006) found that roughly 70 to 80 % of the parents of two- and three-year-olds reported that their children exhibited at least some form of physically aggressive behavior. This matches up with other influential studies that have found similar proportions of youth exhibiting aggressive behavior during toddlerhood (Nærde et al. 2014; Tremblay et al. 2004). Richard Tremblay (2015) has gone so far to note that data from, "[P]rospective studies suggest that the peak in the frequency of physical aggression for most humans is somewhere between two and four years of age" (p. 42). The key insight here is that many young children, indeed the vast majority, can be said to be involved in some degree of physical aggression at some point during toddlerhood and the preschool years. Put simply, there is substantial support for that notion of a normative element to problem behaviors during early childhood.

One crucial element in viewing behavior problems as developmentally normative early on in childhood is that, by and large, for most people, these behaviors tend to go away. Indeed, evidence suggests that for the vast majority of children, such behaviors tend to begin to markedly attenuate by the time they enter the preschool stage. We noted above that Alink et al. (2006) found that roughly three out of four children exhibited some form of aggressive behavior during the toddler stage. It is noteworthy that follow-up data indicate that, despite the stability viewed from age two to age three, aggressive behavior begins a significant decline for many children after their third birthday. This is roughly consistent with other studies documenting significant declines in problem behavior during latter stages of toddlerhood (Nærde et al. 2014) and across the preschool stage and beyond (Côté et al. 2006). This also fits with research suggesting that a substantial proportion of children with elevated levels of physical aggression as toddlers effectively extinguish aggressive behavior by the end of the preschool stage (NICHD Early Child Care Research Network 2004). All this is to say, our understanding of problem behavior during toddlerhood as a normative developmental phenomenon is rooted in evidence that, for many children, behavior problems peak during the toddler stage and decrease markedly as they move into the preschool years and middle childhood.

You might note, however, that not all problem behavior ceases during the toddler stage. Rather, in a salient minority of children, we see a continuation of aggressive and disruptive behaviors during the preschool years and into middle childhood, preadolescence, and beyond. There are a number of really exciting studies in this area, tracing the trajectories of behavior problems from the toddler stage through the preschool years and beyond. The influential developmental psychologist, Richard Tremblay, and his colleagues have carried a number of longitudinal studies focused on physical aggression among youth during early childhood. In one trajectory analysis, Tremblay et al. (2004) identified a subsample of children (14 %) who, not only maintain high levels of physical aggression across the toddler stage, but also exhibit an increase in aggression as they entered the preschool years. Côté et al. (2006) carried out a similar study in which they identified a subgroup of youth (17 %) that showed elevated and stable levels of physical aggression across toddlerhood, the preschool years, and throughout middle childhood.[4] Research lead by Susan Campbell, as part of the National Institute of Child and Human Development (NICHD) Early Child and Youth Development study, points to similar results. For instance, Campbell et al. (2006) found that 15 % of youth exhibit moderate and stable levels of aggression across the spectrum of childhood while an estimated 3 % maintain aggressive behavior from toddlerhood to preadolescence. Together, these and other studies provide compelling evidence that, for an important subset of children, behavior problems begin early on and continue throughout childhood.

We will circle back to the work of Richard Tremblay, Susan Campbell, and other influential researchers who have examined the trajectories of behavior problems among youth as their work sheds important light on the biosocial antecedents of addiction and antisocial behavior. However, their work raises an important issue related to the salience as well as the challenge of distinguishing between normative and non-normative behavior problems during the toddler and preschool stages. Evidence of continuity

---

[4] It is worth noting that, while we do see a steady pattern of high physical aggression among this subset from 17 to 60 months, peak scores were observed for highly aggressive and less aggressive youth at 42 months. In other words, this study also suggests that childhood aggression finds its pinnacle somewhere between the ages of three and four.

between early and later childhood behavior problems for a minority of children suggests that behavioral issues in toddlers and preschool children are not something simply to be dismissed. Certainly, for many young children, exhibiting some aggressive or noncompliant behavior is a normal part of child development; however, for others behavior problems early in life mark the start of a trajectory of behavior that can be highly problematic for the children themselves and others around them. As we will discuss in greater depth later on in this book (see Chap. 8: "Prevention and Treatment"), it is critical that we work to identify and help children whose early behavior problems are most likely to develop into a long-standing pattern of problem behavior.

In the same breath, diagnostically identifying—or, some may say, labeling—toddlers or preschool children as exhibiting behavior that is clinically pathological and marks a potential long-term pattern of problem behavior is no small thing. Toward the end of this chapter (see the section entitled "Salient childhood risk factors") we will delve more into research that has been instrumental in identifying children for whom early problem behavior may represent the beginnings of a non-normative trajectory of behavior problems. A number of high-quality, longitudinal studies have demonstrated that we can prospec-tively identify—based on behavior as well as intrapersonal and con-textual factors—young children that are most at risk of continuing to exhibit behavior problems across childhood and beyond. However, this is no easy task and we also cannot predict long-term behavioral outcomes with anything approaching 100 % accuracy. As such, we are obliged to underscore the importance of taking great care in identifying those youth that truly are at risk. As articulated in a thoughtful editorial published in *The Journal of Child Psychology and Psychiatry*,

The answer should balance between the risk of over-pathologizing normal behavior in young children that represents developmentally deviant but transient manifestations of dysfunction on the one hand, and the risk of missed opportunities for early recognition of clinically significant indica-tors for the later onset of a full-blown disorder and appropriate early intervention on the other. (Banaschewski 2010, p. 2)

The precise details of such diagnoses are beyond the scope of this chapter, but clearly a developmentally specified nosology that looks deeply at the frequency, quality, and context of problem behavior in early childhood is necessary (Wakschlag et al. 2010).

Middle Childhood: Kindergarten to Puberty

Describing problem behavior is perhaps a little bit less tricky during middle childhood. This is a reflection of two interrelated points. First, advances in cognitive, emotional, and social development during middle childhood are such that problem behaviors like physical aggression and other impulse-related outbursts are simply less normative. As described above, physical aggression among a two-and-a-half-year-old who pushes another child in defense of a toy or bites their caretaker in the midst of a pre-nap meltdown is, in relatively low frequency, somewhat to be expected. However, the psychoemotional and verbal capacity of children between roughly the ages of 6 and 12 is such that such problem behavior is far less common and far less developmentally normative (Underwood et al. 2009).

On a related note, defining problem behavior during middle childhood is made easier by the fact that we can rather confidently look to widely accepted diagnostic criteria for relevant disruptive, impulse-control, and conduct disorders as laid out in the American Psychiatric Association's (APA) (2013) *Diagnostic and Statistical Manual of Mental Disorders, Fifth Edition* (DSM-5). The DSM's understanding of conduct disorder—a persistent pattern of behaviors that violate the rights of others or age-appropriate norms—taps into behaviors that begin to really emerge during middle childhood (e.g., serious physical aggression toward people or animals, property destruction, deceitfulness/theft, serious rule-breaking). Indeed, the DSM-5 notes in the description of the development and course of conduct disorder that "The onset of conduct disorder may occur as early as the preschool years, but the first significant symptoms usually emerge during the period from middle childhood through middle adolescence" (p. 473). Simply put, conduct disorder gives us a well-specified framework for understanding behavior problems during middle childhood.

At this point we should note that our discussion of problem behavior up to this point and throughout middle childhood excludes alcohol and drug use. This is noteworthy given that this is a book explicitly about both addiction and antisocial behavior. It is also perhaps noteworthy given that substance misuse is clearly identified as an associated feature of conduct disorder, particularly among females (APA 2013). However, we elected in this chapter to focus our discussion around non-substance-use problem behaviors for several reasons. First, evidence suggests that, by and large, the prevalence of alcohol and drug use among prepubescent children is low. For instance, data from the HBSC study (Iannotti 2013), indicate that—when asked on a questionnaire—98.72 % of 10-year-olds and 98.23 % of 11-year-olds report having never been drunk.[5] Along the same lines, we see that 99.67 % of ten-year-olds and 98.54 % of 11-year-olds report having never used marijuana. Another issue is that there is a dearth of systematic epidemiologic data on drug use among children as most of this type of research is typically conducted on populations age 12 and above. Two of the largest, most important studies of drug use—Monitoring the Future and the National Survey on Drug Use and Health—do not begin collecting data until youth are on the cusp of adolescence. And finally, drug use in adolescence and adulthood has its etiological roots in early problem behavior manifested in childhood. In other words, higher prevalence child problem behaviors such as physical aggression and noncompliance invariably precede substance use initiation by several years. The point here is that we are not dismissing the importance of substance use initiation during the latter childhood years, but that we have elected to focus our attention on such disconcerting behavior as part of our chapter on adolescence.

---

[5] To be fair, we see higher prevalence rates when we look at alcohol *consumption* rather than *intoxication*. For instance, 3.1% of ten-year-olds and 7.69% of 11-year-olds surveyed in the HBSC report having consumed alcohol in the previous 30 days (Iannotti 2013). Drawing from a life-course perspective, such early initiation—even when it is just a sip (see Jackson et al. 2015)—is potentially problematic and may relate to constructs such as timing of lives and cumulative disadvantage.

Childhood Externalizing (Very Often) Sets the Stage

At this point we've described how problem behavior manifests across the spectrum of childhood, but important questions remain unanswered. In particular, what relevance does child problem behavior have for our broader, biosocial understanding of addiction and antisocial behavior across the life course? Above, in our discussion of the life-course perspective, we underscored the insight that childhood experiences often have important implications for our health and behavior across an entire life span—indeed, across generations (Braveman and Barclay 2009). Below we will discuss several important ways in which serious and recurrent childhood externalizing very often sets the stage for drug abuse and delinquency during adolescence as well as addiction and antisocial behavior that persists into the adult years. We will also point to important caveats, including evidence that clearly not all young people who exhibit elevated levels of problem behavior during the first decade are destined for a life of addiction and antisociality.

To begin, let's start by considering the degree to which childhood behavior problems are related to antisocial behavior later on in life. It is not often that Dr. Phil is quoted in scientific books,[6] but his commentary via social media on 24 March 2014 fits well here: "The best predictor of future behavior is relevant past behavior." Dr. Phil's analysis is undoubtedly simplistic, but certainly substantial evidence indicates that problem behavior during childhood does not bode well in terms of adolescent delinquency and adult antisociality. More precisely, multiple longitudinal studies have found that young people who consistently exhibit elevated levels of aggression and/or other forms of problem behavior across early and middle childhood are far more likely than their peers to persist in this behavior into adolescence and, frequently,

---

[6] However, serious researchers have examined the pitfalls of following the advice provided by televised talk shows dedicated to health and well-being. A study published in the *BMJ* in 2014 found that the advice from *The Dr. Oz Show and The Doctors* was often lacking an evidence base or ran counter to consensus medical opinion (Korownyk et al. 2014). The *BMJ* study did not look at *Dr. Phil*, but the findings indicate that it's wise to bring a bit of skepticism to health-related talk shows.

well into adulthood (Aguilar et al. 2000; Broidy et al. 2003; Campbell et al. 2006; Farrington et al. 1998; Moffitt 1993; Piquero et al. 2012; Roisman et al. 2010; Sampson and Laub 2003). In this way we can meaningfully say that there is an important degree of connection between childhood behavior problems and antisocial behavior across the life course.

However, this is no small claim and, consequently, two important points of clarification should be highlighted. First, the proportion of children who exhibit very high levels of childhood problem behavior and, in turn, are most likely to persist in such behavior during later developmental stages is quite small. Across a variety of data sources, we continually see that this subset of individuals comprises roughly 3 to 6 % of the childhood, adolescent, and adult population (Tracy and Kempf-Leonard 1996; Wolfgang et al. 1972). In our own work, we have referred to this subset of offenders who, despite the relative size, account for a substantial proportion of antisocial behavior as the "Severe 5 %" (Vaughn et al. 2011, 2014). Second, we cannot emphasize enough that not all children who exhibit elevated levels of problem behavior during childhood persist in such behavior in later developmental stages. In fact, multiple studies have identified what are deemed "recoveries" or "childhood limiteds"; that is, individuals who show levels of childhood externalizing similar or slightly lower than that of the "Severe 5 %" but desist to low-to-normal levels of problem behavior sometime before the onset of adolescence (Aguilar et al. 2000; Roisman et al. 2010). Typically, this group is relatively small, accounting for anywhere between 5 and 12 % of youth, but it is nevertheless a group that is repeatedly identified in longitudinal trajectory analyses. Simply, it is worth noting that, when we take a close look at subgroups of youth, past childhood problem behavior is an important but not always a perfect predictor of delinquent or antisocial behavior at later developmental stages.

At this point an important question remains: What, if anything, does child problem behavior tell us about drug abuse and addiction? For better or for worse, it seems to tell us quite a bit. The often-cited review by Hawkins et al. (1992) of risk and protective factors describes in substantial detail the developmental link between early and persistent problem behaviors and substance use during adolescence. This matches up with more up-to-date evidence from longitudinal studies examining the predictive power of early behavior problems for adolescent drug abuse (see Lee et al. 2011; Martel et al. 2009; Sitnick et al. 2014; Storr et al. 2004; Wu et al. 2010). For instance, Fergusson et al. (2007) found in a prospective study that conduct problems at ages seven to nine predicted tobacco, alcohol, cannabis, and other illicit drug use use/abuse during the latter stages of adolescence.[7] Similarly, Molina and Pelham (2003) found—in a prospective study of children with attention-deficit/hyperactivity disorder (ADHD) diagnoses—that childhood diagnoses of a behavioral disorder (i.e., oppositional defiant disorder or conduct disorder) uniquely predicted (with large effects) adolescent drug use while controlling for inattention, impulsivity, and hyperactivity. Simply put, we can say quite confidently that problem behavior during childhood, particularly in its more severe and persistent forms, is robustly linked with substance use problems during the adolescent stage.

Evidence also suggests that child behavior problems are related to risk for substance-abuse problems during young adulthood and beyond. For instance, Moffitt et al. (2002), using data from the highly influential Dunedin study, found that individuals who began exhibiting problem behavior during childhood that persisted into adolescence were far more likely to report elevated alcohol and drug use problems as young adults. In the same breath, however, those who showed significant behavior problems during childhood but not thereafter (i.e., "recoveries") were, by the age of 26, no different from the normative comparison group with respect to alcohol or drug-use problems. Moffitt and colleagues are clearly not the only ones to examine this issue using prospective data. Englund et al. (2008), in a study that followed individuals from middle childhood through early adulthood, found that elevated externalizing among boys at the age of nine was significantly associated with the likelihood of meeting criteria for an alcohol use disorder at age 28. Still other studies have found links between early aggressive/externalizing behaviors and drug use outcomes such as alcohol and drug use, problem

---

[7] Please note that in Chapter 6, "Adolescence," we go into greater detail as to the standard age parameters for defining the adolescent stage among American youth in the 21st century.

drinking, drug abuse, drunk driving, and alcohol and other drug-use disorders during adulthood (Farrington 1991; Galéra et al. 2013; Reinke et al. 2012; Robins and Price 1991). All in all, evidence from a variety of studies suggests that childhood behavior problems—particularly those that begin early and stretch into the adolescent stage—often foreshadow alcohol and drug abuse problems later in life.

Salient Childhood Risk Factors

We have laid out the evidence from multiple studies suggesting that child problem behavior is related to drug abuse and antisocial behavior during adolescence and beyond. This evidence is quite clear and compelling, but it still begs a number of important questions. For one, what predicts child problem behavior in the first place? Is there scientific evidence that can help us to understand the intrapersonal and contextual factors related to childhood aggression, noncompliance, and other oppositional and conduct-related issues? If so, are these risk factors also linked with behavior at later developmental stages or are they factors that have relevance only to childhood? Below we will take a close look at these questions in light of state-of-the-art scientific research as we delve into the etiology of childhood problem behavior, as well as the importance of childhood risk factors in the etiology of drug abuse and antisocial behavior across the life course.

Early Childhood Temperament: A Core Intrapersonal Construct

As we took a developmentally specified look at child problem behavior, we began by discussing studies that have examined problem or externalizing behavior among infant children. We noted that many serious scholars believe that externalizing behavior can be examined very early on in life, including as early as the latter part of the first year (Alink et al. 2006; Carter et al. 2003; Tremblay et al. 1999; Van Zeijl et al. 2006). Importantly, however, in our discussion, we focused primarily on observable comportment that could be described as behaviorally akin to externalizing at later developmental stages (e.g., hitting, biting, etc.). Looking at such behaviors is undoubtedly informative, but there are many other early reactive and self-regulatory features—arguably more important than externalizing—that have been demonstrated to be of tremendous importance to a biosocial and developmental understanding of behavior problems during childhood and beyond.

One central feature is temperament. Temperament can be understood as the largely inborn ways in which individuals experience and, in turn, regulate their responses to a wide array of environmental stimuli (DeLisi and Vaughn 2014, 2015). For example, is a child more inclined to passively observe their environment or do they strongly prefer to move their bodies and actively explore the world around them? We see substantial variation in terms of the level of activity observed among children during infancy and toddlerhood (Saudino 2012). Additionally, how does a child tend to respond to new people, objects, or situations? Some children are drawn to novel experiences while others tend to withdraw or avoid novelty (Zentner and Bates 2008). What does a child's mood tend to look like? Some children seem to smile constantly and draw others in while others are quick to cry or be unfriendly with those around them. Responses to these and other kinds of questions looking at infant adaptability, intensity of reaction, task persistence, distractibility, and other constructs tap into to the various dimensions of temperament. Indeed, based on the aforementioned constructs, Alexander Thomas and Stella Chess (1977) developed a highly influential model of temperamental profiles of children. They found that some children are quite "easy" most of the time, others are a bit "slow to warm up," and still others can be said to be markedly "difficult" inasmuch as they are typically slow to adjust to new things and tend to react negatively and intensely to stimuli in their environment (Thomas et al. 1982).

Temperament is typically conceptualized as a largely innate and stable characteristic that is moderately heritable (Tuvblad et al. 2010) and shaped by biological factors relating to central nervous system reactivity and our neuroanatomy (Kagan and Snidman 1991; Whittle et al. 2006, 2008). Mary Rothbart (2011), the developer of several widely used measures of early childhood temperament, provides an in-depth description of temperament, stating:

> We have defined temperament as relatively stable, primarily biologically-based differences in reactivity and self-regulation. By reactivity, we mean the excitability or arousability of behavioral, endocrine, autonomic, and central nervous system responses . . . By self-regulation, we mean processes, such as attention, approach, avoidance, and inhibition that serve to modulate (enhance or inhibit) reactivity. (p. 273)

Temperament is particularly relevant to research on childhood as there is broad consensus that it can be meaningfully measured as early as in infancy. Indeed, psychometric studies using Rothbart's Infant Behavior Questionnaire point to reliable and valid measurement as early as three to six months of age (Gartstein and Rothbart 2003). Beyond measurement, the prospective implications of temperament have been shown to be quite far-reaching. Indeed, evidence suggests that temperament plays an important role in probabilistically predicting the likelihood that children will manifest behavior problems and, in turn, run into issues with drug abuse and antisocial behavior. As it turns out, studying the ways in which six-month-olds react to the world around them can tell us a lot about how they will continue to react to their environment long into the future (McCrae et al. 2000; Rothbart et al. 2000).

Let us go back for a moment to the studies that have tried to measure problem behavior among infants. While we are admittedly a bit reluctant to make too much of hitting, biting, and grabbing at nine to 12 months of age, these studies have found something very interesting that relates to temperament. In the study of early childhood externalizing by Van Zeijl et al. (2006), difficult temperament was found to be far and away the strongest correlate of externalizing among children at 12, 24, and 36 months.[8] This is consistent with other prospective studies that have found difficult temperament at six months of age (i.e., high activity

---

[8] This particular study relied upon the Infant Characteristics Questionnaire (ICQ; Bates et al. 1979). The ICQ is designed to be used with infants as young as four to six months of age and measures constructs such as fussiness, adaptability, mood, predictability, and cuddliness.

level, difficult to soothe, distress due to limitations) to be associated with elevated levels of physical aggression during toddlerhood and the early preschool years (Nærde et al. 2014). Still other studies have found that, while controlling for a variety of parental characteristics, parenting practices, family dysfunction, and socioeconomic status, the link between early childhood temperament and later antisocial behavior ceases to be significant (Tremblay et al. 2004). While results are admittedly somewhat mixed, we can say that—even during the very early stages of child development—it is reasonable to conclude that temperament likely functions as an important factor of relevance to behavior problems.

The importance of temperament is certainly not limited to infancy, toddlerhood, and preschool. Moffitt's (1993) highly influential taxonomy of child- versus adolescent-onset antisocial behavior placed temperament and other neuropsychological risk factors at the heart of its understanding of child problem behavior and the continuity of such behavior across the life course. The study by Caspi et al. (1995) of the developmental links between early childhood temperament (ages 3–5) and antisocial behavior at the tail edge of childhood (ages 9–11) and early-to-mid adolescence (ages 13–15) provides an important source of empirical support for Moffitt's taxonomy. More specifically, an early temperamental "lack of control"—that is, difficulty regulating impulsive behavior, difficulty persisting in problem-solving, and negative reactions in the face of challenge—robustly predicted externalizing roughly a decade later on in life. This is consistent with more recent studies that have found early childhood temperament to be an important construct in understanding antisocial behavior well beyond childhood, particularly in conjunction with other sources of social and contextual risk (Althoff et al. 2010; Fearon et al. 2014). In addition to antisocial behavior, we also see substantial evidence linking early childhood temperament to later substance-use problems. Indeed, Moffitt et al. (2002) found that, in following their sample into the young adult stage, those individuals with child-onset problem behavior (i.e., those most likely to have a difficult temperament early in life) were at markedly greater risk for alcohol and drug problems. Again, these findings cohere with more recent research linking childhood temperament with substance abuse and other neurologically similar outcomes (i.e., pathological gambling) during adolescence and adulthood (Armstrong et al. 2013; Lahat et al. 2012; Rioux et al. 2016; Martel et al. 2009; Slutske et al. 2012).

Let's Be Absolutely Clear: Social and Contextual Factors Matter

There is a risk in discussing temperament—as well as any variety of biologically based or biologically influenced factors—of giving the impression that biology is the sole driver of child problem behavior and, later, addiction and antisocial behavior. It should be stated unequivocally that this is not our position and, perhaps more importantly, it would not be an accurate interpretation of the overarching body of evidence examining child problem behavior and related constructs. As noted above, a number of factors that are undoubtedly related to human biology do seem to be an important part of the puzzle in terms of understanding why some young people exhibit problem behavior early on in life and why some persist in such behavior beyond childhood. However, such findings need to be situated within a broader familial and social context in order to be properly interpreted. Moreover, evidence also seems to indicate that biologically based factors such as temperament influence child problem behavior and risk for later addiction/antisocial behavior primarily by means of *interacting* with social and contextual factors over time. Below we will briefly discuss several well-researched social and contextual factors that have been shown to play an important role in the etiology of child problem behavior, as well as in the etiology of drug abuse and antisocial behavior during adolescence and beyond.

Not surprisingly, parents and parenting are of relevance to child problem behavior. For instance, a number of prospective studies have found that low levels of maternal sensitivity during early childhood—that is, failure to perceive and respond to a child's cues—are related to physical aggression during middle childhood (Campbell et al. 2006, 2010; Roisman et al. 2010). Failure to be in tune with an infant's needs is related to risk for problem behavior, but we also see that active parenting practices are also related with child problem behavior. For instance, Tremblay et al. (2004) found harsh and coercive parenting practices at five months to be significantly associated with a clear pattern of sustained physical aggression across the toddlerhood stage (i.e., 15 to 42 months). Notably, this matches up with more recent studies that have found a developmental link between harsh parenting, including corporal punishment, and problem behavior across the first decade of life (Barnes et al. 2013; Côté et al. 2006; MacKenzie et al. 2014) as well as research suggesting a robust link between adverse childhood experiences and a variety of substance-use disorders and antisocial behavioral problems during adulthood (Anda et al. 2006; Vaughn et al. 2015a, b). Simply put, parental factors, especially parenting practices that are either unresponsive or markedly harsh, clearly are related to problem behavior.

Neither parenting practices nor child problem behavior take place in a vacuum, but rather both play out in the context of families, family stress, and home environments. For instance, Aguilar et al. (2000), in a prospective study ranging from birth to mid-adolescence, found that social and economic stress among parents during childhood (i.e., 12 to 48 months) was significantly associated with offspring early-onset and persistent antisocial behavior. This matches with findings from the Dunedin Study in which family conflict during childhood (i.e., ages seven to nine years) differentiated between childhood onset antisocial behavior versus later onset antisociality (Moffitt and Caspi 2001). Other studies have found a chaotic home environment— defined by lack of routine, regular confusion, and disorder—to be linked with child problem behavior as well as low parental nurturance, dysfunctional parental discipline, and parental stress (Dumas et al. 2005). Collectively, these findings fit well within an ecological systems framework in which parental, household, and, presumably, broader contextual factors reciprocally interact to shape the developmental and problem behavior trajectories of youth (Bronfenbrenner and Ceci 1994; Szapocznik and Coatsworth 1999).

Beyond simply looking independently at intrapersonal (i.e., temperament) and contextual (i.e., family stress, home environment) factors, a number of studies have looked at the concurrent and developmental relationships between these factors in relation to problem behavior. For instance, Martel et al. (2009), in a prospective study of youth from early childhood through adolescence, sought to identify temperamental and child behavioral mechanisms that could explain the relationship between family risk factors (parental alcoholism/antisociality) and adolescent substance abuse. They found that reactive control was related to childhood problem behavior which, in turn, was associated with alcohol and drug abuse during adolescence. Similarly, Fearon et al. (2014), in a study of adoptive mothers and their children, examined the complex interplay of early childhood temperament, maternal negativity towards the child, and marital conflict. Study findings suggest that difficult child temperament is associated with problem behavior during early childhood, but only in the context of family stress (i.e., marital problems among the adoptive parents). Other studies have looked at similarly interesting and complex relationships between temperament, parental factors, and substance use and antisocial behavior to provide fascinating evidence of the ways in which biological and social factors interact over the life course (Armstrong et al. 2013; Mesman et al. 2009; Pickles et al. 2013; Rioux et al. 2016).

Conclusion

We have covered a lot of ground in this chapter as the developmental period of childhood is vast and an astounding amount of research has examined the emergence and development of problem behavior over life's first decade. It is reasonable at this point to ask, what are we to make of all this information related to childhood and behavior problems? The take away here can be reduced to three main points. First, we see evidence of behavior problems across the full spectrum of childhood, but great care needs to be taken to understand such behavior within a developmentally specified framework. While physical aggression is always disconcerting, it may mean something different during toddlerhood than in kindergarten or on the cusp of adolescence. Second, biologically based factors such as temperament clearly seem to be an important part of the equation when it comes to understanding child problem behavior; however, findings from a variety of prospective studies suggest that a "difficult temperament" may be most troublesome when combined with exposure to environmental adversities such as harsh parenting and family stress. In other words, the etiology of child behavior problems is likely more a function of *biosocial* interactions rather than independent biological and/or social risk factors.

Third, child problem behavior is most meaningfully understood from a life-course perspective. The constructs of timing of lives and cumulative disadvantage help us in understanding how early behavioral problems can snowball into larger, more serious outcomes. And with that, let us conclude our discussion of childhood and move into looking at the biosocial bases of drug abuse and delinquent behavior during adolescence.

References

Achenbach, T.M. & Rescorla, L.A. (2000). *ASEBA preschool forms & profiles*. Burlington: University of Vermont, Research Center for Children, Youth and Families.

Aguilar, B., Sroufe, L.A., Egeland, B., & Carlson, E. (2000). Distinguishing the early-onset/persistent and adolescence-onset antisocial behavior types: From birth to 16 years. *Development and Psychopathology, 12*(2), 109–132.

Alink, L.R., Mesman, J., Van Zeijl, J., Stolk, M.N., Juffer, F., Koot, H.M., et al. (2006). The early childhood aggression curve: Development of physical aggression in 10-to 50-month-old children. *Child Development, 77*(4), 954–966.

Althoff, R.R., Verhulst, F.C., Rettew, D.C., Hudziak, J.J., & van der Ende, J. (2010). Adult outcomes of childhood dysregulation: A 14-year follow-up study. *Journal of the American Academy of Child & Adolescent Psychiatry, 49*(11), 1105–1116.

Anda, R.F., Felitti, V.J., Bremner, J.D., Walker, J.D., Whitfield, C.H., Perry, B.D., et al. (2006). The enduring effects of abuse and related adverse experiences in childhood. *European Archives of Psychiatry and Clinical Neuroscience, 256*(3), 174–186.

APA (American Psychiatric Association). (2013). *Diagnostic and statistical manual of mental disorders (DSM-5®)*. Arlington American Psychiatric Publications.

Armstrong, J.M., Ruttle, P.L., Burk, L.R., Costanzo, P.R., Strauman, T.J., & Essex, M.J. (2013). Early risk factors for alcohol use across high school and its covariation with deviant friends. *Journal of Studies on Alcohol and Drugs, 74*(5), 746–756.

Banaschewski, T. (2010). Editorial: Preschool behaviour problems: Over-pathologised or under-identified? A developmental psychopathology perspective is needed. *Journal of Child Psychology and Psychiatry, 51*(1), 1–2.

Barnes, J.C., Boutwell, B.B., Beaver, K.M., & Gibson, C.L. (2013). Analyzing the origins of childhood externalizing behavioral problems. *Developmental Psychology*, *49*(12), 2272–2284.

Bates, J.E., Freeland, C.A.B., & Lounsbury, M.L. (1979). Measurement of infant difficultness. *Child Development*, *50*(3), 794–803.

Beaver, K.M., DeLisi, M., Wright, J.P., & Vaughn, M.G. (2008). Desistance from delinquency: The marriage effect revisited and extended. *Social Science Research*, *37*(3), 736–752.

Braveman, P. & Barclay, C. (2009). Health disparities beginning in childhood: A life-course perspective. *Pediatrics*, *124*(Suppl 3), S163–S175.

Broidy, L.M., Nagin, D.S., Tremblay, R.E., Bates, J.E., Brame, B., Dodge, K.A., et al. (2003). Developmental trajectories of childhood disruptive behaviors and adolescent delinquency: A six-site, cross-national study. *Developmental Psychology*, *39*(2), 222–245.

Bronfenbrenner, U. & Ceci, S.J. (1994). Nature–nuture reconceptualized in developmental perspective: A bioecological model. *Psychological Review*, *101*(4), 568–586.

Bronson, M. (2000). *Self-regulation in early childhood: Nature and nurture*. New York: Guilford Press.

Calkins, S.D. (2015). *Handbook of infant biopsychosocial development*. New York: Guilford Press.

Campbell, S.B. (2006). *Behavior problems in preschool children. Clinical and developmental issues*. New York: Guilford Press.

Campbell, S.B., Spieker, S., Burchinal, M., & Poe, M.D. (2006). Trajectories of aggression from toddlerhood to age 9 predict academic and social functioning through age 12. *Journal of Child Psychology and Psychiatry*, *47*(8), 791–800.

Campbell, S.B., Spieker, S., Vandergrift, N., Belsky, J., & Burchinal, M. (2010). Predictors and sequelae of trajectories of physical aggression in school-age boys and girls. *Development and Psychopathology*, *22*(1), 133–150.

Carter, A.S., Briggs-Gowan, M.J., Jones, S.M., & Little, T.D. (2003). The infant–toddler social and emotional assessment (ITSEA): Factor structure, reliability, and validity. *Journal of Abnormal Child Psychology*, *31*(5), 495–514.

Caspi, A., Henry, B., McGee, R.O., Moffitt, T.E., & Silva, P.A. (1995). Temperamental origins of child and adolescent behavior problems: From age three to age fifteen. *Child Development*, *66*(1), 55–68.

Chumlea, W.C., Schubert, C.M., Roche, A.F., Kulin, H.E., Lee, P.A., Himes, J.H., & Sun, S.S. (2003). Age at menarche and racial comparisons in US girls. *Pediatrics, 111*(1), 110–113.

Côté, S., Vaillancourt, T., LeBlanc, J.C., Nagin, D.S., & Tremblay, R.E. (2006). The development of physical aggression from toddlerhood to pre-adolescence: A nation-wide longitudinal study of Canadian children. *Journal of Abnormal Child Psychology, 34*(1), 68–82.

DeLisi, M. & Vaughn, M.G. (2014). Foundation for a temperament-based theory of antisocial behavior and criminal justice system involvement. *Journal of Criminal Justice, 42*(1), 10–25.

DeLisi, M. & Vaughn, M.G. (2015). Ingredients for criminality require genes, temperament, and psychopathic personality. *Journal of Criminal Justice, 43*(4), 290–294.

DiClemente, C.C. (2006). Natural change and the troublesome use of substances: A life-course perspective. In W.R. Miller & K.M. Carroll (Eds.), *Rethinking substance abuse: What science shows, and what we should do about it* (pp. 81–96). New York: Guilford Press.

Dills, A.K., Jacobson, M., & Miron, J.A. (2005). The effect of alcohol prohibition on alcohol consumption: Evidence from drunkenness arrests. *Economics Letters, 86*(2), 279–284.

Dumas, J.E., Nissley, J., Nordstrom, A., Smith, E.P., Prinz, R.J., & Levine, D.W. (2005). Home chaos: Sociodemographic, parenting, interactional, and child correlates. *Journal of Clinical Child and Adolescent Psychology, 34*(1), 93–104.

Edmonds, E.V. & Pavcnik, N. (2005). Child labor in the global economy. *The Journal of Economic Perspectives, 19*(1), 199–220.

Elder Jr, G.H. (1974). *Children of the Great Depression: Social change in life experience.* Chicago University of Chicago Press.

Elder Jr, G.H. (1985). *Life course dynamics: Trajectories and transitions 1968–1980.* Ithaca Cornell University Press.

Elder Jr, G.H. (1998). The life course as developmental theory. *Child Development, 69*(1), 1–12.

Elder Jr, G.H., Van Nguyen, T., & Caspi, A. (1985). Linking family hardship to children's lives. *Child Development, 56*(2), 361–375.

Englund, M.M., Egeland, B., Oliva, E.M., & Collins, W.A. (2008). Childhood and adolescent predictors of heavy drinking and alcohol use disorders in early adulthood: A longitudinal developmental analysis. *Addiction, 103*(s1), 23–35.

Euling, S.Y., Herman-Giddens, M.E., Lee, P.A., Selevan, S.G., Juul, A., Sørensen, T.I., et al. (2008). Examination of US puberty-timing data from 1940 to 1994 for secular trends: Panel findings. *Pediatrics*, *121*(Suppl 3), S172–S191.

Farrington, D.P. (1991). Childhood aggression and adult violence: Early precursors and later-life outcomes. In D.J. Pepler & K.H. Rubin (Eds.), *The development and treatment of childhood aggression* (pp. 5–29). Hillsdale Lawrence Erlbaum Associates.

Farrington, D.P. (2003). Developmental and life-course criminology: Key theoretical and empirical issues—The 2002 Sutherland Award Address. *Criminology*, *41*(2), 221–225.

Farrington, D.P., Lambert, S., & West, D.J. (1998). Criminal careers of two generations of family members in the Cambridge Study in Delinquent Development. *Studies on Crime and Crime Prevention*, *7*, 85–106.

Fass, P.S. & Mason, M.A. (Eds.) (2000). *Childhood in America*. New York New York University Press.

Fearon, R.M., Reiss, D., Leve, L.D., Shaw, D.S., Scaramella, L.V., Ganiban, J.M., et al. (2014). Child-evoked maternal negativity from 9 to 27 months: Evidence of gene–environment correlation and its moderation by marital distress. *Development and Psychopathology*, *27*(4pt1), 1251–1265.

Fergusson, D.M., Horwood, L.J., & Ridder, E.M. (2007). Conduct and attentional problems in childhood and adolescence and later substance use, abuse and dependence: Results of a 25-year longitudinal study. *Drug and Alcohol Dependence*, *88*(S1), S14–S26.

Galéra, C., Pingault, J.B., Fombonne, E., Michel, G., Lagarde, E., Bouvard, M.P., et al. (2013). Attention problems in childhood and adult substance use. *The Journal of Pediatrics*, *163*(6), 1677–1683.

Gartstein, M.A. & Rothbart, M.K. (2003). Studying infant temperament via the revised infant behavior questionnaire. *Infant Behavior and Development*, *26*(1), 64–86.

Hawkins, J.D., Catalano, R.F., & Miller, J.Y. (1992). Risk and protective factors for alcohol and other drug problems in adolescence and early adulthood: Implications for substance abuse prevention. *Psychological Bulletin*, *112*(1), 64–105.

Herman-Giddens, M.E., Slora, E.J., Wasserman, R.C., Bourdony, C.J., Bhapkar, M.V., Koch, G.G., et al. (1997). Secondary sexual characteristics and menses in young girls seen in office practice: A study from the Pediatric Research in Office Settings network. *Pediatrics*, *99*(4), 505–512.

Hser, Y.I., Longshore, D., & Anglin, M.D. (2007). The life course perspective on drug use: A conceptual framework for understanding drug use trajectories. *Evaluation Review*, *31*(6), 515–547.

Iannotti, R.J. (2013). *Health behavior in school-aged children (HBSC), 2009–2010*. Ann Arbor Inter-University Consortium for Political and Social Research.

Jackson, K.M., Barnett, N.P., Colby, S.M., & Rogers, M.L. (2015). The prospective association between sipping alcohol by the sixth grade and later substance use. *Journal of Studies on Alcohol and Drugs*, *76*(2), 212–221.

Kagan, J. & Snidman, N. (1991). Temperamental factors in human development. *American Psychologist*, *46*(8), 856–862.

Korownyk, C., Kolber, M.R., McCormack, J., Lam, V., Overbo, K., Cotton, C., et al. (2014). Televised medical talk shows—what they recommend and the evidence to support their recommendations: A prospective observational study. *BMJ*, 349, g7346.

Lahat, A., Pérez-Edgar, K., Degnan, K.A., Guyer, A.E., Lejuez, C.W., Ernst, M., et al. (2012). Early childhood temperament predicts substance use in young adults. *Translational Psychiatry*, *2*(9), e157.

Laub, J.H. & Sampson, R.J. (1993). Turning points in the life course: Why change matters to the study of crime. *Criminology*, *31*(3), 301–325.

Laub, J.H. & Sampson, R.J. (2003). *Shared beginnings, divergent lives: Delinquent boys to age 70*. Cambridge, MA: Harvard University Press.

Lee, P.A., Guo, S.S., & Kulin, H.E. (2001). Age of puberty: Data from the United States of America. *APMIS*, *109*(2), 81–88.

Lee, S.S., Humphreys, K.L., Flory, K., Liu, R., & Glass, K. (2011). Prospective association of childhood attention-deficit/hyperactivity disorder (ADHD) and substance use and abuse/dependence: A meta-analytic review. *Clinical Psychology Review*, *31*(3), 328–341.

MacKenzie, M.J., Nicklas, E., Brooks-Gunn, J., & Waldfogel, J. (2014). Repeated exposure to high-frequency spanking and child externalizing behavior across the first decade: A moderating role for cumulative risk. *Child Abuse & Neglect*, *38*(12), 1895–1901.

Martel, M.M., Pierce, L., Nigg, J.T., Jester, J.M., Adams, K., Puttler, L.I., et al. (2009). Temperament pathways to childhood disruptive behavior and adolescent substance abuse: Testing a cascade model. *Journal of Abnormal Child Psychology*, *37*(3), 363–373.

McCrae, R.R., Costa Jr, P.T., Ostendorf, F., Angleitner, A., Hřebíčková, M., Avia, M.D., et al. (2000). Nature over nurture: Temperament, personality, and life span development. *Journal of Personality and Social Psychology*, *78*(1), 173–186.

Mesman, J., Stoel, R., Bakermans-Kranenburg, M.J., van IJzendoorn, M.H., Juffer, F., Koot, H.M., et al. (2009). Predicting growth curves of early child-hood externalizing problems: Differential susceptibility of children with diffi-cult temperament. *Journal of Abnormal Child Psychology*, *37*(5), 625–636.

Miron, J.A., & Zwiebel, J. (1991). *Alcohol consumption during prohibition* (No. w3675). Washington, DC: National Bureau of Economic Research.

Moffitt, T.E. (1993). Adolescence-limited and life-course-persistent antisocial behavior: A developmental taxonomy. *Psychological Review*, *100*(4), 674–701.

Moffitt, T.E. & Caspi, A. (2001). Childhood predictors differentiate life-course persistent and adolescence-limited antisocial pathways among males and females. *Development and Psychopathology*, *13*(02), 355–375.

Moffitt, T.E., Caspi, A., Harrington, H., & Milne, B.J. (2002). Males on the life-course-persistent and adolescence-limited antisocial pathways: Follow-up at age 26 years. *Development and Psychopathology*, *14*(1), 179–207.

Molina, B.S. & Pelham Jr, W.E. (2003). Childhood predictors of adolescent substance use in a longitudinal study of children with ADHD. *Journal of Abnormal Psychology*, *112*(3), 497–507.

Nærde, A., Ogden, T., Janson, H., & Zachrisson, H.D. (2014). Normative development of physical aggression from 8 to 26 months. *Developmental Psychology*, *50*(6), 1710–1720.

NICHD Early Child Care Research Network. (2004). Trajectories of phy-sical aggression from toddlerhood to middle childhood. *Monographs of the Society for Research in Child Development, 69* (Whole No.4, Serial No. 278).

Olson, S.L. & Sameroff, A.J. (2009). *Biopsychosocial regulatory processes in the development of childhood behavioral problems*. New York Cambridge University Press.

Pickles, A., Hill, J., Breen, G., Quinn, J., Abbott, K., Jones, H., et al. (2013). Evidence for interplay between genes and parenting on infant temperament in the first year of life: Monoamine oxidase A polymorphism moderates effects of maternal sensitivity on infant anger proneness. *Journal of Child Psychology and Psychiatry*, *54*(12), 1308–1317.

Piquero, A.R. (2008). Taking stock of developmental trajectories of criminal activity over the life course. In A.M. Liberman (Ed.), *The long view of crime: A synthesis of longitudinal research* (pp. 23–78). New York: Springer.

Piquero, A.R., Jennings, W.G., & Barnes, J.C. (2012). Violence in criminal careers: A review of the literature from a developmental life-course perspec-tive. *Aggression and Violent Behavior*, *17*(3), 171–179.

Qvortrup, J., Corsaro, W., & Honig, M. (2009). *The Palgrave handbook of child studies.* Basingstoke/New York: Palgrave Macmillan.

Reinke, W.M., Eddy, J.M., Dishion, T.J., & Reid, J.B. (2012). Joint trajectories of symptoms of disruptive behavior problems and depressive symptoms during early adolescence and adjustment problems during emerging adulthood. *Journal of Abnormal Child Psychology, 40*(7), 1123–1136.

Rioux, C., Castellanos-Ryan, N., Parent, S., Vitaro, F., Tremblay, R.E., & Séguin, J.R. (2016). Differential susceptibility to environmental influences: Interactions between child temperament and parenting in adolescent alcohol use. *Development and Psychopathology, 28*(1), 265–275.

Robins, L.N. & Price, R.K. (1991). Adult disorders predicted by childhood conduct problems: Results from the NIMH Epidemiologic Catchment Area project. *Psychiatry, 54*(2), 116–132.

Roisman, G.I., Monahan, K.C., Campbell, S.B., Steinberg, L., & Cauffman, E. (2010). Is adolescence-onset antisocial behavior developmentally normative? *Development and Psychopathology, 22*(02), 295–311.

Rothbart, M.K. (2011). *Becoming who we are: Temperament and personality in development.* New York Guilford Press.

Rothbart, M.K., Ahadi, S.A., & Evans, D.E. (2000). Temperament and personality: Origins and outcomes. *Journal of Personality and Social Psychology, 78*(1), 122–135.

Salas-Wright, C.P., Vaughn, M.G., Todic, J., Córdova, D., & Perron, B.E. (2015). Trends in the disapproval and use of marijuana among adolescents and young adults in the United States: 2002–2013. *The American Journal of Drug and Alcohol Abuse, 41*(5), 392–404.

Sampson, R.J. & Laub, J.H. (1996). Socioeconomic achievement in the life course of disadvantaged men: Military service as a turning point, circa 1940–1965. *American Sociological Review, 61*(3), 347–367.

Sampson, R.J. & Laub, J.H. (1997). A life-course theory of cumulative disadvantage and the stability of delinquency. In T.P. Thornberry (Ed.), *Developmental Theories of Crime and Delinquency* (pp. 133–161). New Brunswick Transaction Publishers.

Sampson, R.J., & Laub, J.H. (2003). Life-course desisters? Trajectories of crime among delinquent boys followed to age 70. *Criminology, 41*(3), 555–592.

Saudino, K.J. (2012). Sources of continuity and change in activity level in early childhood. *Child Development, 83*(1), 266–281.

Sitnick, S.L., Shaw, D.S., & Hyde, L.W. (2014). Precursors of adolescent substance use from early childhood and early adolescence: Testing a developmental cascade model. *Development and Psychopathology*, 26(1), 125–140.

Slutske, W.S., Moffitt, T.E., Poulton, R., & Caspi, A. (2012). Undercontrolled temperament at age 3 predicts disordered gambling at age 32: A longitudinal study of a complete birth cohort. *Psychological Science*, 23(5), 510–516.

Steinberg, L. (2014). *Age of opportunity: Lessons from the new science of adolescence*. Boston Houghton Mifflin Harcourt.

Storr, C.L., Reboussin, B.A., & Anthony, J.C. (2004). Early childhood misbehavior and the estimated risk of becoming tobacco-dependent. *American Journal of Epidemiology*, 160(2), 126–130.

Szapocznik, J. & Coatsworth, J.D. (1999). An ecodevelopmental framework for organizing the influences on drug abuse: A developmental model of risk and protection. In M. Glantz & C. R. Hartel (Eds.), *Drug abuse: Origins and interventions* (pp. 331–366). Washington, DC: American Psychological Association Press.

Teruya, C. & Hser, Y.I. (2010). Turning points in the life course: Current findings and future directions in drug use research. *Current Drug Abuse Reviews*, 3(3), 189–195.

Thomas, A. & Chess, S. (1977). *Temperament and development*. Oxford Brunner/Mazel.

Thomas, A., Chess, S., & Korn, S.J. (1982). The reality of difficult temperament. *Merrill-Palmer Quarterly*, 28(1), 1–20.

Tracy, P.E. & Kempf-Leonard, K. (1996). *Continuity and discontinuity in criminal careers*. New York Plenum Press.

Tremblay, R.E. (2000). The development of aggressive behaviour during childhood: What have we learned in the past century? *International Journal of Behavioral Development*, 24(2), 129–141.

Tremblay, R.E. (2015). Antisocial behavior before the age–crime curve: Can developmental criminology continue to ignore developmental origins? In J. Morizot, & L. Kazemian (Eds.), *The development of criminal and antisocial behavior* (pp. 39–49). Cham, Switzerland: Springer International Publishing.

Tremblay, R.E., Japel, C., Perusse, D., McDuff, P., Boivin, M., Zoccolillo, M., et al. (1999). The search for the age of "onset" of physical aggression: Rousseau and Bandura revisited. *Criminal Behaviour and Mental Health*, 9(1), 8–23.

Tremblay, R.E., Nagin, D.S., Seguin, J.R., Zoccolillo, M., Zelazo, P.D., Boivin, M., et al. (2004). Physical aggression during early childhood: Trajectories and predictors. *Pediatrics*, 114(1), e43–e50.

Tuvblad, C., Isen, J., Baker, L.A., Raine, A., Lozano, D.I., & Jacobson, K.C. (2010). The genetic and environmental etiology of sympathetic and parasympathetic activity in children. *Behavior Genetics, 40*(4), 452–466.

Underwood, M.K., Beron, K.J., & Rosen, L.H. (2009). Continuity and change in social and physical aggression from middle childhood through early adolescence. *Aggressive Behavior, 35*(5), 357–375.

United Nations General Assembly (1989). Convention on the Rights of the Child. *United Nations, Treaty Series,* 1577, 3.

Van Zeijl, J., Mesman, J., Stolk, M.N., Alink, L.R., Van IJzendoorn, M.H., Bakermans-Kranenburg, M.J., et al. (2006). Terrible ones? Assessment of externalizing behaviors in infancy with the Child Behavior Checklist. *Journal of Child Psychology and Psychiatry, 47*(8), 801–810.

Vaughn, M.G., DeLisi, M., Gunter, T., Fu, Q., Beaver, K.M., Perron, B.E., et al. (2011). The severe 5 %: A latent class analysis of the externalizing behavior spectrum in the United States. *Journal of Criminal Justice, 39*(1), 75–80.

Vaughn, M.G., Salas-Wright, C.P., DeLisi, M., & Maynard, B.R. (2014). Violence and externalizing behavior among youth in the United States: Is there a severe 5 %? *Youth Violence and Juvenile Justice, 12*(1), 3–21.

Vaughn, M.G., Salas-Wright, C.P., Underwood, S., & Gochez-Kerr, T. (2015a). Subtypes of non-suicidal self-injury based on childhood adversity. *Psychiatric Quarterly, 86*(1), 137–151.

Vaughn, M.G., Salas-Wright, C.P., Huang, J., Qian, Z., Terzis, L.D., & Helton, J.J. (2015b). Adverse childhood experiences among immigrants to the United States. *Journal of Interpersonal Violence.* Advance online publication. doi:10.1177/0886260515589568.

Veenendaal, M.V., Painter, R.C., Rooij, S.R., Bossuyt, P.M., Post, J.A.M., Gluckman, P.D., et al. (2013). Transgenerational effects of prenatal exposure to the 1944–45 Dutch famine. *BJOG: An International Journal of Obstetrics & Gynaecology, 120*(5), 548–554.

Wakschlag, L.S., Tolan, P.H., & Leventhal, B.L. (2010). Research Review: "Ain't misbehavin'": Towards a developmentally-specified nosology for preschool disruptive behavior. *Journal of Child Psychology and Psychiatry, 51*(1), 3–22.

Whittle, S., Allen, N.B., Lubman, D.I., & Yücel, M. (2006). The neurobiological basis of temperament: Towards a better understanding of psychopathology. *Neuroscience & Biobehavioral Reviews, 30*(4), 511–525.

Whittle, S., Yücel, M., Fornito, A., Barrett, A., Wood, S.J., Lubman, D.I., et al. (2008). Neuroanatomical correlates of temperament in early adolescents.

Journal of the American Academy of Child and Adolescent Psychiatry, 47(6), 682–693.

Wolfgang, M.E., Figlio, R.M., & Sellin, T. (1972). *Delinquency in a birth cohort.* Chicago University of Chicago Press.

Wu, J., Witkiewitz, K., McMahon, R.J., Dodge, K.A., & Conduct Problems Prevention Research Group. (2010). A parallel process growth mixture model of conduct problems and substance use with risky sexual behavior. *Drug and Alcohol Dependence, 111*(3), 207–214.

Zentner, M. & Bates, J.E. (2008). Child temperament: An integrative review of concepts, research programs, and measures. *International Journal of Developmental Science, 2*(1–2), 7–37.

6

Adolescent Drug Abuse and Delinquency

Introduction

It is often believed that the topsy-turvy period of adolescence is when all the real problems with drug abuse and antisociality begin. While it is true that the manifestations of these behaviors are clearly above the surface during this period, we have also seen that many of the underlying bio-developmental processes that propel adolescents along various pathways begin much earlier. In the present chapter, we begin by providing a definition of adolescence that accounts for both biological and social factors in defining the period between childhood and adulthood. From there, our objective is to provide an empirical and theoretical foundation for the concurrent relations between adolescent drug abuse and delinquent behavior. In doing so, we take great care to be as thoughtful and nuanced as possible with regard to the thorny and tenuous issues of causality as well as the complexities of the biological and social factors linked with behavior problems in adolescence and beyond.

© The Author(s) 2016   **129**
C.P. Salas-Wright et al., *Drug Abuse and Antisocial Behavior*,
Palgrave's Frontiers in Criminology Theory,
DOI 10.1057/978-1-137-55817-6_6

Adolescence, Problem Behavior, and the Life Course

Defining Adolescence

In the previous chapter, we drew the line between childhood and adolescence at the onset of puberty. We noted that puberty is a *useful* marker because it is universal and relatively easy to measure as well as a *meaningful* marker inasmuch as pubertal onset brings with it a host of developmental changes (Steinberg 2014). Indeed, we witness profound physiological changes in terms of sexual maturation (e.g., menarche, testicular growth), body composition (e.g., increased lean body mass, muscular development), and skeletal development (e.g., increased height, changes in bone mineralization) as young people transition from childhood into the adolescent years (Coleman and Coleman 2002; Lee 1980; Wheeler 1991; Yilmaz et al. 2005). Such readily observable physiological changes truly are an impressive aspect of adolescent development; however, adolescence also brings with it a number of critical biopsychosocial changes that are perhaps a bit more subtle than breakouts of teenage acne or a six-inch summer growth spurt. Indeed, adolescence is a period of pronounced neurobiological, psychological, and social development and the bulk of this chapter will be dedicated to examining the implications of such changes as they relate to adolescent drug abuse and delinquent behavior.

If adolescence begins with the onset of puberty, when does it end? This is a tricky question and there is not absolute consensus as to when we can say adolescence is officially over. The prominent developmental psychologist, Lawrence Steinberg (2014), suggests that, while biological changes (i.e., puberty) mark the beginning of the adolescent stage, the conclusion of adolescence is more meaningfully a reflection of culturally embedded social indicators. For instance, we may look to indicators such as being of a legal voting or drinking age, living independently, supporting oneself economically, or getting married and having children. These are not perfect indicators and, depending on which indicator we select, the endpoint for adolescence can be as low as age 18 (i.e., when young people in the United States can vote) or as high as somewhere in the late

20s as the mean age for first marriage among Americans is now age 27 for women age 29 for men (Cohn et al. 2011). Moreover, a substantial proportion of American adults never get married and many married and unmarried individuals elect not to have children. Beyond nitpicking the social indicators, the point here is that the selection of a meaningful social indicator to mark the end of adolescence is easier said than done.

At this point, we would be remiss were we not to mention Jeffrey Jensen Arnett's influential work on the construct of "emerging adulthood" (Arnett 2000, 2004, 2014). Arnett's work is far-reaching in scope; however, much of his contribution rests upon one particularly salient insight: That is, demographic trends in the latter part of the 20th century with respect to marriage, education, and employment suggest that a meaningfully distinct developmental stage has arisen for many youth in industrialized nations. It is a developmental stage that sits somewhat uncomfortably between the end of adolescence and the onset of adulthood. More precisely, as more and more young people delay marriage, spend more years in higher education, and enter into longer-term career roles later on in life, we see that earlier conceptualizations of the transition from adolescence to adulthood—rooted in an assumption that this happened somewhere around age 18 or 20—may no longer fit for many American youth.[1] In Arnett's (2007) words, "Most young people now spend the period of their late teens to their mid-20s not settling into long-term adult roles, but trying out different experiences and gradually making their way toward enduring choices in love and work" (p. 69). This period of gradual transition, roughly between the ages of 18 and 25, is what Arnett refers to with the term "emerging adulthood."

---

[1] An important point to note here is that the construct of emerging adulthood is, in part, predicated upon social and economic privilege. Arnett himself very clearly notes that young people in many developing nations make something resembling a full transition to adulthood far earlier on in life than do young people in the United States, Canada, Western Europe, and other developed nations. This is due in large part to the fact that, in contexts of relative economic scarcity, young people simply do not have the luxury of prolonged education and identity exploration. Sometime in the teenage years they have to go to work and assume adult roles, and that's that. There is, of course, an analogy to be made between the experiences of developing world youth and those of young people growing up in economically disadvantaged families and communities in developed nations. Simply put, not everyone has the resources in place to extend the adolescent period into the twenties.

Notably, Arnett argues that emerging adulthood not be understood as a developmental period that is categorically distinct from adolescence and adulthood, but rather as one that meaningfully overlaps with the both the adolescent and adult stages.

It is worth noting that both Steinberg and Arnett place the transition into adulthood somewhere in the mid-to-late 20s. While Steinberg's approach directly links adolescence and adulthood and Arnett makes room for a period of transition between the two stages, both fundamentally affirm that our prior understanding of adulthood beginning at the tail end of the teen years simply doesn't fit the 21st-century data. Notably, the placement of the transition from adolescence/emerging adulthood into adulthood coheres in important ways with state-of-the-art developmental neuroscience research. In particular, it matches up with a mounting body of brain-imaging research suggesting that the gradual maturation of the human brain—in particular, prefrontal regions associated with impulse control, complex reasoning, and judgment—continues well into life's third decade (Johnson et al. 2009; Johnson and Giedd 2015; Lenroot and Giedd 2006). In fact, the influential National Institute of Mental Health neuroscientist, Jay Giedd, has divined that adolescent brains may not reach full maturity until roughly age 25 (Wallis and Park 2004). Although not resolved, the point here is to note that converging sociodemographic and neuroscientific evidence suggests that we can meaningfully think of adolescence—or the pre-adult stage of emerging adulthood—as stretching into roughly the mid-20s. With that, we can confidently state that, for our purposes, adolescence begins at the onset of puberty (i.e., roughly age 11–14) and ends somewhere around age 25.

Adolescent Drug Abuse and Delinquency from a Life-Course Perspective

A developmental, life-course perspective is critical to making biosocial sense of drug abuse and delinquency during the adolescent years. That is to say, adolescent trajectories related to drug abuse and antisocial behavior are most fully understood when situated within a broader understanding of the intrapersonal, contextual, and behavioral factors that precede—and, indeed, follow—such behavior. Additionally, life-course principles of timing of lives and cumulative disadvantage have great relevance when we think about the use of alcohol and other drugs during the teenage years, as well as the continuation or initiation of antisocial or criminal behaviors during adolescence. Below we delve into three inter-related issues that are rooted in the framework and logic of a developmental, life-course perspective.

Early Versus Later-Onset Alcohol and Drug Use

As noted in the previous chapter focused on childhood, we have elected to situate our discussion of alcohol and drug-use initiation within the context of adolescence. By no means should this be interpreted as an indication that substance use among teens is a secondary concern. To the contrary, adolescent substance use is a critical issue. Nationally representative evidence from the National Survey on Drug Use and Health (NSDUH) points to disconcerting levels of lifetime alcohol (38 %), marijuana (18 %), and other illicit drug use (11 %) among youth ages 12 to 17 and indicate that experimentation with alcohol (86 %) and marijuana (52 %) may be normative by the time American youth reach young adulthood.[2] Of importance to this text, adolescent substance use is also intimately related to antisocial behavior during the teenage years and beyond. Indeed, recent estimates suggest that more than half ($35 billion) of the overall social costs ($62 billion) associated with underage drinking in the United States can be attributed to alcohol-related violence and delinquency (Pacific Institute for Research and Evaluation 2011). Our recent research also clearly indicates that alcohol, marijuana, and other illicit drug use is markedly elevated among youth reporting lifetime involvement with the criminal justice system (Vaughn et al. 2016a, b).

---

[2] Please note that findings using NSDUH data are highly consistent with studies that have relied upon data from other key sources of youth drug use surveillance in the United States (see Chen & Jacobson 2012; Eaton et al. 2012; Johnston et al. 2015).

While alcohol and drug abuse among young people is an issue in and of itself, it is also important to note that not all young people who initiate substance use do so at the same age. A substantial body of evidence suggests that this is no small issue. Indeed, studies have repeatedly found alcohol and drug use during the first few years of adolescence—typically operationalized as either ages 11/12 to 14 or prior to age 15—to be linked with academic and mental-health issues, later substance use and delinquency, and the diagnosis of substance use disorders during adulthood (Anthony and Petronis 1995; Chen et al. 2009; DeWit et al. 2000; Ellickson et al. 2003; Meier et al. 2016). And concern may not be limited to just higher-risk substance-use activities like binge drinking or illicit drug use. In fact, a recent study by researchers at Brown University's Center for Alcohol and Addiction Studies suggests that a prospective relationship may exist between literally sipping alcohol early on in life and running into alcohol-related problems in the early part of high school. Indeed, Kristina Jackson and her colleagues (Jackson et al. 2015) found that, controlling for a host of temperamental, behavioral, and environmental factors associated with externalizing, youth self-reports of having sipped alcohol by sixth grade significantly predicted intoxication and heavy drinking by ninth grade.

At this point, it's probably fair to say that a fair number of behavior geneticists have begun to roll their eyes and maybe even experience a bit of constricted breathing—and perhaps with good reason. Indeed, a bevy of recent studies have examined the relationship between early substance use and later problems using twin-based designs that allow for the modeling of genetic and environmental influence. Findings, however, are somewhat mixed. Some studies suggest that, when genetic factors are taken into account, we see that early substance-use initiation doesn't seem to cause later addiction, but rather both outcomes are influenced by similar genetic and environmental sources of risk (Kuntsche et al. 2015; Prescott and Kendler 1999; Ystrom et al. 2014). Others present evidence that, while measuring for genetic and shared environmental factors, we still see a meaningful link between early drug use and later drug-use problems (Agrawal et al. 2006; Grant et al. 2006; Lynskey et al. 2003). In lieu of definitive evidence, perhaps the best option is to split the difference, noting that, undoubtedly, genetic factors play a very important role in the etiology of addiction, as well as in the degree to which early substance use is related to later drug-abuse problems and antisocial behavior (Meyers and Dick 2010). Put another way, the two behaviors represent an underlying trait vulnerability that is shared. However, it seems certainly reasonable to conclude that early drug use—and the assorted interpersonal, social, and legal risks that come along with such behavior—likely has a hand in shaping life-course trajectories related to addiction and antisocial behavior.

Childhood-Persistent Versus Adolescent-Onset Behavior Problems

In our previous chapter focused on childhood, we noted that a minority of individuals begin to exhibit serious behavior problems early in life and that, for some, such behaviors persist into the adolescent years and beyond. To state the obvious, severe and persistent childhood-onset problem behavior is not desirable as it portends of life-course-persistent behavior problems and typically reflects both biological and social adversity. Importantly, however, some young people show low-to-moderate levels of behavior problems during childhood, but begin to run into problems for the first time in the teenage years. For instance, Aguilar et al. (2000) found, in their long-term longitudinal study of high-risk youth in Minnesota, that roughly one in three (29 %) young people in their sample exhibited low levels of antisociality throughout childhood but later showed decidedly elevated levels of antisocial behavior during adolescence. In fact, by age 16, self-reported delinquency among adolescent-onset youth was markedly similar to that of youth found to have early-onset and persistent antisocial behavior problems. Such findings are consistent with a broader body of literature suggesting that adolescent-onset problem behavior is, in fact, a phenomenon that can be observed among a substantial proportion of young people (Fairchild et al. 2013; Moffitt 2003, 2006).

Moffitt's (1993) early theorizing suggested that the emergence of problem behaviors during the adolescent years may be best understood as a normative phenomenon. The overall view was that—in contrast with youth manifesting childhood-onset behavior problems—a bit of teenage experimentation with relatively minor property crimes, status offenses, or skirmishes was to be conceptualized as disconcerting, but not entirely unexpected. Moffitt theorized that adolescent-onset problem behaviors were primarily rooted in a gap between biological and social maturity such that young people act out and imitate antisocial peers in an effort to be viewed as full-fledged adults. Whereas child-onset behavior problems were understood to be rooted in biosocial risk (e.g., genetic susceptibility, neurological impairment, elevated social adversity), adolescent-onset problem behavior was viewed more in normative developmental terms. The notion that adolescent problem behavior is normative seems to match up with data from the National Survey on Drug Use and Health (NSDUH) collected between 2002 and 2013. NSDUH data indicate that, by age 17, one in three (33 %) teens report having taken part in one or more low-level problem behaviors (i.e., truancy, theft, fighting) in the previous 12 months. In other words, while clearly not all young people are involved in problem behaviors during adolescence, high-quality epidemiological evidence indicates that a substantial proportion of adolescents are involved in some degree of externalizing. Importantly, Moffitt's original developmental taxonomy posited that adolescent-onset problem behaviors are, by and large, transient and typically should be expected to dissipate by the time young people transition to adulthood.

Moffitt's (1993) developmental taxonomy has had a profound influence on contemporary understandings of antisocial behavior and crime (see Jennings and Reingle 2012). According to Google Scholar, Moffitt's original theoretical article on the topic has been cited more than 7500 times since its publication in the early 1990s. Some have even gone so far as to speak of the profound and far-reaching influence of the developmental taxonomy in terms of "The Moffittization of Criminology" (DeLisi 2013). Additionally, for many of us, the notion that a number of low-grade behavior problems emerge during the teenage years and then go away as we mature not only has face validity, but matches up with our own experience of adolescence. Indeed, the core insights of the developmental taxonomic theory of antisocial behavior have shaped the fundamental formulation of the chapters in this very book. And yet, a number of empirical studies have been conducted over the last several decades that raise important questions about some of the critical details related to the original understanding of adolescent-onset antisocial behavior. In particular, scholars have conducted substantial research examining the degree to which adolescent-onset behavior is best understood as developmentally normative.

So, can we say that adolescent-onset antisocial behavior is developmentally normative? In large part, it depends what we are talking about. If we are describing youth exhibiting adolescent-onset antisocial behavior as those who, beginning sometime after puberty, sometimes bend the truth in conversation with parents, occasionally cut class, or have once stolen a candy bar or gotten into a heated shoving match, then I think we can confidently say that this kind of behavior is normal (Steinberg and Scott 2003). Indeed, there is rather broad consensus that—due to the temporal gap between puberty (and the thrill-seeking tendencies it often brings) and the full maturation of our brain's prefrontal cortex (which is crucial in decision making and self-control)—that we do well to expect young people to take risks, including risks related to drug abuse and delinquent behavior (Steinberg 2007). It is not behavior that you would hope your children take part in, but this type of adolescence-limited, low-grade problem behavior is something we routinely observe and should not raise too much concern. For instance, we conducted a study of truant youth in the United States and found that only a fraction of youth who skip school do so with any regularity (Maynard et al. 2012).[3] Along the same lines, we have found that, for even more severe and potentially consequential acts such as handgun carrying, most youth who enact such behaviors do so very infrequently (Vaughn et al. 2016c). Similarly, in our research examining subtypes of youth offenders during adolescence using national samples, we routinely identify a "normative" class of youth that accounts for the overwhelming majority of young people (Salas-Wright et al. 2014c, 2016b). Even among these normative classes that are empirically derived based on the fundamental absence of problem behavior, we still see at least

---

[3] It is worth noting that we found that most "truant youth" report skipping one to two days of school per month. However, we did identify a small subgroup of youth (6 % of the sample) that reported skipping on average 13 days per month. Youth in this "chronic skipper" class were markedly more likely than their occasionally skipping peers to use drugs and take part in violent and nonviolent criminal behavior. They are also, relative to most other truant youth, more likely to be academically disengaged, report poor grades, and receive little academic help from parents.

occasional involvement in low-grade problem behaviors such as truancy and fighting. All this is to say that some degree of problem behavior certainly appears to be normative and to be expected among a sizable proportion of young people during the adolescent stage.

That being said, let's be unequivocal in stating that growing evidence from a variety of studies indicates quite clearly that it is *not* developmentally normative for youth to begin to frequently take part in serious antisocial behaviors during adolescence. There are a number of reasons why this is the case. First, while a substantial proportion of youth occasionally partake in relatively low-grade antisocial behaviors such as truancy and petty theft, only a stark minority of youth are frequently involved in more serious offenses. For instance, NSDUH data suggest that very few adolescents report involvement in serious offenses such as drug selling (3.3 %) and serious attacks intended to harm others (7.2 %), and only a very small fraction report more than one instance of involvement (1.58 % and 0.9 %, respectively). Our recent research on handgun carrying among adolescents points to a similar pattern, particularly among Hispanic and African American youth (Vaughn et al. 2016c). While the NSDUH data do not allow for us to disentangle child- versus adolescent-onset, they do tell us that involvement in such serious behaviors is highly unusual. Second, evidence from prospective studies has found that youth manifesting adolescent-onset behavior problems report markedly higher levels of life stress and internalizing problems compared to their "never antisocial" peers (Aguilar et al. 2000). In fact, such problems often persist beyond adolescence as adolescent-onset youth are more likely to experience serious psychological and physical problems well on into adulthood (Moffitt et al. 2002; Odgers et al. 2007). In other words, adolescent-onset behavior problems seem to bring with them—or at least co-occur with and are followed by—substantial difficulties. Third, while adolescent-onset youth, by definition, abstain from behavior problems in childhood, evidence suggests that they are nevertheless distinct from their normative peers in terms of salient biosocial risk factors. Specifically, prospective studies have found adolescent-onset antisocial youth to be more likely to have exhibited a difficult early childhood temperament, lower cognitive functioning during early childhood, and to have experienced lower levels of maternal sensitivity, greater levels of parental conflict, and greater family socioeconomic disadvantage (Fergusson et al. 2000;

Roisman et al. 2010). Such evidence also coheres with recent evidence suggesting that adolescent-onset behavior is at least partially influenced by genetic factors (Burt 2009; Burt and Mikolajewski 2008).

All of the above points seem to indicate that adolescent-onset antisocial behavior that is frequent and more severe in nature is not developmentally normative. Such a developmental trajectory is arguably non-normative because: 1) frequent and severe antisocial behavior is quite rare among young people; 2) adolescent-onset youth are more likely to experience significant internalizing problems during adolescence and beyond; and 3) the onset of problem behaviors in adolescence is robustly predicted by risk factors that are similar to that of child-onset antisocial behavior. In our estimation, these three points alone make a compelling argument; however, it is a fourth point that seems to put the nail in the coffin, so to speak. Namely, longitudinal data has made it increasingly clear that youth classified into adolescent-onset antisocial behavior trajectories are likely to have behavior problems well beyond adolescence. For instance, Odgers et al. (2007) found, using long-term follow up data from the Dunedin Study in New Zealand, that adolescent-onset youth were no different from child-onset/persistent youth with respect to conduct problems at age 26 (however, they did fare better than child-onset offenders by age 32). Nagin et al. (1995) report similar findings as "adolescent-limited" offenders in London were found to be substantially more at risk for alcohol and drug abuse, interpersonal violence, and criminal behavior at age 32 compared to those never involved in the criminal justice system. This also matches up with findings from Moffitt et al. (2002) suggesting that adolescent-onset problem behavior is linked with manifold issues during young adulthood, including mental illness and substance-use disorders.

Adolescent Drug Abuse and Delinquency: Does One Cause the Other?

It is well-established that adolescent drug abuse and juvenile delinquency co-occur. We have found this to be the case again and again in our research on adolescents in the United States and beyond. For instance, we have found a robust association between adolescent involvement in violent and nonviolent antisocial behaviors such as truancy, drug selling, group fighting, and serious violent crimes and a host of substance use outcomes, including alcohol and drug-use disorders (DeLisi et al. 2015a, b; Shook et al. 2013; Vaughn et al. 2013). Turning the relationship around, we have also found that adolescent alcohol and drug users are at similarly elevated risk for involvement in violent and nonviolent delinquent behavior (Salas-Wright et al. 2014a, 2016a; Vaughn et al. 2016a). We also see very compelling evidence that youth involved in the juvenile justice system are far more likely to have substance-use problems both during the adolescent years and across the life course (Vaughn et al. 2015b, 2016b). We reference our own work above, but such findings are by no means unique to our research. Fundamentally, evidence is quite compelling that young people who take part in antisocial behavior are more likely to abuse alcohol and other drugs, and vice versa.

Two important points should be noted. First, while evidence is clear that there is a strong probabilistic link between drug abuse and juvenile delinquency, by no means does this mean that all youth who take part in one problem behavior also take part in the other. In fact, we have published several recent studies in which we modeled subtypes of adolescent externalizing on the basis of drug use and antisocial behavior. In one such study, we identified four subtypes of American youth, including: a *normative* class (73 %) characterized by low levels of involvement in drug use and delinquency; a *substance-user* class (13 %) characterized by very elevated levels of tobacco, alcohol, and marijuana use in combination with low involvement in violent and nonviolent antisocial behavior; a *violent-offender* class (9 %) characterized by modest levels of tobacco, alcohol, and marijuana use in combination with very high levels of fighting, group fighting, and violent attacks; and a *severe* class (5 %) characterized by elevated levels of substance use and antisocial behavior (Vaughn et al. 2014). We have identified similar variation in studies with juvenile-offender youth in the United States and youth residing in high-risk neighborhoods in San Salvador, El Salvador (Salas-Wright et al. 2015). We have found comparable findings again and again in that we routinely see that, while a noteworthy proportion of youth partake in both drug abuse and antisocial behavior, many do not and a small number may appear to "specialize" in one or the other.

The second point is equally if not more important than the first; namely, the identification of cross-sectional—and even longitudinal—associations between drug abuse and delinquency does not mean that we can necessarily talk about a causal relationship. Causality is more complex inasmuch as it demands association, temporality (i.e., that one precedes the other), and evidence that changes in one variable leads to changes in the other variable while ruling out confounds (e.g., genetic) and selection bias (e.g., randomization) as well as a variety of other criteria that help us to confidently conclude that one thing truly influences another (Bradford Hill 1965). There are, of course, a number of good reasons to believe that the use of alcohol and some drugs might play a direct role in influencing both nonviolent and violent antisocial behavior among youth. The first is primarily a biological reason: it has been clearly demonstrated that alcohol and drug use and abuse have implications for our short-term and long-term neurological functioning. A variety of experimental and observational studies provide strong evidence suggesting that consuming alcohol and other drugs can impair executive functioning and alter neurochemical systems critical to self-control (Heinz et al. 2011; Witt 2010). Such impairment can have important implications for disinhibited behavior and, potentially, interpersonal violence and other antisocial acts (DeWall et al. 2010). Notably, this point is largely consistent with Goldstein's (1985) conceptualization of violent behavior that is influenced by the pharmacological effects of alcohol and drug use.

A second plausible reason to believe that drug abuse influences adolescent antisocial behavior can also be borrowed from Goldstein, particularly with respect to his "economic compulsive" model. Specifically, adolescents who use alcohol and other drugs and develop a substance-use disorder may turn to criminal behaviors in order to get money and, in turn, purchase alcohol or drugs. A third reason that may have particular salience for adolescents relates to peer social networks. That is, youth who use alcohol and other drugs may be more likely to be involved in antisocial peer groups that endorse and take part in antisocial behaviors. Some of our research with high-risk youth in El Salvador has documented the importance of antisocial peer affiliation with respect to involvement in both drug abuse and delinquency (Salas-Wright et al. 2013a, 2013b). Such reasoning is also consistent with the social development model and behavior genetic findings which highlight the role of peer affiliation and non-shared environmental factors in the etiology of both substance use and antisocial behavior (Hawkins and Weis 1985; Catalano et al. 1996).

The aforementioned points suggest that a causal relationship between adolescent drug abuse and antisocial behavior is certainly plausible, but what do actual prospective studies tell us? First, a growing number of prospective studies—including some of our own—have demonstrated rather convincingly that substance use during the teenage years is linked with antisocial behavior further down the road in adolescence and beyond (see Boden et al. 2012; Maldonado-Molina et al. 2010; Popovici et al. 2012; Reingle et al. 2011, 2013; White et al. 2012). For instance, several influential studies examining the prospective links between substance use and antisocial behavior have emerged from the Dunedin Multidisciplinary Health and Development Study. Using the Dunedin data, Odgers et al. (2008) found that—utilizing a propensity-score-matching approach that accounted for a variety of childhood, family, and social-risk factors—alcohol and illicit drug use early on in adolescence (i.e., for age 15) was strongly related to the likelihood and frequency of criminal conviction during the latter stages of adolescence and into adulthood (i.e., ages 17–32). Hussong et al. (2004) also utilized the Dunedin data in a study examining the influence of adolescent alcohol and drug use on antisocial behavior across young adulthood. They found that substance use during late adolescence (i.e., age 18) seems to have the capacity to "launch" young people into a trajectory of antisocial behavior during the young adult st age (i.e., ages 21–26). This matches up with recent studies from the Cambridge Study in Delinquent Development that found adolescent binge drinking, particularly binge drinking that persisted into adulthood, to be linked with criminal convictions during early adulthood and beyond (Craig et al. 2015; Jennings et al. 2015). Simply put, it seems that, however you slice it, alcohol and drug use during the early teenage years seem to have important implications for antisocial behavioral trajectories.

Now, before we come to any definitive conclusions about substance use causing antisocial behavior, how about a few more quick caveats to the causality argument? For one, we should point out that longitudinal research indicates that antisocial behavior during adolescence also predicts subsequent alcohol and drug use. This is an important point to underscore inasmuch as it indicates that the relationship between substance use and antisocial behavior is not simply a one-way affair; rather, both seem to influence one another. For instance, a recent study by

Cho et al. (2014) found that antisocial behavior—including theft, violence, and truancy— predicted alcohol use among youth over the course of mid- to late adolescence (i.e., ages 13–17). They also found that alcohol use at age 15 was predictive of antisocial behavior at age 17, but only among males. These findings cohere with those of an often-cited study by White et al. (1999) that systematically examined the developmental associations between substance use and violence among adolescent participants in the Pittsburgh Youth Study. White and her colleagues found longitudinal evidence that alcohol and, to a lesser extent, marijuana use predicts violent behavior, but also found that violent behavior strongly predicts both alcohol and marijuana use across much of adolescence. In other words, such findings suggest that substance use and antisocial behavior likely influence one another in a reciprocal fashion as youth develop during the adolescent stage.

There seem to be two reasonable interpretations here. First, it is possible that data suggesting either a cross-sectional or longitudinal link between substance use and violence simply points to the influence of an underlying shared etiological trait factor (or factors) that influence both outcomes. Certainly, there is ample evidence to suggest that there is a substantial degree of overlap in the etiological factors that influence substance use and violence (Hawkins et al. 2002; Resnick et al. 1997). In our own research, we have often found that psychosocial and cultural factors, such as religiosity, foreign birth, and victimization, are related to both adolescent drug abuse and delinquency (Maynard et al. 2016; Salas-Wright et al. 2012, 2013a, b, c, 2014b, 2016a, 2014c). This is also in line with research that has highlighted the genetic influences on constructs such as self-control, impulsivity, and risk-taking that are of great importance to understanding adolescent experimentation with alcohol and drugs as well as involvement in violent and nonviolent delinquent behaviors (DeLisi 2011; Kreek et al. 2005). Research documenting a maturational gap between socioemotional and cognitive control networks in the adolescent brain and the salience of this gap in terms of involvement in risky behaviors also seems to lend credence to the importance of considering underlying neurodevelopmental factors linked with both substance use and impulse-driven antisocial behaviors (Bava and Tapert 2010; Casey and Jones 2010; Steinberg 2004, 2007).

Simply put, it is certainly possible that drug use actually does not facilitate antisocial behavior (or the other way around), but rather people who use drugs are more likely to be also antisocial, and vice versa.

A second reasonable interpretation is that drug abuse and antisocial behavior are related, but that these constructs do not relate to one another in a causal faction per se. For instance, it may be that adolescent drug abuse and delinquency are developmentally interrelated phenomena that, for many youth, evolve together in a reciprocal fashion. White et al. (1999) describe this possibility in discussing their findings of a bi-directional relationship between adolescent alcohol use and violence, noting:

> [O]ur data do not support a unidirectional causal association between heavy drinking and subsequent violence. Rather, other more complicated mediation and moderation models are probably more applicable to the alcohol–violence relationship. For example, the developmental associations probably occur because heavy drinking individuals compared to less heavy drinkers or abstainers are more likely to emerge from those who already are somewhat higher in prior aggression. In addition, heavy drinkers often select settings such as bars in which other inebriated individuals tend to congregate and in which intrapersonal conflicts are more likely to occur and to escalate into violence. (p. 788–799)

This matches up with some of our recent findings that suggest that youth involvement in violent behavior may be related to drug-abuse risk by introducing youth to peer groups made up of young people who, in addition to enacting violence, are also more likely to have lenient substance-use views and also use drugs (Monahan et al. 2014; Salas-Wright et al. 2015). Along the same lines, our recent research on the links between violence, substance use, and drug-selling also suggest that involvement in antisocial peer networks may increase adolescent drug access and the likelihood of receiving drug offers (Shook et al. 2013; Vaughn et al. 2015a). In other words, involvement in one problem behavior is developmentally related to the likelihood of involvement in another problem behavior. From this vantage point, we might say that drug abuse, violence, and crime are—to some degree—all part of the same developmental soup.

The Take Away: Biosocial and Life-Course Insights

We've presented quite a bit of material in the above sections. In particular, we have looked in depth that the adolescent onset of drug abuse and antisocial behavior and presented evidence for and against a causal relationship between these behaviors. Literally hundreds of peer-reviewed journal articles have been written on the aforementioned topics and numerous scholars have weighed in on these very important biosocial and developmental discussions. That being said, having laid out the arguments above, what are we to make of all of this? Fundamentally, to what degree are adolescent drug abuse and antisocial behavior causally or developmentally related to one another? Our take is that biosocial and life-course developmental logic can be very useful in terms of pulling all this information together.

Let us begin with the biosocial argument. At this point, we can say with confidence that biosocial factors are related to both the onset of antisocial behavior and drug use during adolescence. Whereas early theorizing was rooted in the understanding that adolescent-onset antisocial behavior was best understood as primarily a socially influenced phenomenon, a mounting body of evidence indicates that there is, in part, a genetic basis to the emergence of serious conduct problems during the teenage years. Similarly, evidence certainly seems to indicate that the prevention of alcohol and drug use initiation during adolescence is important with respect to the development of later behavior problems, including adult drug abuse, addiction, and criminal offending. Importantly, however, research also seems to indicate that using alcohol and other drug use at an early age may be best understood not as a cause of addiction in adulthood, but rather as a reflection of underlying genetic risk related to both early-onset use and addiction. Similarly, evidence also suggests that drug abuse and other high-risk and delinquent behaviors may be related to overlapping genetic and neurological vulnerabilities related to risk taking and externalizing in general.

Life-course theory can also shed an important degree of light on the often simultaneous and reciprocal development of adolescent drug use and antisocial behavior. In particular, early-onset behavior problems—be they antisocial behaviors that emerge in childhood or thereafter or substance-related issues that emerge around the time of puberty—do not take place in isolation, but rather in the lives of youth that are embedded in family, school, and community contexts. Life-course theorists, as well as ecological systems theorists, would note that young people's behavior not only is influenced by the social systems they inhabit, but also young people have the power to shape the way that people and systems around them behave. Indeed, while an initial set of biological and social factors may place young people at risk for using drugs or enacting physical aggression, such behaviors can re-shape a child's world in profound ways. For some, it may literally mean that their environment changes in the case that they are sent to an alternative school or placed into a youth detention facility, but more often this reshaping begins by simply causing others to treat them differently. Oftentimes, such reshaping is quite negative and can serve to further isolate young people with behavioral issues. Young people who use substances or behave antisocially are more likely to elicit hostile reaction from their parents, experience strained relationships with their teachers, and be rejected by their prosocial peers.[4] In the face of such hostility and rejection, youth may be tempted to spiral into continued externalizing or to seek out other young people who have also been rejected due to their substance use or antisocial behavioral issues. In this way, behavior problems can be said to initiate a process of *cumulative disadvantage* in which behavior problems early on limit one's options down the road. One bad thing seems to lead quite readily to another. To quote Glen Elder (1998), early-onset drug abuse and antisocial behavior provide yet another example of the ways in which "changing lives alter developmental trajectories" (p. 1).

Conclusion

In this chapter, we examined research suggesting that early-onset alcohol and drug use is, at best, a bad sign and, at worst, an important step in a downward cascade toward adult persistent drug abuse and antisocial

---

[4] See Robert Sampson and John Laub's (1997) chapter on "A life course theory of cumulative disadvantage and the stability of delinquency" for a rich discussion of the ways in which cumulative disadvantage plays out in the lives of youth exhibiting early-onset behavior problems.

behavior. Next, we made the case that a foray into a limited degree of low-grade antisocial behavior can be said to be somewhat normative during adolescence; that is, although undoubtedly disconcerting, an important proportion of adolescents seem to dabble in status offenses and petty crime at some point during the teen years and are likely none the worse for it down the road. But we also presented evidence to support the notion that adolescent-onset antisocial behavior that is frequent and severe in nature is anything but normative and portents of negative outcomes related to addiction and crime. Finally, we examined the ways in which drug abuse and antisocial behavior co-occur in the lives of many adolescents and considered the degree to which these behaviors may or may not cause one another.

Fundamentally, our assessment of the interrelatedness of adolescent drug abuse and antisocial behavior during adolescence is in keeping with the overall position we take throughout this text. There is little doubt that biological factors influence the likelihood of early-onset alcohol and drug use as well as behavior problems that began either in childhood or adolescence. Biosocial explanations clearly also play an important role in understanding the ways in which drug abuse and antisocial behavior influence one another across the span of adolescence and beyond. Indeed, biosocial factors clearly matter, but biosocial theorizing is at its best when it is, indeed, both biological and social in nature. That is, biosocial explanations must be placed into a broader developmental and ecological framework if they are to begin to explain complex biological, interpersonal, and social phenomena such as drug abuse and antisocial behavior.

References

Agrawal, A., Grant, J.D., Waldron, M., Duncan, A.E., Scherrer, J.F., Lynskey, M.T., et al. (2006). Risk for initiation of substance use as a function of age of onset of cigarette, alcohol and cannabis use: Findings in a Midwestern female twin cohort. *Preventive Medicine, 43*(2), 125–128.

Aguilar, B., Sroufe, L.A., Egeland, B., & Carlson, E. (2000). Distinguishing the early-onset/persistent and adolescence-onset antisocial behavior types: From birth to 16 years. *Development and Psychopathology, 12*(2), 109–132. doi: 10.1017/S0954579400002017.

Anthony, J.C. & Petronis, K.R. (1995). Early-onset drug use and risk of later drug problems. *Drug and Alcohol Dependence, 40*(1), 9–15.

Arnett, J.J. (2000). Emerging adulthood: A theory of development from the late teens through the twenties. *American Psychologist, 55*(5), 469–480.

Arnett, J.J. (2004). *Emerging adulthood: The winding road from the late teens through the twenties.* New York: Oxford University Press.

Arnett, J.J. (2007). Emerging adulthood: What is it, and what is it good for? *Child Development Perspectives, 1*(2), 68–73.

Arnett, J.J. (2014). *Adolescence and emerging adulthood.* Upper Saddle River Pearson Education Limited.

Bava, S. & Tapert, S.F. (2010). Adolescent brain development and the risk for alcohol and other drug problems. *Neuropsychology Review, 20*(4), 398–413.

Boden, J.M., Fergusson, D.M., & Horwood, L.J. (2012). Alcohol misuse and criminal offending: Findings from a 30-year longitudinal study. *Drug and Alcohol Dependence, 128*(1), 30–36.

Bradford Hill, A. (1965). The environment and disease: Association or causation? *Proceedings of the Royal Society of Medicine, 58*(5), 295–300.

Burt, S.A. (2009). Are there meaningful etiological differences within antisocial behavior? Results of a meta-analysis. *Clinical Psychology Review, 29*(2), 163–178.

Burt, S.A. & Mikolajewski, A.J. (2008). Preliminary evidence that specific candidate genes are associated with adolescent-onset antisocial behavior. *Aggressive Behavior, 34*(4), 437–445.

Casey, B.J. & Jones, R.M. (2010). Neurobiology of the adolescent brain and behavior: Implications for substance use disorders. *Journal of the American Academy of Child & Adolescent Psychiatry, 49*(12), 1189–1201.

Catalano, R.F., Kosterman, R., Hawkins, J.D., Newcomb, M.D., & Abbott, R. D. (1996). Modeling the etiology of adolescent substance use: A test of the social development model. *Journal of Drug Issues, 26*(2), 429–455.

Chen, C.Y., Storr, C.L., & Anthony, J.C. (2009). Early-onset drug use and risk for drug dependence problems. *Addictive Behaviors, 34*(3), 319–322.

Chen, P. & Jacobson, K.C. (2012). Developmental trajectories of substance use from early adolescence to young adulthood: Gender and racial/ethnic differences. *Journal of Adolescent Health, 50*(2), 154–163.

Cho, S.B., Heron, J., Aliev, F., Salvatore, J.E., Lewis, G., Macleod, J., et al. (2014). Directional relationships between alcohol use and antisocial behavior across adolescence. *Alcoholism: Clinical and Experimental Research, 38*(7), 2024–2033.

Cohn, D., Passel, J.S., Wang, W., & Livingston, G. (2011). Barely half of US adults are married—A record low. Retrieved March 2016 from www.pewsocialtrends. org/2011/12/14/barely-half-of-u-s-adults-are-married-a-record-low/.

Coleman, L. & Coleman, J. (2002). The measurement of puberty: A review. *Journal of Adolescence, 25*(5), 535–550.

Craig, J.M., Morris, R.G., Piquero, A.R., & Farrington, D.P. (2015). Heavy drinking ensnares adolescents into crime in early adulthood. *Journal of Criminal Justice, 43*(2), 142–151.

DeLisi, M. (2011). Self-control theory: The Tyrannosaurus rex of criminology is poised to devour criminal justice. *Journal of Criminal Justice, 39*(2), 103–105.

DeLisi, M. (2013). The moffittization of criminology. *International Journal of Offender Therapy and Comparative Criminology, 57*(8), 911–912.

DeLisi, M., Vaughn, M.G., & Salas-Wright, C.P. (2015a). Rumble: Prevalence and correlates of group fighting among adolescents in the United States. *Behavioral Sciences, 5*(2), 214–229.

DeLisi, M. Vaughn, M.G., Salas-Wright, C.P., & Jennings, W.G. (2015b). Drugged and dangerous: Prevalence and variants of substance use comorbidity among seriously violent offenders in the United States. *Journal of Drug Issues, 45*(3), 232–248.

DeWall, C.N., Bushman, B.J., Giancola, P.R., & Webster, G.D. (2010). The big, the bad, and the boozed-up: Weight moderates the effect of alcohol on aggression. *Journal of Experimental Social Psychology, 46*(4), 619–623.

DeWit, D.J., Adlaf, E.M., Offord, D.R., & Ogborne, A.C. (2000). Age at first alcohol use: A risk factor for the development of alcohol disorders. *American Journal of Psychiatry, 157*(5), 745–750.

Eaton, D.K., Kann, L., Kinchen, S., Shanklin, S., Flint, K.H., Hawkins, J., et al. (2012). Youth risk behavior surveillance—United States, 2011. *Morbidity and mortality weekly report. Surveillance Summaries, 61*(4), 1–162.

Elder Jr, G.H. (1998). The life course as developmental theory. *Child Development, 69*(1), 1–12.

Ellickson, P.L., Tucker, J.S., & Klein, D.J. (2003). Ten-year prospective study of public health problems associated with early drinking. *Pediatrics, 111*(5), 949–955.

Fairchild, G., Goozen, S.H., Calder, A.J., & Goodyer, I.M. (2013). Research review: Evaluating and reformulating the developmental taxonomic theory of antisocial behaviour. *Journal of Child Psychology and Psychiatry, 54*(9), 924–940.

Fergusson, D.M., Horwood, L., & Nagin, D.S. (2000). Offending trajectories in a New Zealand birth cohort. *Criminology, 38*(2), 525–552.

Goldstein, P.J. (1985). The drugs/violence nexus: A tripartite conceptual framework. *Journal of Drug Issues*, *15*(4), 493–506.

Grant, J.D., Scherrer, J.F., Lynskey, M.T., Lyons, M.J., Eisen, S.A., Tsuang, M.T., et al. (2006). Adolescent alcohol use is a risk factor for adult alcohol and drug dependence: Evidence from a twin design. *Psychological Medicine*, *36*(1), 109–118.

Hawkins, J.D., Catalano, R.F., & Arthur, M.W. (2002). Promoting science-based prevention in communities. *Addictive Behaviors*, *27*(6), 951–976.

Hawkins, J.D. & Weis, J.G. (1985). The social development model: An integrated approach to delinquency prevention. *Journal of Primary Prevention*, *6*(2), 73–97.

Heinz, A.J., Beck, A., Meyer-Lindenberg, A., Sterzer, P., & Heinz, A. (2011). Cognitive and neurobiological mechanisms of alcohol-related aggression. *Nature Reviews Neuroscience*, *12*(7), 400–413.

Hussong, A.M., Curran, P.J., Moffitt, T.E., Caspi, A., & Carrig, M.M. (2004). Substance abuse hinders desistance in young adults' antisocial behavior. *Development and Psychopathology*, *16*(4), 1029–1046.

Jackson, K.M., Barnett, N.P., Colby, S.M., & Rogers, M.L. (2015). The prospective association between sipping alcohol by the sixth grade and later substance use. *Journal of Studies on Alcohol and Drugs*, *76*(2), 212–221.

Jennings, W.G., Piquero, A.R., Rocque, M., & Farrington, D.P. (2015). The effects of binge and problem drinking on problem behavior and adjustment over the life course: Findings from the Cambridge Study in Delinquent Development. *Journal of Criminal Justice*, *43*(6), 453–463.

Jennings, W.G. & Reingle, J.M. (2012). On the number and shape of developmental/life-course violence, aggression, and delinquency trajectories: A state-of-the-art review. *Journal of Criminal Justice*, *40*(6), 472–489.

Johnson, S.B., Blum, R.W., & Giedd, J.N. (2009). Adolescent maturity and the brain: The promise and pitfalls of neuroscience research in adolescent health policy. *The Journal of Adolescent Health*, *45*(3), 216–221.

Johnson, S.B. & Giedd, J.N. (2015). Normal brain development and child/adolescent policy. In J. Clausen & N. Levy (Eds.), *Handbook of neuroethics* (pp. 1721–1735). New York Springer.

Johnston, L.D., O'Malley, P.M., Miech, R.A., Bachman, J.G., & Schulenberg, J.E. (2015). *Monitoring the future national survey results on drug use: 1975–2014: Overview, key findings on adolescent drug use*. Ann Arbor Institute for Social Research, The University of Michigan.

Kreek, M.J., Nielsen, D.A., Butelman, E.R., & LaForge, K.S. (2005). Genetic influences on impulsivity, risk taking, stress responsivity and vulnerability to drug abuse and addiction. *Nature Neuroscience, 8*(11), 1450–1457.

Kuntsche, E., Rossow, I., Engels, R., & Kuntsche, S. (2015). Is "age at first drink" a useful concept in alcohol research and prevention? We doubt that. *Addiction, 111*(6), 957–965.

Lee, P.A. (1980). Normal ages of pubertal events among American males and females. *Journal of Adolescent Health Care, 1*(1), 26–29.

Lenroot, R.K. & Giedd, J.N. (2006). Brain development in children and adolescents: Insights from anatomical magnetic resonance imaging. *Neuroscience & Biobehavioral Reviews, 30*(6), 718–729.

Lynskey, M.T., Heath, A.C., Bucholz, K.K., Slutske, W.S., Madden, P.A., Nelson, E.C., et al. (2003). Escalation of drug use in early-onset cannabis users vs co-twin controls. *Journal of the American Medical Association, 289*(4), 427–433.

Maldonado-Molina, M.M., Reingle, J.M., & Jennings, W.G. (2010). Does alcohol use predict violent behaviors? The relationship between alcohol use and violence in a nationally representative longitudinal sample. *Youth Violence and Juvenile Justice, 9*(2), 99–111.

Maynard, B.R., Salas-Wright, C.P., Vaughn, M.G., & Peters, K.E. (2012). Who are truant youth? Examining distinctive profiles of truant youth using latent profile analysis. *Journal of Youth and Adolescence, 41*(12), 1671–1684.

Maynard, B.R., Vaughn, M.G., Salas-Wright, C.P., & Vaughn, S.R. (2016). Bullying victimization among school-aged immigrant youth in the United States. *Journal of Adolescent Health, 58*(3), 337–344.

Meier, M.H., Hall, W., Caspi, A., Belsky, D.W., Cerdá, M., Harrington, H.L., et al. (2016). Which adolescents develop persistent substance dependence in adulthood? Using population-representative longitudinal data to inform universal risk assessment. *Psychological Medicine, 46*(4), 877–889.

Meyers, J.L. & Dick, D.M. (2010). Genetic and environmental risk factors for adolescent-onset substance use disorders. *Child and Adolescent Psychiatric Clinics of North America, 19*(3), 465–477.

Moffitt, T.E. (1993). Adolescence-limited and life-course persistent antisocial behavior: A developmental taxonomy. *Psychological Review, 100*(4), 674–701.

Moffitt, T.E. (2003). Life-course persistent and adolescence-limited antisocial behavior: A 10-year research review and research agenda. In B. B. Lahey, T. E. Moffitt, & A. Caspi (Eds.), *Causes of conduct disorder and juvenile delinquency* (pp. 49–75). New York: Guilford Press.

Moffitt, T.E. (2006). Life-course-persistent versus adolescence-limited antisocial behavior. In D. Cicchetti & D. J. Cohen (Eds.), *Developmental psychopathology: Risk, disorder, and adaptation* (Vol. 3, pp. 570–598). Hoboken John Wiley & Sons.

Moffitt, T.E., Caspi, A., Harrington, H., & Milne, B.J. (2002). Males on the life-course-persistent and adolescence-limited antisocial pathways: Follow-up at age 26 years. *Development and Psychopathology, 14*(1), 179–207.

Monahan, K.C., Rhew, I.C., Hawkins, J.D., & Brown, E.C. (2014). Adolescent pathways to co-occurring problem behavior: The effects of peer delinquency and peer substance use. *Journal of Research on Adolescence, 24*(4), 630–645.

Nagin, D.S., Farrington, D.P., & Moffitt, T.E. (1995). Life-course trajectories of different types of offenders. *Criminology, 33*(1), 111–139.

Odgers, C.L., Caspi, A., Broadbent, J.M., Dickson, N., Hancox, R.J., Harrington, H., et al. (2007). Prediction of differential adult health burden by conduct problem subtypes in males. *Archives of General Psychiatry, 64*(4), 476–484.

Odgers, C.L., Caspi, A., Nagin, D.S., Piquero, A.R., Slutske, W.S., Milne, B.J., et al. (2008). Is it important to prevent early exposure to drugs and alcohol among adolescents? *Psychological Science, 19*(10), 1037–1044.

Pacific Institute for Research and Evaluation (PIRE) (2011). Underage drinking costs. Calverton PIRE. Retrieved 14 August 2016 from www.pire.org/documents/UnderageDrinking.doc.

Prescott, C.A. & Kendler, K.S. (1999). Age at first drink and risk for alcoholism: A noncausal association. *Alcoholism: Clinical and Experimental Research, 23*(1), 101–107.

Popovici, I., Homer, J.F., Fang, H., & French, M.T. (2012). Alcohol use and crime: Findings from a longitudinal sample of US adolescents and young adults. *Alcoholism: Clinical and Experimental Research, 36*(3), 532–543.

Reingle, J.M., Jennings, W.G., Lynne-Landsman, S.D., Cottler, L.B., & Maldonado-Molina, M.M. (2013). Toward an understanding of risk and protective factors for violence among adolescent boys and men: A longitudinal analysis. *Journal of Adolescent Health, 52*(4), 493–498.

Reingle, J.M., Jennings, W.G., & Maldonado-Molina, M.M. (2011). The mediated effect of contextual risk factors on trajectories of violence: Results from a nationally representative, longitudinal sample of Hispanic adolescents. *American Journal of Criminal Justice, 36*(4), 327–343.

Resnick, M.D., Bearman, P.S., Blum, R.W., Bauman, K.E., Harris, K.M., Jones, J., et al. (1997). Protecting adolescents from harm: Findings from the

National Longitudinal Study on Adolescent Health. *Journal of the American Medical Association, 278*(10), 823–832.

Roisman, G.I., Monahan, K.C., Campbell, S.B., Steinberg, L., & Cauffman, E. (2010). Is adolescence-onset antisocial behavior developmentally normative? *Development and Psychopathology, 22*(02), 295–311.

Salas-Wright, C.P., Vaughn, M.G., Hodge, D.R., & Perron, B.E. (2012). Religiosity profiles of American youth in relation to substance use, violence, and delinquency. *Journal of Youth and Adolescence, 41*(12), 1560–1575.

Salas-Wright, C.P., Olate, R., & Vaughn, M.G. (2013a). Religious coping, spirituality, and substance use and abuse among youth in high-risk communities in San Salvador, El Salvador. *Substance Use and Misuse, 48*(9), 769–783.

Salas-Wright, C.P., Olate, R., & Vaughn, M.G. (2013b). The protective effects of religious coping and spirituality on delinquency: Results among high-risk and gang-involved Salvadoran youth. *Criminal Justice and Behavior, 40*(9), 988–1008.

Salas-Wright, C.P., Olate, R., Vaughn, M.G., & Tran, T.V. (2013c). Direct and mediated associations between religious coping, spirituality, and youth violence in El Salvador. *Pan American Journal of Public Health, 34*(3), 183–189.

Salas-Wright, C.P., Hernandez, L., Maynard, B.R., Saltzman, L.Y., & Vaughn, M.G. (2014a). Alcohol use among Hispanic early adolescents in the United States: An examination of behavioral risk and protective profiles. *Substance Use & Misuse, 49*(7), 864–877.

Salas-Wright, C.P., Lombe, M., Vaughn, M.G., & Maynard, B.R. (2014b). Do adolescents who regularly attend religious services stay out of trouble? Results from a national sample. *Youth & Society*. Advance online publication. doi:10.1177/0044118X14521222.

Salas-Wright, C.P., Vaughn, M.G., Maynard, B.R., Clark, T.T., & Snyder, S. (2014c). Public or private religiosity: Which one is protective for adolescent substance use and by what pathways? *Youth & Society*. Advance online publication. doi:10.1177/0044118X14531603.

Salas-Wright, C.P., Olate, R., & Vaughn, M.G. (2015). Substance use, violence, and HIV risk behavior in El Salvador and the United States: Cross-national profiles of the SAVA Syndemic. *Victims & Offenders, 10*(1), 95–116.

Salas-Wright, C.P., Olate, R., & Vaughn, M.G. (2016a). Preliminary findings on the links between violence, crime, and HIV risk among young adults with substance use disorders in El Salvador. *Journal of Substance Use, 21*(1), 35–40.

Salas-Wright, C.P., Vaughn, M.G., Schwartz, S.J., & Córdova, D. (2016b). An "immigrant paradox" for adolescent externalizing behavior? Evidence from a national sample. *Social Psychiatry and Psychiatric Epidemiology*, *51*(1), 27–37.

Sampson, R.J., & Laub, J.H. (1997). A life-course theory of cumulative disadvantage and the stability of delinquency. In T. P. Thornberry (Ed.), *Developmental theories of crime and delinquency* (pp. 133–161). Piscataway Transaction Publishers.

Shook, J.J., Vaughn, M.G., & Salas-Wright, C.P. (2013). Exploring the variation in drug selling among adolescents in the United States. *Journal of Criminal Justice*, *41*(6), 365–374.

Steinberg, L. (2004). Risk taking in adolescence: What changes, and why? *Annals of the New York Academy of Sciences*, *1021*(1), 51–58.

Steinberg, L. (2005). Cognitive and affective development in adolescence. *Trends in Cognitive Sciences*, *9*(2), 69–74.

Steinberg, L. (2007). Risk taking in adolescence new perspectives from brain and behavioral science. *Current Directions in Psychological Science*, *16*(2), 55–59.

Steinberg, L. (2014). *Age of opportunity: Lessons from the new science of adolescence*. Boston Houghton Mifflin Harcourt.

Steinberg, L. & Scott, E.S. (2003). Less guilty by reason of adolescence: Developmental immaturity, diminished responsibility, and the juvenile death penalty. *American Psychologist*, *58*(12), 1009–1018.

Vaughn, M.G., Maynard, B.R., Salas-Wright, C.P., Perron, B.E., & Abdon, A. (2013). Prevalence and correlates of truancy in the US: Results from a national sample. *Journal of Adolescence*, *36*(4), 767–776.

Vaughn, M.G., Salas-Wright, C.P., DeLisi, M., & Maynard, B.R. (2014). Violence and externalizing behavior among youth in the United States: Is there a severe 5 %? *Youth Violence and Juvenile Justice*, *12*(1), 3–21.

Vaughn, M.G., Salas-Wright, C.P., DeLisi, M., Shook, J.J., & Terzis, L. (2015a). A typology of drug selling among young adults in the United States. *Substance Use & Misuse*, *50*(3), 403–413.

Vaughn, M.G., Salas-Wright, C.P., DeLisi, M., Maynard, B.R., & Boutwell, B.B. (2015b). Prevalence and correlates of psychiatric disorders among former juvenile detainees in the United States. *Comprehensive Psychiatry*, 59, 107–116.

Vaughn, M.G., Nelson, E.J., Salas-Wright, C.P., DeLisi, M., & Qian, Z. (2016a). Handgun carrying among white youth increasing in the United States: New evidence from the National Survey on Drug Use and Health 2002–2013. *Preventive Medicine*, 88, 127–133. doi:10.1016/j.ypmed.2016.03.024.

Vaughn, M.G., Nelson, E.J., Salas-Wright, C.P., Shootman, M., & Qian, Z. (2016b). Racial and ethnic trends and correlates of non-medical use of prescription opioids among adolescents in the United States 2004–2013. *Journal of Psychiatric Research, 73*, 17–24.

Vaughn, M.G., Salas-Wright, C.P., Boutwell, B.B., DeLisi, M., & Curtis, M. P. (2016c). Handgun carrying among youth in the United States: An analysis of subtypes. *Youth Violence and Juvenile Justice.* Advance online publication. doi:10.1177/1541204016629721.

Vaughn, M.G., Salas-Wright, C.P., Córdova, D., Nelson, E.J. (2016d). Racial and ethnic trends in binge alcohol and illicit drug use among arrestees 2002–2013. *Journal of Criminal Justice* http://yvj.sagepub.com/content/early/2016/02/18/1541204016629721.abstract.

Wallis, C., & Dell, K. (2004). What makes teens tick. *Time Magazine, 163* (19), 56–65.

Wheeler, M.D. (1991). Physical changes of puberty. *Endocrinology and metabolism clinics of North America, 20*(1), 1–14.

White, H.R. (2012). Substance use and crime. In K. J. Sher (Ed.), *Psychology and substance abuse.* Oxford Oxford University Press.

White, H.R., Loeber, R., Stouthamer-Loeber, M., & Farrington, D.P. (1999). Developmental associations between substance use and violence. *Development and Psychopathology, 11*(4), 785–803.

White, H.R., Lee, C., Mun, E.Y., & Loeber, R. (2012). Developmental patterns of alcohol use in relation to the persistence and desistance of serious violent offending among African American and Caucasian young men. *Criminology, 50*(2), 391–426.

Witt, E.D. (2010). Research on alcohol and adolescent brain development: Opportunities and future directions. *Alcohol, 44*(1), 119–124.

Yilmaz, D., Ersoy, B., Bilgin, E., Gümüşer, G., Onur, E., & Pinar, E.D. (2005). Bone mineral density in girls and boys at different pubertal stages: Relation with gonadal steroids, bone formation markers, and growth parameters. *Journal of Bone and Mineral Metabolism, 23*(6), 476–482.

Ystrom, E., Kendler, K.S., & Reichborn-Kjennerud, T. (2014). Early age of alcohol initiation is not the cause of alcohol use disorders in adulthood, but is a major indicator of genetic risk. A population-based twin study. *Addiction, 109*(11), 1824–1832.

7

Adulthood, Addiction, and Antisocial Behavior

Introduction

Whether we like it or not, we all grow up someday. Regretfully, however, getting over the hump of childhood, adolescence, and emerging adulthood does not mean that our problems go away during the adult years. In the present chapter, we will look at what national data tells us about the prevalence of drug abuse, addiction, and antisocial behavior during the several decades that have come to constitute adulthood. Additionally, having laid an epidemiological foundation in terms of what we know about behavior problems in the general population, we will focus on what can be gathered from the long-term, life-course research conducted with adults who continue to struggle with alcohol and drug abuse and, quite frequently, criminal behavior. In doing so, we will extend our developmental focus to consider the ways in which addiction and antisocial behavior influence one another over the span of adulthood.

© The Author(s) 2016
C.P. Salas-Wright et al., *Drug Abuse and Antisocial Behavior*,
Palgrave's Frontiers in Criminology Theory,
DOI 10.1057/978-1-137-55817-6_7

Adulthood, Addiction, and Antisocial Behavior

A Broad Developmental Window

We have already noted that a tremendous amount of development takes place during the first decade or so that constitutes childhood. And we have also observed that biological, psychological, and social growth continues at a remarkable rate as adolescents experience the profound changes of puberty and, later, the neurological and social vicissitudes that mark the transition to the adult stage. That being said, as developmentally impressive as childhood and adolescence are, adulthood is nothing to shake your head at. Our own experience makes clear that we continue to evolve long after the myelination and synaptic pruning of the mid-twenties. In the same vein, although something developmentally important certainly happens as young people transition into adult roles of marriage, career, and family, there can be no doubt that human growth and development persist well beyond the mid- to late twenties. Importantly, this is not simply the case in a broad developmental sense, but also with respect to the biosocial phenomena that are the central focus of this text.

Thinking developmentally about adulthood is critical for several important reasons. The first relates to the broad manner in which we tend to think about adulthood. Indeed, the term "adulthood" is often used, by laypersons and scientists alike, to refer to the bulk of human experience, stretching from the end of adolescence to the end of life. In the previous chapter, we suggested that adolescence ends somewhere in the mid- to late twenties. This means that—given that the life expectancy at birth has stretched to nearly age 79 in the United States—we can safely say that, on average, adulthood spans a period of five or six decades (Xu et al. 2016).[1] This is no small point as, despite being frequently lumped together into a singular

---

[1] While the Centers for Disease Control and Prevention (CDC) places the life expectancy for Americans at 78.8 years, we do see noteworthy differences across gender and race/ethnicity. On average, women live roughly five years longer than men (81.2 years versus 76.4 years) and non-Hispanic whites live, on average, four years longer than do African-Americans (78.9 years versus 75.1 years). The life expectancy for Hispanics (81.6 years) is greater than that of all other major racial/ethnic groups and nobody seems to live longer than Hispanic females who, on average live 83.8 years. All this is to say, adulthood is a broad window, but one that is broader for some than for others.

category, we can see really important differences between adults at different ages. Indeed, few would deny that 30-year-olds are quite different than 50-year-olds or, say, 70-year-olds with respect to any number of biological, psychological, and social factors. We might even go so far as note that biosocial differences between a 30-year-old and a 70-year-old are no less marked than the difference between an adolescent and a young adult. Beyond specifics, the point here is to note that, while we will refer to adulthood in its broadest sense, certainly we must also take care to differentiate young adulthood (ages 26–34), middle adulthood (ages 35–64), and older adulthood (65 and older) as important developmental subperiods.

A second and related point is that research has helped us to increasingly appreciate the ways in which adulthood is a time of profound biosocial change (Elder Jr 1975; Erikson1959; Levinson 1978, 1986). Longitudinal research on cognitive development suggests that our intellectual abilities such as inductive reasoning, spatial orientation, and vocabulary develop throughout adulthood, typically finding their pinnacle somewhere around the time of middle adulthood (Schaie 1996; Willis and Schaie 2005). At the same time, during middle adulthood we tend to see declines in our capacity to quickly perform mathematical computations and make judgments based on visual stimuli, and many cognitive abilities decline as we move closer and closer to old age (Craik and Bialystok 2006). We also see other changes such as progressive losses in muscle mass, decreases in bone-mineral density, and reduced capacity to metabolize alcohol and other drugs of abuse (Blow and Barry 2002; Evans 2010; Riggs et al. 2004). Certainly, behavioral and social factors play an important role in many of the changes experienced during adulthood. Indeed, cognitive development and declines are influenced by manifold factors such as educational opportunities, parental education level, diet and physical activity, and socioeconomic status (Féart et al. 2009; Hackman and Farah 2009; Schaie et al. 2005; Yaffe et al. 2001). Similarly, while sarcopenia—that is, age-related loss in skeletal muscle mass and function—is to be expected, ample evidence demonstrates that losses in muscle mass during adulthood can be attenuated by means of dietary, exercise-related, and other therapeutic interventions (Waters et al. 2010). All this is to say that our brains, our bodies, and our overall functioning continue to be a biosocial work in progress across the adult stage. As such, while here we choose to use the broad term of adulthood, we are clear that development does not stop after one's mid-twenties and, consequently, it is of vital importance that we maintain a developmental orientation towards our discussion of adulthood.

The Drug-Abuse and Antisocial-Behavior Curve During Adulthood

A number of critically important changes can be observed with respect to drug abuse, addiction, and antisocial behavior across the span of adulthood. We will look at this step-by-step, beginning first with what information can be gleaned from epidemiological surveillance data in terms of the prevalence of drug abuse and antisocial behavior in the general population. In particular, we will present prevalence estimates from the National Survey on Drug Use and Health (NSDUH), a long-standing, nationally representative survey conducted by the United States Federal Government (Substance Abuse and Mental Health Services Administration [SAHMSA] 2014). The NSDUH is administered annually to more than 50,000 non-institutionalized individuals living in communities in all 50 states and the District of Columbia. It is a powerful data source in that it allows us to examine the prevalence of drug abuse as well as a number of violent and nonviolent antisocial behaviors in a very large national sample. However, it is limited in the sense that NSDUH data are cross-sectional and the survey excludes homeless persons who do not live in shelters as well as individuals living in institutional settings such as jails or hospitals. Nevertheless, the NSDUH is undoubtedly one of the nation's primary sources of drug use surveillance and provides high-quality data that can be examined in conjunction with findings from other national surveys.

Drug Use, Addiction, and the Life Course

Let us first take a look at what the NSDUH data tell us with respect to changes in the prevalence in alcohol and drug use across the life course. In looking at Fig. 7.1, we can tell at first glance that the prevalence of alcohol use—at all ages from adolescence to older adulthood—is markedly greater

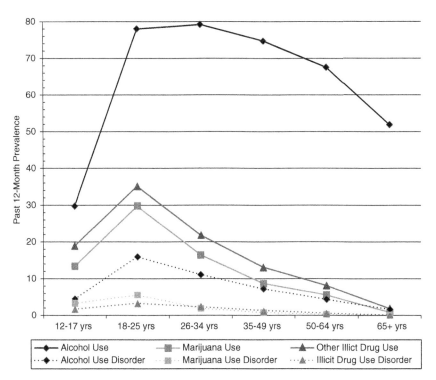

Fig. 7.1 Prevalence of past year alcohol and drug use/DSM substance use disorders by age categories in the National Survey on Drug Use and Health, 2002–2013

than that of marijuana and other illicit drugs. This is perhaps unsurprising given that alcohol is legal for purchase and consumption across the United States whereas, despite a few noteworthy exceptions, the same cannot be said of marijuana and other illicit drugs. Notably, in addition to differences in overall prevalence, we also see a different pattern, compared to marijuana and other illicit drugs, with respect to changes in the prevalence of alcohol use across adulthood. For alcohol, marijuana, and other illicit drug use we see a substantial spike in use between adolescence (ages 12–17) and emerging adulthood (ages 18–25). However, for marijuana and illicit drug use, we see steep declines beginning during young adulthood (ages 26–34) that continue steadily throughout the adult stage. This is not the case for alcohol. We do not see a steep drop in alcohol use during young adulthood; rather, the prevalence of past 12-month alcohol use actually increases to reach its pinnacle during young adulthood (ages 26–34) before only gradually decreasing between ages 35 and 49 and continuing a downward trajectory in the second half of middle adulthood (ages 50–64) and arriving at an adult low of 52 % during older adulthood (ages 65 and older).[2] Simply put, the alcohol use "curve" is nowhere near as steep as that of marijuana or other illicit drug use.

Before moving on to look at substance-use disorders, let us dedicate our attention to one important critique of the content presented in the previous paragraph. Namely, reliance on a *past year* measure of *any alcohol use* might potentially mask tremendous differences relating to changes in the frequency or severity of alcohol consumption across the adult life course. To address this possibility, we looked at the data on alcohol use from a number of different angles. First, we looked at changes in the past-month use of any alcohol across adulthood to assess the degree to which applying a more circumscribed temporal window might yield different results. Overall, these results tell a very similar story in which past month use reaches its pinnacle during young adulthood (ages 26–34; 63 %), declines only gradually during middle adulthood (ages 35–64; 57 %), and then drops substantially during older adulthood (ages 65 and older; 40 %). In other words, the proportion of the adult population that can be categorized as "drinkers" is elevated and remains as such for much of adulthood. Second, we also looked at changes in the prevalence of frequent drinking (i.e., 20–30 drinking days in the last month) across the developmental spectrum of adulthood. NSDUH evidence suggests that the prevalence of frequent drinking among alcohol users increases steadily with age, rising from 11 % among young adults (i.e., ages 26–34) to 18 % in middle adulthood

---

[2] This pattern of results is consistent with recent findings for past-year alcohol use based in nationally representative survey data from the National Epidemiologic Study on Alcohol and Related Conditions (NESARC; Dawson et al., 2015) as well as prospective data from the United Kingdom (Britton et al., 2015). It is noteworthy, however, that the recent NESARC-based study suggests that the proportion of adult alcohol users in the United States has increased by roughly 7% to 10% since the early 2000s.

(i.e., ages 35–64) and reaching a pinnacle of 29 % among older adults. That being said, drinking nearly every day does not necessarily imply problem drinking. This is consistent with NSDUH evidence that— among past-year drinkers—the prevalence of alcohol-use disorder decreases steadily from young adulthood (14 %) through middle adulthood (8 %) and into the older adult stage (3 %). All in all, NSDUH data seem to suggest that alcohol use remains quite steady throughout adulthood, but more alcohol-related problems are observed among younger than among older drinkers.

The use of alcohol and drugs is one thing, but what about the prevalence of substance-use disorders across the span of adulthood? As with alcohol use, the prevalence of alcohol-use disorder is markedly greater than that of marijuana or other illicit-drug-use disorders. However, the changes in the prevalence of alcohol, marijuana, and other illicit-drug-use disorders are more similar than was the case with substance use. More precisely, for all substance-use disorders, we see peak prevalence during the emerging adult stage (ages 18–25) and a clear downward trajectory as we move further and further into adulthood. Notably, this pattern of results matches up nicely with recent findings from the National Epidemiologic Study of Alcohol and Related Conditions (NESARC) study, which was sponsored by the National Institute on Alcohol Abuse and Alcoholism (see Grant et al. 2015, 2016; Hasin et al. 2015, 2016). For instance, recent studies by Hasin et al. (2015, 2016) provide compelling evidence that marijuana use as well as marijuana-use disorders are substantially more common among emerging adults (i.e., 18–24) and attenuate both in terms of prevalence and severity during the young, middle, and older adult stages. Along the same lines, Grant et al. (2016) report similar findings with respect to drug-use disorders in general with a clear drop in prevalence and severity of disorder observed among individuals at later stages of adulthood.

Antisocial Behavior and Adulthood

In addition to self-report data on substance use and substance-use disorders, the NSDUH also includes a number of items related to antisocial behavior. In particular, respondents are asked about nonviolent antisocial

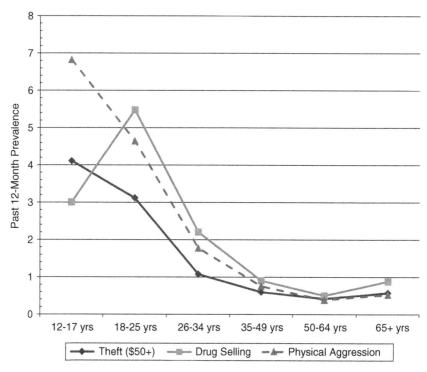

Fig. 7.2 Prevalence of past year antisocial behavior by age categories in the National Survey on Drug Use and Health, 2002–2013

behavior such as theft of something worth more than $50 and the sale of illegal drugs as well as violent behaviors such as attacking another person with the intent to inflict serious harm. As shown in Fig. 7.2, the pattern of results is quite clear. Specifically, we see consistent decreases in the prevalence of theft and physical aggression from the teenage years (ages 12–17) all the way through the emerging adult years (ages 18–25) and into young (ages 26–34), middle (ages 35–64), and older (ages 65 and older) adulthood. Drug-selling follows essentially the same pattern with the exception that we see an increase in drug-selling between the teenage years (ages 12–17) and the young adult stage (ages 18–25) followed by a pattern of reductions in prevalence that is similar to that of theft and physical aggression.

These findings are consistent with other population-based estimates of violent and nonviolent crime (Shulman et al. 2013) and converge nicely with prior research on the "age–crime curve" which suggests that criminal offending peaks during adolescence before attenuating during the young adult stage and across adulthood (Farrington 1986; Farrington et al. 2013; Laub and Sampson 2003; Piquero et al. 2007). While some variation can be noted in the timing of the age–crime curve for particular offenses and across demographic groups, the developmental pattern has been identified again and again in life-course studies of violent and nonviolent antisocial behavior. That is, the evidence is compelling that, in the general population, the prevalence of violent and nonviolent criminal behavior drops dramatically at the outset of adulthood and continues to move ever closer to zero during the later adult stages.

One additional point is worth making here. There is little debate that theft, drug-selling, and physical attacks are clear manifestations of overt criminal behaviors that are unquestionably antisocial. However, not all antisocial behaviors—that is, behaviors that demonstrate a lack of concern for right and wrong or the well-being of others—represent criminal offenses and many are far more subtle than the behaviors examined above. For example, behaviors such as frequent lying or the use of a fake name or alias are not necessarily illegal, but they certainly are in keeping with diagnostic criteria used to identify those with antisocial personality disorder. Additionally, some antisocial behaviors such as scamming others for money require less physical prowess than others, which would presumably impact the ability of adults to enact them with age. While, regretfully, the NSDUH does not collect information on such behaviors, the highly respected National Epidemiologic Study on Alcohol and Related Conditions (NESARC) study looks at a number of such behaviors as part of their antisocial behavior personality diagnostic module. Interestingly enough, the NESARC data on the aforementioned behaviors tell a very similar story to the one we see in the NSDUH data. Namely, we see a marked drop in prevalence of lying, fake names, and scamming as young people transition from emerging adulthood into the young adult years as well as a continual pattern of reductions as individuals move across adulthood (see Fig. 7.3). Simply, these findings seem to suggest that—at least in

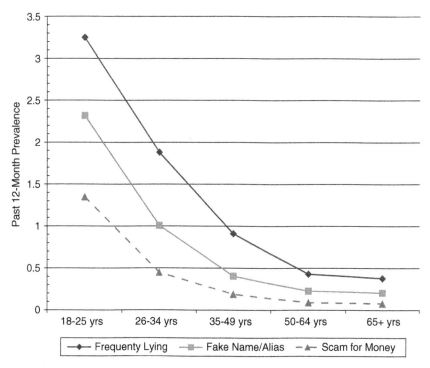

Fig. 7.3 Prevalence of past year antisocial behavior by age categories in the "National Epidemiologic Survey on Alcohol and Related Condidtions" Survey on Drug Use and Health, 2002–2013

the general population—adulthood is a time of substantial reductions in prevalence for a wide range of legal and illegal, violent and nonviolent, physically demanding and non-physical antisocial behaviors.

Adult Trajectories of Addiction, Recovery, and Crime

Looking at the changes in the prevalence of drug abuse, addiction, and antisocial behavior in the general population undoubtedly provides important information. Understanding that both phenomena tend, in general, to dissipate as people move from the latter part of adolescence or emerging adulthood and enter fully into the adult stage tells us that the transition to adulthood is a normative time for many drug users and offenders to desist.

And yet, looking only at aggregate, surveillance data—that is, looking at data that is primarily cross-sectional and is primarily comprised of abstainers— also misses something really important. Indeed, it tells us little about the behavioral and developmental trajectories of the minority of individuals for whom drug abuse and antisocial behavior are quite severe and persist well beyond childhood, adolescence, and the emerging adult years. To learn about trajectories, it is necessary that we look at long-term, prospective studies that draw from a developmental, life-course perspective.

A number of important questions arise when we think about adult drug abuse and addiction from a life-course perspective. For instance, what do the drug-abuse and behavioral trajectories of adults with sub-stance-use disorders look like over time? We know that drug abuse and addiction have immediate consequences, but what do the lives of indi-viduals living with addiction look like several years or even several decades down the road? Do most adults with serious alcohol and drug-use problems seek help and get better with time? Does treatment work? What about criminal behavior among those with long-standing alcohol and drug problems? Fortunately, a number of very powerful, prospective studies have been conducted that shed light on such ques-tions. Below we discuss a number of key insights that have emerged from life-course studies of adult trajectories in addiction, recovery, and crime.

The Duration of Addiction

First, let us look at what we know about the *duration of addiction*. Prospective studies of adults with alcohol and other drug-use disorders illustrate quite clearly that, for many, drug-abuse and addiction issues persist for years. Indeed, George Vaillant's longitudinal research on alcohol use suggests that alcohol problems quite often stretch on for decades. Vaillant (1996), in his multi-decade study of a cohort of Harvard undergraduates, found that more than half of the young men he studied who had alcohol problems during college were still struggling with serious alcohol-related problems at age 60. Now, you might say that this is a really interesting finding, but also note that a study of Harvard undergraduates has serious limitations when it comes to generalizability. We certainly agree. And it appears that Vaillant was aware of this critique as well as he conducted a parallel study focused on a community sample comprised of the "healthy controls" interviewed in the original Glueck and Glueck (1950) study of delinquent youth. In his community sample we see similarly disconcerting evidence with respect to the link between young adult alcohol abuse and later alcohol-related problems during middle adulthood and late life (Vaillant 1996, 2003). Specifically, among those found to have alcohol problems as young adults, more than two in five (43 %) reported alcohol problems at age 60 and one in three (33 %) reported persistent problems at age 70. In a word, these studies point to a great degree of continuity when it comes to alcohol problems across adulthood.

Similarly disconcerting evidence can be found for those who struggle with addiction to illicit drugs. For instance, Yih-Ing Hser and her colleagues at the University of California at Los Angeles conducted a 33-year follow-up study of heroin-dependent criminal offenders who received compulsory drug treatment in the early 1960s (Hser et al. 1993, 2001). They found that nearly one in three (32 %) participants tested positive for heroin two decades later and more than one in five participants (21 %) tested positive for heroin more than three decades after receiving drug-use treatment. In fact, it is likely that far more than 21 % of Hser's study participants were struggling with heroin addiction at the 33-year follow-up as 9 % of study participants refused to provide a urine sample and an additional 14 % were incarcerated and, therefore, unable to provide a urine sample. Indeed, self-reported past-year heroin use was over 40 % among study participants and sizeable proportions reported daily alcohol use (22 %) as well as past year use of marijuana (35 %), cocaine (19 %), and amphetamines (12 %). Notably, Hser and colleagues' research is very much in keeping with a number of long-term follow-up studies suggesting that, for many opiate addicts, the struggle with the ongoing use of heroin and other drugs of abuse is one that lasts a lifetime (see Goldstein and Herrera 1995; Kimber et al. 2010; Oppenheimer et al. 1994; Vaillant 1973, 1988).

Given that the aforementioned studies all focus on heroin use, it is reasonable to wonder if the long-term trajectories of heroin users might be distinct—that is, marked by more severe and persistent patterns of use—from those who use other drugs. Indeed, we know that, despite the neurobiological and behavioral similarities observed among those addicted to any number of substances, not all addictions are created equal. Upon closer inspection, we do find longitudinal research suggesting that heroin users are more, in fact, more likely to have longer-term, persistent drug-use problems compared to users of other drugs (Hser et al. 2008a, b; Vaillant 1988). In the same breath, however, evidence is also quite clear that drug addiction tends to be, on average, a condition that is long-lasting whether the primary drug of abuse is cocaine, cannabis, heroin, methamphetamine, or something else (see Brecht et al. 2008; Chen and Kandel 1995; Hser et al. 2008; Perkonigg et al. 2008). Evidence suggests that—among those meeting criteria for any substance-use disorder—the average time lag between first use of drugs and sustained abstinence is nearly 30 years (Dennis et al. 2005). In essence, the evidence is quite clear that, similar to prospective life-course research focused on alcohol-use disorder, drug addiction is, for a disconcerting proportion of individuals, a condition that can persist for decades after problems first appear.

Seeking Out Treatment for Addiction

A related point has to do with to what we know about *individuals seeking out treatment for substance-use disorders*. Regretfully, what we know is mostly bad news. To begin, many people with alcohol and drug-use disorders do not pursue treatment. Indeed, evidence from the NESARC suggest that only a very small fraction—fewer than one in four—of individuals who meet lifetime criteria for alcohol-use disorder ever seek out treatment, including self-help groups (Cohen et al. 2007; Hasin et al. 2007). Other studies examining treatment-seeking among those meeting diagnostic criteria for an alcohol or drug-use disorder have found higher rates of lifetime treatment and suggest that treatment varies by drug type, but we nevertheless see a clear pattern in which the majority of people with an addiction do not seek out treatment (Kessler et al. 2001).

The low levels of treatment-seeking may exist for a number of reasons. For one, epidemiological evidence suggests that only a minority people with substance-use disorders believe that they are in need of help (Mojtabai et al. 2002). If you do not believe you need addictions treatment, you are highly unlikely to seek out such treatment unless required to do so by your employer, friends or family, or the criminal justice system. Additionally, seeking treatment is not easy in psychological or practical terms and many avoid receiving professional help on account of factors such as stigma, feelings of embarrassment, or negative attitudes toward drug treatment (Cunningham et al. 1993; Mancini et al. 2015). Finally, a large proportion of people do not seek treatment because they get better without ever attending an Alcoholics Anonymous meeting or meeting with a health professional (DiClemente 2006; Hall et al. 2015). While this is certainly the case, leading voices in addictions research and treatment have argued that such "natural recovery" is far more common among those with less severe addictions and that the majority of individuals with severe addictive disorders will struggle to achieve recovery without specialized, professional assistance (Volkow et al. 2016).

Many people, of course, do seek treatment at some point in their lives. However, it is well documented that, on average, there is typically a *substantial lag in treatment-seeking*. For example, evidence from a variety of large-scale, epidemiological studies suggests that the lag between the first experiences of alcohol and drug-related problems and first-time substance-abuse treatment is, on average, between one and two decades with the longest delays observed among those who begin using alcohol and drugs early in life (Chapman et al. 2015; Hasin et al. 2007; Kessler et al. 2001; Keyes et al. 2010). While disconcerting, it is, perhaps, understandable that we would see a lag between the onset of a few substance-related problems and treatment. It is reasonable to suspect that the lag would be less in terms of the onset of full-blown addiction and help-seeking. In fact, it is; however, evidence also points to a substantial delay—typically, five to ten years—between the onset of alcohol or drug dependence and help seeking (Borges et al. 2007; Keyes et al. 2010, Kessler et al. 2001). Given such delays, many in addictions research and treatment have made the case that drug treatment be made widely and easily available in institutional settings such as juvenile detention facilities, jails, and prisons where rates of drug abuse and addiction are exceedingly high (Chandler et al. 2009; Golzari et al. 2006; Mitchell et al. 2007, 2012).

Treatment Effects and Long-Term Recovery

A relevant question when discussing treatment-seeking relates to the degree to which substance-use treatment results in long-term, positive outcomes. Regretfully, evidence suggests that *even state-of-the-art treatments are by no means a panacea.* For instance, evidence from the National Treatment Outcome Research Study in the United Kingdom found that, although various approaches to treatment led to long-term reductions in the frequency of heroin and intravenous drug use, only a minority of those who received treatment (25–38 %) were found to be absent five years later (Gossop et al. 2003). This is consistent with the overall outcomes for large-scale intervention projects led by NIAAA in which noteworthy reductions in alcohol use were observed but sustained abstinence was far from the norm (Anton et al. 2006; Project MATCH Research Group 1998). We see similar treatment outcomes for individuals with cannabis, cocaine, and methamphetamine-use disorders (Kadden et al. 2007; Roll et al. 2006; Simpson et al. 2002). Such results also match up with evidence indicating that, on average, there is nearly a decade-long delay between beginning treatment and achieving long-term abstinence[3] (Dennis et al. 2005). Simply put, even when people pursue professional assistance for the treatment of addiction, it is difficult—but by no means impossible—to achieve a long-term recovery characterized by sustained abstinence.

Let us be absolutely clear: treating addiction is very challenging and one or more instances of relapse are to be expected, but there is no doubt that *many people with alcohol and drug-use disorders achieve a long-term recovery.* Moreover, those who are able to stop using and, in turn, put together a sustained period of abstinence are quite likely to continue to experience recovery long into the future. Vaillant's (1996) long-term follow-up study of

---

[3] There is debate as to the use of long-term abstinence as a primary marker of a positive outcome for the treatment of alcohol and drug use disorders. Noting the chronic nature of addiction and highlighting the likelihood of relapse for many people, serious thinkers in the field of addiction consider meaningful reductions in alcohol and drug use to be a positive outcome for those with addictive disorders. We fully affirm that relapse is a high probability event for many people in recovery and that relapse along the road to recovery should not be viewed as a treatment failure; however, we also concur with those noting that abstinence is generally to be understood as the optimal goal for a lasting recovery (DuPont et al., 2016).

Harvard undergraduates and inner-city youth in Boston found that relapse was a rare phenomenon among men with alcohol problems who were able to abstain from drinking for several years. This is consistent with more recent research from Dennis et al. (2007) who found a rather robust relationship between past and future abstinence. Specifically, among those who had been abstinent for one to three years, two out of three (66 %) remained abstinent for an additional year or more and, among those reporting three or more years of abstinence, more than four in five (86 %) maintained abstinence for at least an additional year. In other words, abstinence predicts continued abstinence, particularly after one gets over the initial challenges of early recovery. Predictably, sustained abstinence has been found to be substantially more likely among those who regularly attend 12-step groups, establish friendships with others in recovery, and are actively involved in aftercare programs designed to support recovery (Dennis et al. 2007; Scott et al 2003; Vaillant 2003). All this is to say that long-term recovery is certainly possible, particularly when individuals are able to sustain abstinence beyond the first few months and are committed to participation in activities designed to foster sobriety and prevent relapse.

Addiction, Recovery, and Crime

Finally, let us discuss what prospective evidence tells us about *long-term addiction, recovery, and criminal offending across adulthood*. We have discussed at length in the text the cross-sectional association between drug abuse and nonviolent and violent antisocial behavior. We have noted that those who abuse alcohol and other drugs tend to be more likely to also take part in behaviors that reflect a lack of concern for others, and vice versa. In addition, we have noted that there appears to be a reciprocal relationship between drug abuse and antisocial behavior across the developmental period of adolescence. In this section, however, we are looking at the relationship between these factors from a different angle; namely, we are concerned with the degree to which adults with long-standing substance-use disorders are involved in crime and the criminal justice system. We know what cross-sectional and adolescent data tell us, but what about longitudinal data on adults? Do we see a drug abuse/antisocial behavior link among the minority of adults who suffer from addictive disorders that persist for years or decades? Do people who recover from addiction tend to abstain from both drug use and antisocial behavior? Such questions are central to a life-course understanding of drug abuse, addiction and antisocial behavior.

Regretfully, the longitudinal evidence is quite clear: multiple studies point to very high levels of antisocial behavior and criminal-justice-system involvement among those suffering from long-standing addictive disorders. Hser et al. (2001) found, in their 33-year follow-up study of heroin addicts in California, that substantial proportions of long-term drug users reported past year property offenses (12 %), drug-selling (26 %), and criminal-justice-system involvement (31 %). While this level of antisocial behavior is problematic at any age, these numbers are all the more remarkable when one considers that Hser's sample had a mean age of 57 years at the time of long-term follow-up. As a point of reference, the prevalence of past year theft (0.42 %), drug-selling (0.51 %), and arrest (1.20 %) among adults ages 50 to 64 in the NSDUH was close to non-existent. Perhaps even more interesting, Hser reports the prevalence of these behaviors among men in her sample who had been abstinent from heroin—but not necessarily alcohol or other drugs—for five or more years. Among those in long-term recovery, we see far lower levels of property crime (1.8 %), drug-selling (0 %), and incarceration (8 %).

Notably, this pattern of results does not appear to be unique to heroin users. For instance, Dennis et al. (2007) observed, in a large-scale, prospective study of adult drug abusers recruited from a treatment sample in Chicago, substantial decreases in illegal activity and illegal income during the first year of recovery. This alone is interesting; however, even more striking is that illegal activity ceased entirely among those reporting one to three, three to five, or five or more years of abstinence. Moreover, Hser et al. (2006), in a 12-year follow-up study of individuals treated for cocaine dependence, identified marked differences between those who achieved stable recovery and those who had not with respect to past-year arrests (8 % versus 34 %) and incarceration (7 % versus 22 %). Still other studies suggest that abstinence may not be necessary in order to see reductions in criminal behavior as there exists evidence that drug treatment—independent of abstinence or other drug-use outcomes—may be linked with drops in the frequency of acquisitive crime as far as five years after care is received (Gossop et al. 2003). Simply put, long-term drug-addiction portents of major issues with respect to antisocial behavior and criminal justice involvement across adulthood, but rather remarkable changes can be observed among those who are able to achieve a sustained recovery.

Conclusion

We began this chapter by emphasizing the importance of bringing a developmental, biosocial lens to our understanding of drug abuse, addiction, and antisocial behavior during adulthood. We presented epidemiological surveillance data from large-scale, nationally representative studies focused on drug abuse and related constructs, including violent and nonviolent antisocial behavior. These data point to a clear pattern in which we see—in the general population—a steady decline in the prevalence of drug abuse and antisocial behavior across the spectrum of young, middle, and older adulthood. While highlighting the utility of large-scale epidemiological studies, we also affirm the fundamental importance of prospective studies focused on the long-term trajectories of those with persistent alcohol and drug-use problems. In delving into such research we see that, for many, addictive disorders can last for decades; individuals with addictive disorders are often reluctant to seek treatment and, even among those who do, there is often a substantial lag between serious drug-related problems and help-seeking. Regretfully, while many certainly do seek treatment and, in turn, achieve a lasting recovery, treatment data nevertheless makes evident that even state-of-the-art treatments are far from a cure-all.

Over the last few chapters, we have seen that childhood very often sets the stage for later drug abuse and antisocial behavior and that adolescence and emerging adulthood are the developmental periods where such behaviors are most commonly observed. However, for most of us, life does not end at age 25 and we see quite clearly that the entry into adulthood is the time when the vast majority of people cease drinking and drugging and taking part in criminal and antisocial behavior. Yet a very important subset of the population continues to have serious problems with addiction and antisocial behavior during young and middle adulthood and sometimes into late life. Research has made quite clear that those dealing with long-term drug-use disorders are disproportionately likely to take part in crime and to be incarcerated, but also that remarkable drops in criminal activity can be observed among those who achieve a sustained recovery. The beauty of a life-course perspective is that it allows us to take the long view when it comes to understanding addiction and antisocial behavior, and to observe the profound interrelatedness of addiction, recovery, and crime over time.

References

Anton, R.F., O'Malley, S.S., Ciraulo, D.A., Cisler, R.A., Couper, D., Donovan, D.M., et al. (2006). Combined pharmacotherapies and behavioral interventions for alcohol dependence: The COMBINE study: A randomized controlled trial. *Journal of the American Medical Association, 295*(17), 2003–2017.

Blow, F.C. & Barry, K.L. (2002). Use and misuse of alcohol among older women. *Alcohol Research and Health, 26*(4), 308–315.

Borges, G., Wang, P.S., Medina-Mora, M.E., Lara, C., & Chiu, W.T. (2007). Delay of first treatment of mental and substance use disorders in Mexico. *American Journal of Public Health, 97*(9), 1638–1643.

Brecht, M.L., Huang, D., Evans, E., & Hser, Y.I. (2008). Polydrug use and implications for longitudinal research: Ten-year trajectories for heroin, cocaine, and methamphetamine users. *Drug and Alcohol Dependence, 96*(3), 193–201.

Britton, A., Ben-Shlomo, Y., Benzeval, M., Kuh, D., & Bell, S. (2015). Life course trajectories of alcohol consumption in the United Kingdom using longitudinal data from nine cohort studies. *BMC Medicine, 13*(1), 47.

Chandler, R.K., Fletcher, B.W., & Volkow, N.D. (2009). Treating drug abuse and addiction in the criminal justice system: Improving public health and safety. *Journal of the American Medical Association, 301*(2), 183–190.

Chapman, C., Slade, T., Hunt, C., & Teesson, M. (2015). Delay to first treatment contact for alcohol use disorder. *Drug and Alcohol Dependence, 147*, 116–121.

Chen, K., & Kandel, D.B. (1995). The natural history of drug use from adolescence to the mid-thirties in a general population sample. *American Journal of Public Health, 85*(1), 41–47.

Cohen, E., Feinn, R., Arias, A., & Kranzler, H.R. (2007). Alcohol treatment utilization: Findings from the National Epidemiologic Survey on Alcohol and Related Conditions. *Drug and Alcohol Dependence, 86*(2), 214–221.

Craik, F.I. & Bialystok, E. (2006). Cognition through the lifespan: Mechanisms of change. *Trends in Cognitive Sciences, 10*(3), 131–138.

Cunningham, J.A., Sobell, L.C., Sobell, M.B., Agrawal, S., & Toneatto, T. (1993). Barriers to treatment: Why alcohol and drug abusers delay or never seek treatment. *Addictive Behaviors, 18*(3), 347–353.

Dawson, D.A., Goldstein, R.B., Saha, T.D., & Grant, B.F. (2015). Changes in alcohol consumption: United States, 2001–2002 to 2012–2013. *Drug and Alcohol Dependence, 148*, 56–61.

Dennis, M.L., Foss, M.A., & Scott, C.K. (2007). An eight-year perspective on the relationship between the duration of abstinence and other aspects of recovery. *Evaluation Review, 31*(6), 585–612.

Dennis, M.L., Scott, C.K., Funk, R., & Foss, M.A. (2005). The duration and correlates of addiction and treatment careers. *Journal of Substance Abuse Treatment, 28*(2), S51–S62.

DiClemente, C.C. (2006). Natural change and the troublesome use of substances: A life-course perspective. In W. R. Miller, & K. M. Carroll (Eds.), *Rethinking substance abuse: What the science shows, and what we should do about it* (pp. 81–96). New York Guilford Press.

DuPont, R.L., Seppala, M.D., & White, W.L. (2016). The three missing elements in the treatment of substance use disorders: Lessons from the physician health programs. *Journal of Addictive Diseases, 35*(1), 3–7.

Elder Jr, G.H. (1975). Age differentiation and the life course. *Annual Review of Sociology, 1*, 165–190.

Erikson, E.H. (1959). Identity and the life cycle: Selected papers [Review]. *Psychological Issues, 1*(1), 1–171.

Evans, W.J. (2010). Skeletal muscle loss: Cachexia, sarcopenia, and inactivity. *The American Journal of Clinical Nutrition, 91*(4), 1123S–1127S.

Farrington, D.P. (1986). Age and crime. In M. Tonry, & N. Morris (Eds.), *Crime and justice: An annual review of research* (Vol. 7, pp. 189–250). Chicago: University of Chicago Press.

Farrington, D.P., Piquero, A.R., & Jennings, W.G. (2013). *Offending from childhood to late middle age: Recent results from the Cambridge study in delinquent development.* New York Springer.

Féart, C., Samieri, C., Rondeau, V., Amieva, H., Portet, F., Dartigues, J.F., et al. (2009). Adherence to a Mediterranean diet, cognitive decline, and risk of dementia. *Journal of the American Medical Association, 302*(6), 638–648.

Glueck, S. & Glueck, E.T. (1950). *Unraveling juvenile delinquency.* New York: Commonwealth Fund.

Goldstein, A. & Herrera, J. (1995). Heroin addicts and methadone treatment in Albuquerque: A 22-year follow-up. *Drug and Alcohol Dependence, 40*(2), 139–150.

Golzari, M., Hunt, S.J., & Anoshiravani, A. (2006). The health status of youth in juvenile detention facilities. *Journal of Adolescent Health, 38*(6), 776–782.

Gossop, M., Marsden, J., Stewart, D., & Kidd, T. (2003). The National Treatment Outcome Research Study (NTORS): 4–5 Year follow-up results. *Addiction, 98*(3), 291–303.

Grant, B.F., Goldstein, R.B., Saha, T.D., Chou, S.P., Jung, J., Zhang, H., et al. (2015). Epidemiology of DSM-5 alcohol use disorder: Results from the National Epidemiologic Survey on Alcohol and Related Conditions III. *JAMA Psychiatry, 72*(8), 757–766.

Grant, B.F., Saha, T.D., Ruan, W.J., Goldstein, R.B., Chou, S.P., Jung, J., et al. (2016). Epidemiology of DSM-5 drug use disorder: Results from the National Epidemiologic Survey on Alcohol and Related Conditions-III. *JAMA Psychiatry, 73*(1), 39–47.

Hackman, D.A. & Farah, M.J. (2009). Socioeconomic status and the developing brain. *Trends in Cognitive Sciences, 13*(2), 65–73.

Hall, W., Carter, A., & Forlini, C. (2015). The brain disease model of addiction: Is it supported by the evidence and has it delivered on its promises? *The Lancet Psychiatry, 2*(1), 105–110.

Hasin, D.S., Stinson, F.S., Ogburn, E., & Grant, B.F. (2007). Prevalence, correlates, disability, and comorbidity of DSM-IV alcohol abuse and dependence in the United States: Results from the National Epidemiologic Survey on Alcohol and Related Conditions. *Archives of General Psychiatry, 64*(7), 830–842.

Hasin, D.S., Saha, T.D., Kerridge, B.T., Goldstein, R.B., Chou, S.P., Zhang, H., et al. (2015). Prevalence of marijuana use disorders in the United States between 2001–2002 and 2012–2013. *JAMA Psychiatry, 72*(12), 1235–1242.

Hasin, D.S., Kerridge, B.T., Saha, T.D., Huang, B., Pickering, R., Smith, S. M., et al. (2016). Prevalence and correlates of DSM-5 cannabis use disorder, 2012–2013: Findings from the National Epidemiologic Survey on Alcohol and Related Conditions-III. *American Journal of Psychiatry*. Advance online publication. doi: http://dx.doi.org/10.1176/appi.ajp.2015.15070907.

Hser, Y.I., Anglin, M.D., & Powers, K. (1993). A 24-year follow-up of California narcotics addicts. *Archives of General Psychiatry, 50*(7), 577–584.

Hser, Y.I., Hoffman, V., Grella, C.E., & Anglin, M.D. (2001). A 33-year follow-up of narcotics addicts. *Archives of General Psychiatry, 58*(5), 503–508.

Hser, Y.I., Stark, M.E., Paredes, A., Huang, D., Anglin, M.D., & Rawson, R. (2006). A 12-year follow-up of a treated cocaine-dependent sample. *Journal of Substance Abuse Treatment, 30*(3), 219–226.

Hser, Y.I., Evans, E., Huang, D., Brecht, M.L., & Li, L. (2008a). Comparing the dynamic course of heroin, cocaine, and methamphetamine use over 10 years. *Addictive Behaviors, 33*(12), 1581–1589.

Hser, Y.I., Huang, D., Brecht, M.L., Li, L., & Evans, E. (2008b). Contrasting trajectories of heroin, cocaine, and methamphetamine use. *Journal of Addictive Diseases, 27*(3), 13–21.

Kadden, R.M., Litt, M.D., Kabela-Cormier, E., & Petry, N.M. (2007). Abstinence rates following behavioral treatments for marijuana dependence. *Addictive Behaviors, 32*(6), 1220–1236.

Kessler, R.C., Aguilar-Gaxiola, S., Berglund, P.A., Caraveo-Anduaga, J.J., DeWit, D.J., Greenfield, S.F., et al. (2001). Patterns and predictors of treatment seeking after onset of a substance use disorder. *Archives of General Psychiatry, 58*(11), 1065–1071.

Keyes, K.M., Martins, S.S., Blanco, C., & Hasin, D.S. (2010). Telescoping and gender differences in alcohol dependence: New evidence from two national surveys. *American Journal of Psychiatry, 167*(8), 969–976.

Kimber, J., Copeland, L., Hickman, M., Macleod, J., McKenzie, J., De Angelis, D., & Robertson, J.R. (2010). Survival and cessation in injecting drug users: Prospective observational study of outcomes and effect of opiate substitution treatment. *British Medical Journal, 341*, c3172.

Laub, J.H. & Sampson, R.J. (2003). *Shared beginnings, divergent lives: Delinquent boys to age 70*. Cambridge, MA: Harvard University Press.

Levinson, D.J. (1978). *The seasons of a man's life*. New York Ballantine Books.

Levinson, D.J. (1986). A conception of adult development. *American Psychologist, 41*(1), 3–13.

Mancini, M.A., Salas-Wright, C.P., & Vaughn, M.G. (2015). Drug use and service utilization among Hispanics in the United States. *Social Psychiatry and Psychiatric Epidemiology, 50*(11), 1679–1689.

Mitchell, O., Wilson, D.B., & MacKenzie, D.L. (2007). Does incarceration-based drug treatment reduce recidivism? A meta-analytic synthesis of the research. *Journal of Experimental Criminology, 3*(4), 353–375.

Mitchell, O., MacKenzie, D., & Wilson, D. (2012). The effectiveness of incarceration-based drug treatment on criminal behavior: A systematic review. *Campbell Systematic Reviews, 8*(18), 1–58. www.campbellcollaboration.org/lib/project/20/

Mojtabai, R., Olfson, M., & Mechanic, D. (2002). Perceived need and help-seeking in adults with mood, anxiety, or substance use disorders. *Archives of General Psychiatry, 59*(1), 77–84.

Oppenheimer, E., Tobutt, C., Taylor, C., & Andrew, T. (1994). Death and survival in a cohort of heroin addicts from London clinics: A 22-year follow-up study. *Addiction, 89*(10), 1299–1308.

Perkonigg, A., Goodwin, R.D., Fiedler, A., Behrendt, S., Beesdo, K., Lieb, R., & Wittchen, H.U. (2008). The natural course of cannabis use, abuse and dependence during the first decades of life. *Addiction, 103*(3), 439–449.

Piquero, A.R., Farrington, D.P., & Blumstein, A. (2007). *Key issues in criminal careers research: New analysis from the Cambridge study in delinquent development.* Cambridge, UK: Cambridge University Press.

Project MATCH Research Group (1998). Matching alcoholism treatments to client heterogeneity: Project MATCH three-year drinking outcomes. *Alcohol Clinical and Experimental Research, 22*(6), 1300–1311.

Riggs, B.L., Melton, L.J., Robb, R.A., Camp, J.J., Atkinson, E.J., Peterson, J.M., et al. (2004). Population-based study of age and sex differences in bone volumetric density, size, geometry, and structure at different skeletal sites. *Journal of Bone and Mineral Research, 19*(12), 1945–1954.

Roll, J.M., Petry, N.M., Stitzer, M.L., Brecht, M.L., Peirce, J.M., McCann, M. J., et al. (2006). Contingency management for the treatment of methamphetamine use disorders. *American Journal of Psychiatry, 163*(11), 1993–1999.

Schaie, K.W. (1996). *Intellectual development in adulthood: The Seattle longitudinal study.* New York Cambridge University Press.

Schaie, K.W., Willis, S.L., & Pennak, S. (2005). An historical framework for cohort differences in intelligence. *Research in Human Development, 2*(1–2), 43–67.

Scott, C.K., Foss, M.A., & Dennis, M.L. (2003). Factors influencing initial and longer-term responses to substance abuse treatment: A path analysis. *Evaluation and Program Planning, 26*(3), 287–295.

Shulman, E.P., Steinberg, L.D., & Piquero, A.R. (2013). The age–crime curve in adolescence and early adulthood is not due to age differences in economic status. *Journal of Youth and Adolescence, 42*(6), 848–860.

Simpson, D.D., Joe, G.W., & Broome, K.M. (2002). A national 5-year follow-up of treatment outcomes for cocaine dependence. *Archives of General Psychiatry, 59*(6), 538–544.

Substance Abuse and Mental Health Services Administration (SAHMSA). (2014). *Results from the 2013 National Survey on Drug Use and Health: Summary of national findings*. Rockville Substance Abuse and Mental Health Services Administration.

Vaillant, G.E. (1973). A 20-year follow-up of New York narcotic addicts. *Archives of General Psychiatry, 29*(2), 237–241.

Vaillant, G.E. (1988). What can long-term follow-up teach us about relapse and prevention of relapse in addiction? *British Journal of Addiction, 83*(10), 1147–1157.

Vaillant, G.E. (1996). A long-term follow-up of male alcohol abuse. *Archives of General Psychiatry, 53*(3), 243–249.

Vaillant, G.E. (2003). A 60-year follow-up of alcoholic men. *Addiction, 98*(8), 1043–1051.

Volkow, N.D., Koob, G.F., & McLellan, A.T. (2016). Neurobiologic advances from the brain disease model of addiction. *New England Journal of Medicine, 374*(4), 363–371.

Waters, D.L., Baumgartner, R.N., Garry, P.J., & Vellas, B. (2010). Advantages of dietary, exercise-related, and therapeutic interventions to prevent and treat sarcopenia in adult patients: An update. *Clinical Interventions in Aging, 5*, 259–270.

Willis, S.L. & Schaie, K.W. (2005). Cognitive trajectories in midlife and cognitive functioning in old age. In S. Willis, & M. Martin (Eds.), *Middle adulthood: A lifespan perspective* (pp. 243–276). Thousand Oaks Sage.

Xu, J., Murphy, S.L, Kochanek, K.D., & Bastian, B.A. (2016). Deaths: Final data for 2013. *National vital statistics reports: From the Centers for Disease Control and Prevention, National Center for Health Statistics, National Vital Statistics System, 64*(2), 1–119.

Yaffe, K., Barnes, D., Nevitt, M., Lui, L.Y., & Covinsky, K. (2001). A prospective study of physical activity and cognitive decline in elderly women: Women who walk. *Archives of Internal Medicine, 161*(14), 1703–1708.

8

Prevention and Treatment

Introduction

After reviewing this text, you have likely developed an opinion about the relevance and importance of biosocial theory in understanding addiction. In our opinion, there is little doubt that addiction is a biosocial process. As a result, neither the genetic underpinnings of disease nor social processes related to addiction may be ignored when attempting to prevent and treat addictive disorders. The treatment of chronic disorders, including addiction, calls for not only short-term and intensive interventions (such as detoxification and inpatient treatment) but also the provision of ongoing services such as therapeutic case management, regular attendance of a support group or group-therapy sessions, regular appointments with a healthcare provider or psychiatrist to discuss medication adherence, and booster sessions designed to provide follow-up to the initial inpatient rehabilitation interventions. In the words of Dackis and O'Brien (2005), "Treatment for this chronic disorder is labor-intensive, requiring a comprehensive assessment by qualified practitioners, as well as ongoing individual, group and family interventions" (p. 1436).

© The Author(s) 2016
C.P. Salas-Wright et al., *Drug Abuse and Antisocial Behavior*,
Palgrave's Frontiers in Criminology Theory,
DOI 10.1057/978-1-137-55817-6_8

Fig. 8.1 Depiction of intervention approaches designed to maximize the likelihood of abstinence through multi-dimensional treatment

As concisely stated by Komro et al. (2016), "most health outcomes have 'multiple interacting influences crossing socio-ecological levels' and require complex, multi-level strategies," including biosocial targets, as a result. Multifactorial approaches to treating addiction encompass a broad array of techniques—all of which engage neural substrates to some degree–including: pharmacotherapies, lifestyle changes, cognitive behavioral therapies, family training and education to reduce risk of relapse. Figure 8.1 depicts several approaches to maximize the likelihood of abstinence through multi-dimensional treatment. In the absence of one domain (e.g., medication management), the treatment program will not address the comprehensive needs of someone suffering from an addictive disease.

To illustrate this point, consider a patient newly diagnosed with type-II diabetes. The patient is diagnosed with the disease at age 15, so he is trained to monitor his blood sugar levels and administer insulin as needed (symptom management). Given the very strong relationship between diabetes and depression (e.g., depressive symptoms so severe that they may have led to development of the disease), he will likely visit a clinical psychologist or counselor on a regular basis (Eaton et al. 1996). Without this therapy, his symptoms may worsen and cause neuropathy, heart problems or even death. Despite all of these efforts to manage our patient's diabetes, his family is unable to purchase healthy foods, and they live in a high-crime neighborhood that limits his physical activity. This limits lifestyle modifications needed for disease control, and as a result, his symptoms never improve. In the presence of a healthy lifestyle, it is likely that our patient could effectively manage his disease well into the future. Our intent is not to say that addiction is comparable to diabetes or a liver transplant that have strong biological ties. Instead, we are attempting to highlight the need for multi-dimensional therapies to converge to treat addiction just as these therapies are used to treat other chronic diseases. We believe that use of multi-factorial addiction treatment programs are far more effective and have long-term effects when compared to single forms of therapy.

But treatment is costly. According to the National Institute on Drug Abuse, substance abuse costs $600 billion annually (National Institute on Drug Abuse 2012). One year of methadone maintenance treatment costs between $5,000 and $10,000 (Cartwright 2000). Of course, this cost is far less than the cost associated with incarcerating a drug offender, which can range from $24,000 to $60,076 per person-year (Henrichson and Delaney 2012). A comprehensive cost-benefit analysis by Cartwright (2000) provided ratios representing the societal cost and associated benefits of various forms of drug treatment. A positive ratio reflects funds saved due to treatment expenditures (e.g., 4.1 = $4.1 saved per $1 spent on treatment); a negative ratio reflects a deficit associated with treatment, or cost. Very few negative ratios were documented in the scientific literature, and benefit ratios ranged from −2.98 (for methadone detoxification) (Gerstein et al. 1994) to 26.3 for residential heroin treatment (Tabbush 1986). Although these precise ratios are sensitive to study design and "benefit" (and "cost") measurement, nearly all studies found that dollars were saved through drug treatment. This is true even when a small percentage of the population relapses and needs additional treatment. The take-home message from this study was that the *long-term* benefits accumulated over decades, while the costs were expended over a (relatively) brief time frame.

As discussed in Chap. 2, addiction does not resolve itself immediately with treatment. In fact, it is relatively uncommon for persons seeking treatment for a substance-use disorder to achieve a lasting recovery after only a single treatment episode (Friedmann 2013). Evidence from state-of-the-art treatment studies consistently indicate that a minority of people seeking first-time treatment for alcohol or other drug-use disorders ceases use and remain completely abstinent for the duration of their lifespan (Cacciola et al. 2005;

Flynn et al. 2003; Hser et al. 1999; Miller et al. 2001; Simpson and Sells 1990). Further, persons who seek out treatment and are able to achieve sustained abstinence are at substantial risk for relapse. In fact, as pointed out by the former Deputy Director of the White House Office of National Drug Control Policy, only 40 to 60 % of individuals who complete drug-abuse treatment remain abstinent one year after discharge (McLellan et al. 2005). By any metric, this relapse rate is high.

Risk of relapse is an issue in the treatment of addiction, but approaching the treatment of addiction from a chronic-disease perspective leads to outcomes that are far superior to short-term, one-time approaches that frame addiction as an acute condition (McLellan et al. 2005). Rather than conceptualizing a single episode of relapse as a treatment failure, the chronic-disease-management model emphasizes the importance of taking a broader view of recovery. For instance, a relapse episode can be used as "grist for the mill" that can foster learning about the components of addiction (e.g., triggers, craving, etc.) that can present challenges to long-term recovery. Along the same lines, success is not limited to cases in which individuals achieve a sustained and unwavering period of abstinence, but rather it also includes the experiences of individuals who occasionally experience relapse as part of a long-term pattern of recovery and treatment adherence.

Prevention Versus Treatment: A Public Health Framework

One of the real advances of the brain disease model of addiction is that it facilitates the framing of drug abuse and addiction with in the language of public health. The World Health Organization (2016) has defined public health as referring to organized efforts to "prevent disease, promote health, and prolong life among the population as a whole. Its activities aim to provide the conditions in which people can be healthy and focus on entire populations, not on individual patients or diseases." Along the same lines, the American Public Health Association (APHA 2013) notes that while the task of physicians and other health professionals has traditionally been the treatment of those experiencing illness or disease, the task of public health is to "prevent people from getting sick or injured in the first place . . . [and to] promote wellness by encouraging healthy behaviors." Fundamentally, public health efforts are oriented around the surveillance of health conditions, the design and implementation of public policies intended to address health concerns, and ensuring access to preventive, health promotion, and treatment services.

The chronic nature of addiction calls for intensive and long-term treatment strategies (Dackis and O'Brien 2005). As such, while substantial time and money has been dedicated to developing evidence-based drug-abuse treatment protocols, scientists and health professionals have become increasingly interested in learning how to effectively prevent young people from initiating substance use and circumvent the development of addiction among those who have begun to misuse alcohol and other drugs (Hawkins et al. 1992). Earlier we discussed the Obama administration's use of the language of "disease" on the White House webpage, *A Drug Policy for the Twenty-first Century* (White House 2014). If we go back to that webpage, we see clear evidence that the Executive Branch of the United States federal government draws a connection between the disease conceptualization and the vital importance of prevention. In particular, we see statements regarding the importance of "emphasizing prevention over incarceration" and "training healthcare professionals to intervene early before addiction develops." In a word, the chronic disease framework underscores the importance of preventing addiction before it starts.

Application of the public health framework to drug abuse and addiction has several important advantages and implications that move the field of prevention forward. First, this movement shifts the addiction prevention and treatment agenda away from the criminal justice system (e.g., tertiary prevention and treatment, which is costly) and toward health behavior, risk reduction and policy (e.g., primary and secondary prevention, which is less costly). To this end, a recent APHA (2013) policy statement entitled, "Defining and implementing a public health response to drug use and misuse" identified the movement to shift away from the criminalization of drug possession and use as a core component of a public health approach. Specifically, the APHA statement highlights how the mass incarceration of drug users in the criminal justice system has made treatment more difficult, created other public health problems, and—not inconsequentially—contributed to the problem of mass incarceration in the United States. Because the majority of persons housed in United States jails and prisons are incarcerated for drug-related offenses (Carson and Golinelli 2013), even a small dent in the rate of substance use at the population-level will result in great cost-savings in criminal justice.

Understanding addiction within the framework of public health allows us to leverage the strengths of epidemiology and public-health practice and policy to address the challenges of drug abuse and addiction. For instance, situating drug abuse and addiction within the framework of public health, we have seen exciting advances in the epidemiology of substance use. The subdiscipline of genetic epidemiology is beginning to profoundly enhance our capacity to understand, prevent, and treat drug abuse and addiction (Kendler et al. 2012; Merikangas and McClair 2012). Social epidemiology has helped us to appreciate the way in which social and contextual factors —such as family and social network norms, neighborhood characteristics and community violence, discrimination and segregation—influence risk for substance abuse and addiction (Galea et al. 2004; Winstanley et al. 2008). Beyond epidemiology, a public health approach to drug abuse and addictions opens up exciting possibilities with respect to large-scale health-promotion efforts designed to prevent drug abuse before it starts, increase treatment access, and reduce drug-related health consequences among active users.

Of course, framing addiction as a public health issue is not a particularly new idea. In 1914, Charles E. Terry published a commentary in the *American Journal of Public Health* in which he states unequivocally, "I believe that few ... [challenges] confronting us affect more seriously the public health than this of drug addictions. It directly and indirectly increases the death rate and ... closely resembles, in its dissemination, contact infection of disease" (p. 37). While a public health framework for conceptualizing addiction may not be new, it is certainly powerful. It constitutes, in part, a potential alternative to models rooted primarily in a criminal justice framework and offers many tools that are helpful for the prevention and treatment of drug abuse and addiction.

Evidence-Based Biosocial Prevention Techniques

While neurobiology is indispensable to a state-of-the-art understanding of addiction, there is simply no getting around the fact that drug abuse and addiction are phenomena that are also profoundly social in nature. Leshner (1997) notes quite clearly in his seminal piece on addiction as a brain disease that "Addiction is not just a brain disease. It is a brain disease for which the social contexts in which it has both developed and is expressed are critically important" (p. 46). Similarly, McLellan et al. (2000), in their original article casting addiction as a chronic medical illness, unequivocally underscore the critical importance of factors such as socioeconomic status and social supports in the successful treatment of addiction and other chronic illnesses. Along the same lines, even a cursory review of the neurobiological model proposed by Volkow and Baler (2014) points to the foundational impact of factors in the economic, social, and built environment in influencing risk for drug-use disorders. In brief, theorists have continually recognized that the genetic and neurobiological understanding of addiction must be situated within a social, economic, and environmental context.

As a result, some of the most effective prevention programs target multiple layers of influence to maximally optimize protective factors and reduce (or mitigate) risk. This framework is commonly known as the social-ecological model (also referred to more generally as ecological models). The individual (or micro) level is the most common prevention target, including demographic factors, personality and attitudes. This level would include modifiable (e.g., amenable to prevention or intervention) biological targets. Among adolescents, life-skills training and educational programs targeting individual-level risk and protective factors are common.

Relationships include peer groups, families and partners (this level of influence is also referred to as the "meso" level) that influence a person's behavior and decision-making. To illustrate the importance of targeting interpersonal relationships, put yourself in the shoes of someone (let's call her Jean) exiting a residential drug-treatment facility. Although this treatment thoroughly targeted individual-level factors, including self-efficacy, attitudes, decision-making skills, and knowledge, her social environment was left unchanged. When Jean returns to her regular job, her drug-using friends show up and invite her to a friend's party. She is able to refuse the first time, but given the strong cravings and situational cues that present in her daily life, how long will she continue to turn down these invitations? As you can imagine, this partially explains why relapse is common. This point also illustrates the interaction between multiple levels of influence (National Research Council and Institute of Medicine 2009), a reason why multi-dimensional and multi-component intervention and prevention programs are among the most effective. In this scenario, treatment taught Jean the harms of substance use and some techniques for refusal. As a result, her attitudes, beliefs, knowledge, and even behavior have changed. Her cravings were also reduced after treatment, making abstinence more tolerable for Jean. But, Jean's friends weren't involved in this treatment and are less than supportive of her decision to remain drug-free. Because her new environment is not conducive to abstinence, all of this individual-level treatment may have little or no long-term effect.

To further discuss the impact of cross-level influence, gene–environment (G*E) interactions represent the amplification of an environmental factor due to an underlying genetic risk. Although the literature in this area is in its infancy, some genetic polymorphisms like MAOA have repeatedly been found to interact with family adversity to produce externalizing behavior. Because the research on many of these gene–environment interactions remains inconclusive, it is important to consider the mechanisms of action to move this field of research beyond exploration and towards causational modeling. For example, are deviant peers directly related to antisocial behavior? Or, is this relationship, which is particularly strong among males, driven by testosterone? These are important considerations for future research to continue considering the effect of biological, in addition to psychosocial, effects on addiction.

Returning to the social-ecological model, the third level of influence is referred to as community, or "exo." Substance-use programs that target the community level seek to change school environments, neighborhoods, workplaces, or any other settings so they may become less conducive to substance use. Common examples of community-level programs include social marketing campaigns, zero-tolerance housing, or workplace drug testing.

Prevention programs targeting the societal (or "macro") level are typically policies or social movements designed to shift the entire culture surrounding substance use. A prime example of a societal prevention target is raising of the legal alcohol consumption age from 18 to 20 (and later, 21) (Wagenaar and Toomey 2002). As a result of this increased drinking age, alcohol consumption and alcohol-related fatal car crashes significantly decreased. Similarly, raising the cost of cigarettes by $0.25 per pack resulted in sale of 819 million fewer packs of cigarettes (Hu et al. 1995). Given the large effects of these policies, the impact of substance-related policy changes that increase the age of onset or cost of substance use are difficult to ignore when considering the totality of the evidence on addiction prevention.

What Does Biosocial Theory Say About All of This?

Informed by the theories and biological research discussed above, there is little doubt that biological and social factors interact to cause addiction. In other words, no amount of genetic predisposition will cause someone to become addicted after a single dose of alcohol, although some people may be more susceptible to addiction. Conversely, this is not to say that those who are not biologically susceptible will never become addicted. With repeated drug administrations and development of contextual or environmental cues, even a non-susceptible person can—and will—become addicted.

This is not to say that the biosocial model, or any simplistic combination of biological and social factors, will perfectly predict one's propensity to become addicted. In fact, there is some concern that this conceptualization of addiction as a brain disease has resulted in a disproportionate investment in research focused on the brain and on the treatment of individuals with severe addiction (Hall et al. 2015). In this paper, the authors argue that the focus on research related to only the most severe manifestations of addiction has been at the cost of research into the role of population-based policies, including epidemiologic studies, that have been repeatedly shown to reduce addiction-related problems (Hall et al. 2015). A related critique focuses on the assertion that loss of control and compulsive behavior are the hallmarks of addiction. Citing the demonstrated effectiveness of contingency management interventions—that is, interventions that offer financial rewards to incentivize abstinence from alcohol and drug use (e.g., payment for negative drug screens)—critics argue that addiction does not seem to fully extinguish self-control in all people (Prendergast et al. 2006).

Model Prevention Programs

The potential cost savings associated with substance-use prevention are great, and hundreds—if not thousands—of "evidence-based" substance-use and addiction prevention programs exist. The Substance Abuse and Mental Health Services Administration (SAMHSA) maintains a registry of evidence-based programs to maximize dissemination of programs deemed effective after scientific evaluation (www.samhsa.gov/nrepp). Although this list is comprehensive, it suggests that a "shelf" program might be universally effective when effects have only been observed among a specific subset of the population. For example, the same program deemed effective in rural Minnesota was not effective in Chicago (Komro et al. 2008; Perry et al. 1996). Further, some programs are universal (e.g., may be administered to a population without restriction) while others are intended for "indicated" populations (e.g., the program should be administered only to those identified as at-risk). Therefore, the literature should be carefully scrutinized before adopting a prevention program from this list, as the adoptee should ensure that the program has been validated in a similar population.

As discussed in Chap. 5, the first eight to 12 years of life are critical for healthy development (National Institutes of Health 2016). The detrimental effects of substance-use onset during these critical years could have collateral consequences that persist into and throughout adulthood. As a result, many of the most effective prevention programs seek to delay onset age. According to a comprehensive review of the literature on school-based prevention programs, interactive programs, those that focus on social norms, individual commitments to abstain, and multiple-components (e.g., addition of community-based elements) increase program effectiveness (Cuijpers 2002). Programs, including peer leaders as agents of change, are particularly effective.

In light of the social-ecological model discussed above, it is not surprising that multi-component intervention and prevention programs are among the most common forms of substance-use programs available today. These programs recognize that a problem as complex and multi-dimensional as substance use cannot be prevented through targeting of a single layer of influence. As a result, many programs seek to mobilize communities and parents, train teachers, and provide skills to youth in an attempt to target all possible layers of influence. Targeting multiple layers of influence has been demonstrated as effective in reducing alcohol use in some contexts (Perry et al. 1996), although meta-analyses suggest that overall results of these programs are mixed (Foxcroft and Tsertsvadze 2011).

Conclusion

Noticeably absent from this chapter is a discussion of how biosocial theory fits into current prevention (and intervention) programs. A long-lasting criticism of biosocial theories of crime relates to their implications, as if "bad apple" youth would be identified and assigned a scarlet letter to follow them through life. This premonition could not be further from the intent of biosocial theories, which are derived from sound clinical research and applied to social science in an effort to *improve,* not detract from, population health. The role of biosocial theory in prevention remains unclear, and the undeniable biological underpinnings of addiction and deviant behavior have not yet been optimally incorporated into our evidence-based programs. However, there is little doubt that innovators in prevention science will one day integrate fundamental biologic elements, including susceptibility, into indicated (or targeted) substance-use-prevention programs.

To illustrate this point, consider genetic testing for chronic diseases (such as Huntington's, which has no cure). This test was highly controversial given its implications—the patient testing positive will have a high likelihood of developing a debilitating chronic disease, which will result in premature mortality and severe morbidity. Considering these circumstances, why would someone get this test? Although the prognosis is poor, Huntington's may be prevented through use of creatine (*Science Daily* 2014), healthy behaviors, exercise, and diligently following a restrictive diet (Marder et al. 2013). Or, a person might wish to prepare themselves cognitively to live with the disorder. If a susceptibility test for addiction or criminality were created, results might be sought by diligent parents who wish to gain training to ensure all protective measures are optimized in their home. A positive test does not indicate that a child will become addicted; instead, it is a call to maximize all possible protective factors and minimize risks. The conversation must be shifted away from labeling children and towards expanding our capacity for prevention, acknowledging the strong evidence in support of biological roots for problem behavior.

References

APHA. (2013). *Defining and implementing a public health response to drug use and misuse*. Washington, DC: APHA.

Cacciola, J.S., Dugosh, K., Foltz, C., Leahy, P., & Stevens, R. (2005). Treatment outcomes: First time versus treatment-experienced clients. *Journal of Substance Abuse Treatment, 28*(Suppl 1), S13–S22.

Carson, E.A. & Golinelli, D. (2013). *Prisoners in 2012: Trends in admissions and releases, 1991–2012*. Washington, DC: Bureau of Justice Statistics.

Cartwright, W.S. (2000). Cost–benefit analysis of drug treatment services: Review of the literature. *Journal of Mental Health Policy and Economics, 3*(1), 11–26.

Cuijpers, P. (2002). Effective ingredients of school-based drug prevention programs. A systematic review. *Addictive Behaviors, 27*(6), 1009–1023.

Dackis, C., & O'Brien, C. (2005). Neurobiology of addiction: Treatment and public policy ramifications. *Nature Neuroscience, 8*(11), 1431–1436.

Eaton, W.W., Armenian, H., Gallo, J., Pratt, L., & Ford, D.E. (1996). Depression and risk for onset of type II diabetes. A prospective population-based study. *Diabetes Care, 19*(10), 1097–1102.

Flynn, P.M., Joe, G.W., Broome, K.M., Simpson, D.D., & Brown, B.S. (2003). Looking back on cocaine dependence: Reasons for recovery. *The American Journal on Addictions, 12*(5), 398–411.

Foxcroft, D.R. & Tsertsvadze, A. (2011). Universal multi-component prevention programs for alcohol misuse in young people. *Cochrane Database of Systematic Reviews, 9*, Cd009307.

Friedmann, P.D. (2013). Alcohol use in adults. *New England Journal of Medicine, 368*(4), 365–373.

Galea, S., Nandi, A., & Vlahov, D. (2004). The social epidemiology of substance use. *Epidemiologic Reviews, 26*(1), 36–52.

Gerstein, D.R., Johnson, R.A., Harwood, H.J., Fountain, K., Suter, N., & Malloy, K. (1994). *Evaluating recovery services: The California Drug and Alcohol Treatment Assessment (CALDATA) general report.* Sacramento: California Department of Alcohol and Drug Programs.

Hall, W., Carter, A., & Forlini, C. (2015). The brain disease model of addiction: Is it supported by the evidence and has it delivered on its promises? *The Lancet Psychiatry, 2*(1), 105–110.

Hawkins, J.D., Catalano, R.F., & Miller, J.Y. (1992). Risk and protective factors for alcohol and other drug problems in adolescence and early adulthood: Implications for substance abuse prevention. *Psychological Bulletin, 112*(1), 64–105.

Henrichson, C. & Delaney, R. (2012). *The price of prisons: What incarceration costs taxpayers.* New York: VERA Institute of Justice, Center on Sentencing and Corrections.

Hser, Y.I., Joshi, V., Anglin, M.D., & Fletcher, B. (1999). Predicting post-treatment cocaine abstinence for first-time admissions and treatment repeaters. *American Journal of Public Health, 89*(5), 666–671.

Hu, T.W., Sung, H.Y., & Keeler, T.E. (1995). Reducing cigarette consumption in California: Tobacco taxes vs an anti-smoking media campaign. *American Journal of Public Health, 85*(9), 1218–1222.

Kendler, K.S., Chen, X., Dick, D., Maes, H., Gillespie, N., Neale, M. C., et al. (2012). Recent advances in the genetic epidemiology and molecular genetics of substance use disorders. *Nature Neuroscience, 15*(2), 181–189.

Komro, K.A., Perry, C.L., Veblen-Mortenson, S., Farbakhsh, K., Toomey, T. L., Stigler, M. H., et al. (2008). Outcomes from a randomized controlled trial of a multi-component alcohol use preventive intervention for urban youth: Project Northland Chicago. *Addiction, 103*(4), 606–618.

Komro, K.A., Flay, B.R., Biglan, A., & Wagenaar, A.C. (2016). Research design issues for evaluating complex multicomponent interventions in neighborhoods and communities. *Translational Behavioral Medicine, 6*(1), 153–159.

Leshner, A.I. (1997). Addiction is a brain disease, and it matters. *Science, 278*(5335), 45–47.

Marder, K., Gu, Y., Eberly, S., Tanner, C. M., Scarmeas, N., Oakes, D., et al. (2013). Relationship of Mediterranean diet and caloric intake to phenoconversion in Huntington disease. *JAMA Neurology, 70*(11), 1382–1388.

McLellan, A.T., Lewis, D.C., O'Brien, C.P., & Kleber, H.D. (2000). Drug dependence, a chronic medical illness: Implications for treatment, insurance, and outcomes evaluation. *Journal of the American Medical Association, 284*(13), 1689–1695.

McLellan, A.T., Weinstein, R.L., Shen, Q., Kendig, C., & Levine, M. (2005). Improving continuity of care in a public addiction treatment system with clinical case management. *American Journal on Addictions, 14*(5), 426–440.

Merikangas, K.R. & McClair, V.L. (2012). Epidemiology of substance use disorders. *Human Genetics, 131*(6), 779–789.

Miller, W.R., Walters, S.T., & Bennett, M.E. (2001). How effective is alcoholism treatment in the United States? *Journal of Studies on Alcohol, 62*(2), 211–220.

National Institute on Drug Abuse. (2012). *Principles of drug addiction treatment: A research-based guide.* Washington, DC: National Institutes of Health, US Department of Health and Human Services.

National Institutes of Health. (2016). A child's first eight years critical for substance abuse prevention. Retrieved 17 August 2016 from www.nih.gov/news-events/news-releases/childs-first-eight-years-critical-substance-abuse-prevention.

National Research Council and Institute of Medicine. (2009). Using a developmental framework to guide prevention and promotion. In M. E. O'Connell, T. Boat, & K. E. Warner (Eds.), *Preventing mental, emotional, and behavioral disorders among young people: Progress and possibilities.* Washington, DC: National Academies Press.

Perry, C.L., Williams, C.L., Veblen-Mortenson, S., Toomey, T.L., Komro, K.A., Anstine, P.S., et al. (1996). Project Northland: Outcomes of a communitywide alcohol use prevention program during early adolescence. *American Journal of Public Health, 86*(7), 956–965.

Prendergast, M., Podus, D., Finney, J., Greenwell, L., & Roll, J. (2006). Contingency management for treatment of substance use disorders: A meta-analysis. *Addiction*, *101*(11), 1546–1560.

Science Daily. (2014). Huntington disease prevention trial shows creatine safe, slows progression. Retrieved 16 August 2016 from www.sciencedaily.com/releases/2014/02/140208080705.htm.

Simpson, D.D. & Sells, S.B. (1990). *Opioid addiction and treatment: A 12-year follow-up*. Malabar: Krieger Publishing Co.

Tabbush, V. (1986). *The effectiveness and efficiency of publicly funded drug abuse treatment and prevention programs in California: A benefit–cost analysis*. Los Angeles: Economic Analysis Corporation.

Terry, C.E. (1914). Drug addictions, a public health problem. *American Journal of Public Health*, *4*, 28–37.

Volkow, N.D. & Baler, R.D. (2014). Addiction science: Uncovering neuro-biological complexity. *Neuropharmacology*, *76*(Pt. B), 235–249.

Wagenaar, A.C. & Toomey, T.L. (2002). Effects of minimum drinking age laws: Review and analyses of the literature from 1960 to 2000. *Journal of Studies on Alcohol Supplement*, *14*, 206–225.

White House. (2014). *A drug policy for the 21st century*. www.whitehouse.gov/ondcp/drugpolicyreform.

Winstanley, E.L., Steinwachs, D.M., Ensminger, M.E., Latkin, C.A., Stitzer, M.L., & Olsen, Y. (2008). The association of self-reported neighborhood disorganiza-tion and social capital with adolescent alcohol and drug use, dependence, and access to treatment. *Drug and Alcohol Dependence*, *92*(1–3), 173–182.

World Health Organization (2016). Public health. Retrieved 5 February 2016 from www.who.int/trade/glossary/story076/en/.

9

The Road Ahead

Introduction

We began this book by providing an overview of the pervasiveness of alcohol and drug abuse and, in turn, describing the interrelatedness of drug abuse and antisocial behavior. Next, we made the case that scientific research has made clear that drug abuse and addiction are best understood not as evidence of moral failing or a deeply flawed character, but rather as chronic medical conditions that are primarily—but certainly not entirely—situated in the human brain. Building upon this conceptual foundation, we explored the ways in which genetics and neurobiology play a critical role in our understanding of both drug abuse and antisocial behavior. We then examined drug abuse and antisocial behavior from a life-course perspective, examining the ways in which biosocial and developmental factors help us to understand the onset, escalation, and cessation of these intersecting behavioral phenomena. Finally, we built upon all of the aforementioned content by examining the ways in which a biosocial, life-course approach can shed light on the prevention and treatment of drug abuse and antisocial behavior.

© The Author(s) 2016   **197**
C.P. Salas-Wright et al., *Drug Abuse and Antisocial Behavior*,
Palgrave's Frontiers in Criminology Theory,
DOI 10.1057/978-1-137-55817-6_9

As stated at the outset, the foundational arguments presented in this book were rooted in seven guiding principles related to drug abuse and antisocial behavior. These principles are, at their core, situated in bio-social logic as well as a developmental, life-course perspective as it is our conviction that these complex phenomena are profoundly influenced by biological and social factors that often unfold over the course of a lifetime. These principles are not necessarily to be set in any particular order, but rather touch upon various facets of a biosocial, developmental understanding of drug abuse and antisocial behavior. Here, in this final chapter, we revisit these guiding principles in order to highlight key points of insight that have been gleaned and, subsequently, consider salient empirical and theoretical questions that remain unanswered. Simply put, we conclude this text by revisiting what has been learned, acknowledging what remains unanswered, and looking forward to the road ahead.

Guiding Principles, Revisited

Principle One

There is no gene for drug use and crime, but there is a genetic vulnerability that underlies both substance-use disorders and antisocial behavior. This first principle is important for several reasons. For one, it affirms unequivocally that—based in the state-of-the-art research on the genetics of drug abuse and antisociality—our biosocial understanding of drug abuse and antisocial behavior rejects any facile and over-simplified notions of genetic determinism. While certainly there are disorders that we know to be caused by a single gene inherited from ones' mother or father, drug abuse and antisocial behavior are simply not in this category. Rather, they are complex, polygenic phenomena that are influenced by many genes as well as a multitude of social, developmental, and environmental factors. That being said, while we are cautious to note that strict genetic determinism does not apply to drug abuse and antisocial behavior, it is imperative that we also be clear in stating that there is little doubt that genes are critically important when it comes to understanding these phenomena. Indeed, research has made it quite evident that genes play an important role in the risk of developing substance-use disorders and becoming involved in antisocial behavior. Moreover, we have increasingly come to understand that a number of genetic factors are likely related to risk for both drug abuse and antisocial behavior.

These genetic factors play out within a context of gene–environment interplay. For example, several genetic polymorphisms have been found to interact with environmental adversity to increase the probability of substance-related problem behaviors. Our research, and that of others, has also shed light on genetic and environmental interactions related to antisocial behavioral outcomes such as violent and nonviolent criminal offending. Beyond gene–environment interaction, there is also substantial research underscoring the phenomenon of gene–environment correlation. That is, empirical studies strongly suggest that a person's genetic makeup can shape and influence environmental exposure. For example, if we are genetically predisposed to sensation-seeking, we may seek out environments that provide greater novelty and risk. In turn, inserting ourselves into risky environments can function as positive reinforcement to the original genetic attribute. All this is to say that, when it comes to drug abuse and antisocial behavior, genes clearly matter; however, the complexity of the relationship between genetics, the social environment, and polygenic phenomena should not be underestimated.

Principle Two

Drugs of abuse hijack the reward pathway. There is little debate among drug-abuse researchers that addiction is a special kind of brain disease that involves key neural circuits and socio-environmental inputs. One of the most important of these neural circuits is the mesolimbic reward system or, simply, the reward pathway. This ancient system evolved to provide reinforcement for basic survival functions such as eating, drinking, and sex; however, drugs of abuse have the capacity to stimulate the reward pathway to supernormal levels which, in turn, can cause us to mistakenly prioritize drug use over other "natural" rewards necessary for our survival. This is precisely what is meant when we speak of drug addiction "hijacking the brain" and significantly limiting our ability to exercise free will and make healthy decisions. For those individuals who are susceptible to addiction, compulsive drug-seeking and craving often are observed. As such, the changes to the mesolimbic reward system—and the problematic behaviors that often follow suit—represent one of the major pathways by which addiction can lead to antisocial behavior. Any biosocial theory of drugs and crime must come to grips with the importance of drugs of abuse in stimulating this critically important area of the brain.

The powerful effects of drugs on the reward pathway lead to profoundly strong reward responses that act as a driver for continued stimulation. After repeated drug use, an individual reaches a stage known as tolerance, which is characterized by the need for larger doses of a drug to obtain a desired psychoactive effect. Further, due to hyper-stimulation of the nucleus accumbens, increased quantities of the drug are often needed for a user to simply feel normal or to avoid experiencing withdrawal. As one might imagine, this powerful drive for continued stimulation can end in any number of undesirable outcomes. Even with strong will-power and intact executive control, the drive to consume drugs of abuse quite often over-powers people living with addiction. When combined with diminished executive governance or an immature or poorly developed capacity for inhibitory control, it is easy to see the ways in which a "hijacked" rewards system can result in involvement in illegal behaviors or exposures to harmful situations. In short, a strong reward response tied to a weak control system can be quite problematic.

Principle Three

Addiction alters brain function long-term. These cognitive modifications could explain ongoing criminal behavior. Drugs of abuse have been shown to significantly alter the prefrontal cortex, which is the brain center responsible for executive function and self-regulation. Regrettably, neurobiological and cognitive neuroscience research has made clear that our capacity for rational decision-making and inhibitory control can become significantly impaired as a result of long-term drug abuse and addiction. In the beginning of an addiction career, higher than normal levels of dopamine activate a person's risk-taking capacity. Over the long-term, reward-seeking behavior taxes our self-control resources. Specific functions such as attention, monitoring, planning, problem-solving, memory, and judgment and decision-making become compromised and a host of problem behaviors often follow. A substantial body of research has documented a relationship between impairment in the frontal regions and antisocial and risky behavior. Of course, we should also note that many drug users possess neuropsychological deficits prior to initiating drug-abuse careers which highlights the ways in which spurious conclusions about the effects of drug abuse might be confounded.

One of the mechanisms by which diminished executive functioning is tied to antisocial behavior is via social cognitive processes. As many drug-treatment professionals and criminal-justice practitioners can likely attest, drug abusers and criminal offenders often struggle with decision-making and the accurate perception of the world around them. Over-reaction to environmental stimuli, such as cues tied to drugs and the misinterpretation of other people's intentions, often results in strained relationships or interpersonal conflict. These challenges frequently persist even after extensive cognitive therapy as well as informal (e.g., advice from loved ones) or formal treatment. While the ultimate cause of such struggles is likely is rooted in neurobiology, social-cognitive processes are nevertheless helpful in explaining many of the self-defeating behaviors that, unfortunately, constitute a cardinal feature of drug abuse and antisocial behavior.

Principle Four

Early manifestations of child behavior problems that persist into adulthood could result from a combination of biologic susceptibility and social conditioning. Many children can be said to exhibit some degree of problem behavior at some point over the first decade or so of life that constitutes childhood. Among toddlers and preschool children, these may be behaviors such as temper tantrums, noncompliance, hyperactivity, difficulty controlling impulses, and physical aggression. Notably, it is quite normal for children to exhibit some degree of the aforementioned behaviors, particularly during these early years in which impulse control and language skills are still developing. Indeed, anxious parents should remind themselves that empirical research suggests that the peak of physical aggression among human beings occurs somewhere between two and four years of age. Most children exhibit some problem behaviors, but then seem to simply grow out of them as they move into middle childhood and beyond.

Notably, however, this is not the case for all children. To be sure, a small—but critically important—minority of individuals exhibit elevated levels of problem behavior that begin early in childhood and continue into the adolescent and, quite often, adult years. Longitudinal studies of this severe subset have revealed several important findings consistent with a biosocial, life-course perspective. To begin, children who have serious and persistent behavior problems are substantially more likely to evince a difficult temperament very early on in life as compared to children without behavior problems. That is, such children are more likely—by as early as four to six months of age—to have marked difficulty adjusting to new things and to react negatively and intensely to the world around them. Such findings, and other research into the neurobiological and genetic underpinnings of temperament, suggest that child problem behavior is very likely influenced by biological factors. That being said, research is also quite clear that social and contextual factors such as unresponsive or harsh parenting practices, family stress and conflict, and chaotic home environments also play a critically important role in the etiology of severe and persistent child problem behavior. In fact, there is general scholarly consensus that biological and social/contextual factors interact to influence child behavioral outcomes.

It is also important that we note that a number of longitudinal studies suggest that severe and persistent child problem behaviors—particularly those that continue on into adolescence—are a portent not only of later antisocial behavioral problems, but also of drug abuse and addiction. In other words, while alcohol and drug use is exceedingly rare among pre-school children or during middle childhood, behaviors such as physical aggression and noncompliance that precede substance use nevertheless provide information related to risk for drug abuse and addiction later on in life. All in all, we see that child behavior problems are profoundly influenced by the interaction of both biological and social/contextual sources of risk, and that—while some degree of behavior problems are to be expected—severe and persistent childhood problem behavior is by no means something to be dismissed.

Principle Five

Delayed onset of drug use is critical, as developmental neuroplasticity among adolescents and young adults is easily disrupted by substance use. Child-behavior problems such as noncompliance, hyperactivity, and physical aggression invariably precede the onset of alcohol and drug use among young people. Really, this should come as no surprise as it is far easier for a preschooler to, say, push or hit another child in a day-care setting than it is for them to access and consume alcohol, marijuana, or other illicit drugs. In this way, it makes sense for researchers and practitioners to be more on the lookout for nondrug problem behaviors for much of the first decade of life. However, epidemiological surveillance data makes clear that, by the end of middle childhood and certainly by the onset of puberty, a disconcerting proportion of young people have begun to experiment with alcohol and other drugs. Early-onset substance use is problematic in and of itself, but we also know that the consumption of alcohol, marijuana, and other substances is related in very important ways to a slew of adverse behavioral and health outcomes down the road.

The negative impact of early-onset substance use is very likely due in part to social factors that come along with early risk-taking. For instance, it is likely that young people who begin using alcohol and/or other drugs early on in their teenage years will be spending time with other young people who are also taking part in other risk behaviors (e.g., delinquency, violence, etc.) as well as those who experience social and contextual risk (e.g., limited parental monitoring, parental substance-use problems, etc.). And, it is, of course, well established that spending time—and establishing friendships and bonds—with young people who are risk-takers and who face social/contextual adversity does not bode well for the health and well-being of young people. That being said, while social factors undoubtedly explain part of why early-onset substance use is linked with poor outcomes later on in life, there is little doubt that biosocial factors are also in play. In particular, we can state quite confidently that the ingestion of psychoactive substances during childhood and adolescence—that is, critical periods in terms of neurological development—has the potential to negatively impact our brains and, in turn, our capacity for self-regulation and decision-making. Simply put, it is well-established that using alcohol and other drugs early on in life is related to biological and social factors that can, in turn, place young people at risk for any number of problems later on in life.

Principle Six

Crime and antisocial behavior are asymmetrical. Studies of crime and antisocial behavior have consistently found that a relatively small subset of people—approximately 5 % of the general population—account for the lion's share of offending. Indeed, in our own examination of antisocial behavior using several large, nationally representative epidemiological samples, we have found that a "severe 5 %" of American adolescents are responsible for close to one in three violent attacks (29 %), one in two thefts (48 %), and nearly three in four drug sales (70 %) among youth aged 12 to 17. Along the same lines, longitudinal studies have consistently identified a severe subset which comprises roughly 3 to 6 % of the childhood, adolescent, and adult population. Importantly, while further research is needed, the current evidence seems to suggest that both biological and social/contextual factors play an important role in distinguishing this severe subset from less severe offenders and from the broader population of individuals who simply abstain from antisocial behavior in general.

In addition to violent and nonviolent antisocial behavior, it is evident that many of the chronic offenders that comprise the severe subset have a history of alcohol and drug abuse and, at various points in their lives, meet criteria for substance-use disorders. To some degree, this should come as no surprise as we have pointed repeatedly to the comorbidity of drug abuse and antisocial behavior, as well as the disproportionate prevalence of substance-use disorders among criminal offenders. It is an important observation, however, because it underscores the fact that drug abuse is not only a critical issue with respect to crime in general, but also among the fraction of the general population that is responsible for an overwhelming proportion of nonviolent and violent criminal offenses.

Principle Seven

All substance-use and crime-prevention or treatment strategies are inherently overlapping and biosocial. The public health prevention model fits well when applied to addiction, and there is little doubt that biosocial influences play a substantial role in addiction prevention and treatment. A multifactorial prevention and treatment approach must incorporate one's biologic susceptibility, or at least behavioral and cognitive manifestations, to be effective in maintaining abstinence. This is particularly important when biologic susceptibility interacts with environmental and social cues to result in prolonged addiction characterized by recurrent relapse; a cycle difficult to terminate.

Biosocial influences represent a critical component of the notorious gene–environment (or G*E) interactions on behavior. Some genetic polymorphisms like MAOA have repeatedly been found to interact with family adversity to produce externalizing behavior, although the literature as a whole in this area is in its infancy and remains largely inconclusive. However, there is little doubt that the fields of epidemiology, genetics, and criminology must work together to inform how we can work with—not against—genetic susceptibility to most efficiently identify, prevent, and treat those at risk for addiction.

The Road Ahead

We have learned a tremendous amount over the last few decades when it comes to understanding drug abuse and antisocial behavior from a biosocial, life-course perspective. Advances in research that have integrated genetics, neuroimaging, and other biological measures into the study of drugs and crime have opened up new possibilities and made space for salient, biosocial questions. Similarly, our depth of understanding has been profoundly enhanced by prospective studies that begin collecting data very early on in life as well as long-term follow-up studies that provide information on drug abuse and antisocial behavior over many decades. We believe that optimism is certainly warranted as it is quite possible that emerging research could transform the way we understand, prevent, and treat drug abuse and antisocial behavior. And yet, the road ahead is one full of uncertainty as many unanswered empirical and theoretical questions remain. Below we offer several observations as to how addictions and criminological research might best move forward in the study of these interrelated phenomena.

Biosocial Measurement

The integration of biosocial measures into research on drug abuse and antisocial behavior has allowed researchers to explore and provide answers to a number of critical biosocial questions. For instance, the collection of saliva samples as part of The National Longitudinal Study of Adolescent to Adult Health (Add Health) has allowed researchers to explore the role of genetics in the etiology of both drug abuse and antisocial behavior in a nationally representative cohort study. Similarly, the inclusion of genetic data in the National Institute on Alcohol Abuse and Alcoholism's National Epidemiologic Survey on Alcohol and Related Conditions (NESARC-III) promises to advance our understanding of the complexities of gene–environment interplay with respect to substance-use disorders and antisocial behavior as well. Along the same lines, the forthcoming Adolescent Brain Cognitive Development (ABCD) study—drawing from the support of the National Institutes of Health—which aims to collect neuroimaging, genetic, and survey data from a cohort of roughly 10,000 children between middle childhood and young adulthood, will clearly constitute a rich data source that promises to shed new light on the biosocial bases of drug abuse and other health-risk behaviors.

These are several highly promising and exciting examples of how biosocial measures can be meaningfully integrated into the study of drug abuse and antisocial behavior. However, beyond large-scale epidemiological studies, it is also incumbent upon individual researchers, research teams, and funding sources to prioritize research that integrates a biosocial approach when examining drugs and crime. To be sure, as we have mentioned at numerous points in this text, a biosocial lens tends to come easier to addictions researchers than to criminologists. Many criminologists may feel reluctant to look at genetic or neuroimaging data in attempting to understand violent and nonviolent antisocial behavior; however, genes, the brain, and other biological measures are simply part and parcel of addiction research. That being said, addiction researchers can also be critiqued for being a bit myopic when it comes to focusing purely on drug use and drug-use disorders without also considering comorbid violence and crime. Indeed, if anything is to be gleaned from this book, it is that drug abuse and antisocial behavior very often go hand-in-hand to influence and, frequently, reinforce one another in the lives of individuals and communities. This point of fact alone seems to underscore the importance of asking biosocial questions related to not just drugs *or* crime, but rather to the interrelatedness of drugs *and* crime.

Starting Earlier, Following Longer

One can only think about drug abuse and antisocial behavior from a life-course perspective for so long before coming to the conclusion that researchers interested in drugs and crime need to start collecting data earlier and following people longer. It is astounding how much can be learned by conducting careful assessments of infant temperament, early parental responsiveness, home environment, and other variables that can relatively easily be measured during the first year of life. The same goes for intrapersonal, behavioral, familial, and contextual variables that can be measured during toddlerhood, the preschool years, middle childhood, and beyond. In fact, it is not only astounding how much can be learned, but it is quite disconcerting to think about how much is typically missed when we study drug abuse and antisocial behavior in samples that begin at, say, ages 12 and older. It's a bit like trying to study the factors that predict car accidents based solely on data collected seconds prior to or even after crashes take place. Or studying weather patterns by only looking out the window to consider what is immediately in sight. We recognize that we ourselves—inasmuch as we have drawn from large, national samples that invariably exclude small children—are often guilty of missing a tremendous part of the story. And we know that this important shortcoming is by no means unique to our research alone. Indeed, the exclusion of biologically based and contextual variables from early life in studies of drug abuse and antisocial behavior is common enough to be considered the *de facto* approach.

In the same way that we miss much when we overlook early childhood, a critical part of the story of drug abuse and antisocial behavior is simply omitted in the absence of long-term follow-up data. As we have described at length, it is not unusual for drug-abuse and antisocial behavioral trajectories to stretch for years or even decades. Similarly, an important percentage of people who use alcohol and drugs or get involved in violence and petty crime do so for only a short period of time before leaving these problems behind. There are many twists and turns that take place in the real lives of people who struggle with drug abuse and crime, but many—if not all—of these critical changes are overlooked in studies that are either cross-sectional or only follow study participants for four or five or even ten years. Indeed, studies that include follow-up points three, four, five, or six decades later simply tell a far more complex and compelling story about drugs and crime across the life course. Research has made clear that these are not, on average, short-term problems but rather pesky and persistent issues that unfold over decades, lifetimes, and even generations.

Of course, it is easy for us to simply extol the benefits of study designs that begin with in utero assessments and stretch across generations, but it is far more challenging to actually conduct research that is truly reflective of life-course measurement. Believe us when we say we know it is hard enough to get funded to conduct a pilot study, let alone string together a series of grants that can allow us to dedicate a decade or more to the study drug abuse and antisociality. In truth, most of us will simply not be afforded the opportunity to conduct such research or even access extant data that can give us the chance to explore the richest of life-course questions. Nevertheless, some people have and will conduct such research and we would do well to pay careful attention to such studies and to integrate the insights garnered from developmental, life-course designs into our own studies (be they cross-sectional or longitudinal). Fundamentally, a core insight from this book is that, whatever studies we conduct or data we use, we would do well to approach questions related to drugs and crime in a way that thinks not only in the short term but also across the lifespan.

A Transdisciplinary Approach

One practical consideration for criminologists interested in biosocially informed etiological or prevention research is the necessity of being a part of transdisciplinary research teams. Big science needs experts from many fields and being open to working with others who have had different disciplinary training can sometimes be frustrating but also enlightening. We realize disciplinary insularity is comforting, but the rewards are potentially great when incorporating knowledge from the natural sciences or biomedical sciences into the social sciences. It might be encouraging to know that most scholars in traditional social science fields such as criminology that engage in biosocial research have had very little formal training in genetics, neurobiology, or even biology in general. They are essentially self-taught. We encourage predoctoral and postdoctoral criminological training not only in biosocial approaches but in addiction science, translational and implementation science, and intervention research. Just a few areas worth exploring are Bayesian statistical simulations that incorporate biological estimates and newer experimental designs that feature Mendelian randomization. The paradigm is shifting in these aforementioned directions and, while skepticism is a necessity in science, so is an open mind.

In conclusion, we believe the present volume enriches both criminological and addiction science. Although much has been learned regarding the biosocial foundations of drug abuse and antisocial behavior, there is little doubt that important discoveries lie ahead. We invite students, early-career and seasoned scholars to consider, question, and extend some of our points. Be sure that we plan to continue to examine and test the biosocial and life-course principles laid out in this text, and to reach for new ways to study and prevent drug abuse and antisocial behavior. In the end, our hope is that readers will find the issues and findings examined in this book as interesting and exciting as we do.

Index

© The Author(s) 2016   **211**
C.P. Salas-Wright et al., *Drug Abuse and Antisocial Behavior*,
Palgrave's Frontiers in Criminology Theory,
DOI 10.1057/978-1-137-55817-6